FUNDAMENTAL LAWS

FUNDAMENTAL LAWS

A Report of the 68th Convocation of the Rose Cross Order

Giving a resume of the proceedings of the Convocation, together with most of the lectures that were delivered during the time of the Convocation, by the several delegates present.

Also a report of the work of ancient Initiation in the Grove of Osiris as especially prepared for the occasion.

TRY

KALPAZ

ISBN: 978-93-5128-879-4(HB)

First Published in 1916
Indian Reprint in 2017

Published by

Kalpaz Publications
C-30, Satyawati Nagar,
Delhi – 110052
E-mail: kalpaz@hotmail.com
Website: kalpazpublications.com
Ph.: +91-9212142040

Cataloging in Publication Data—DK
Courtesy: D.K. Agencies (P) Ltd. <docinfo@dkagencies.com>

Fundamental laws : a report of the 68th convocation of the Rose Cross Order, giving a resume of the proceedings of the convocation, together with most of the lectures that were delivered during the time of the convocation, by the several delegates present, also a report of the work of ancient initiation in the grove of Osiris as especially prepared for the occasion.

pages cm

Reprint. Originally published: Allentown, Pa. : The Philosophical Publishing Co., 1916.

ISBN 9789351288794

1. Rosicrucians. I. Rose Cross Order, issuing body.

BF1623.R7F86 2017 DDC 135.43092 23

THE ROLL OF HONOR

During the sessions of the Rose Cross Order, the delegates came to the conclusion that the lectures which had been given in open session, should be published in book form, and with that idea in mind, subscribed to a fund for the publication of the book. The following were subscribers to this fund and are therefore found on the Roll of Honor:

Charles C. Brown
H. M. Baasch
A. W. Witt
Grace Kincaid Morey
Clara T. Grove
Clara Witt
J. C. Cake
Dr. Ira K. Kepperling
Daisy T. Grove
Gertrude Cosgrove
Julia A. Hauck
Kathryn T. Cake
Emma Schmeiser
Kansas City Center
Marcia Greene
Joseph A. Walter
Elizabeth Walter
Gertrude W. Pelot
Dr. Henry J. Frank
Dr. Thomas B. Henderson
DeLos Ackley
Ferdinand H. Peterman
Charlotte F. Peterman
Blanche B. Stearns
Josephine A. Willis
Minnie W. Pleister
Lars Hansen
Buffalo, N. Y., Center

IN EXPLANATION

In explanation of the contents of this book, it is to be stated that these articles do not give the INNER work of the Rose Cross Order but simply the outer, the public teachings.

The Illuminati and its Soul Science work may be called the child of the Rose Cross Order. Years ago it was found that where there was one person who desired to follow the work with heart and soul, in other words, who was willing to LIVE the life as taught by the Order, there were an hundred others who desired teachings from the Order but who were not willing to dedicate their lives to the Sublime Work.

These thousands had to be taken care of, and as a result, the Illuminati and its Soul Science work was born.

When, in April, the order went forth to the brethren, that a Sacred Convocation was to be held, all delegates were requested to prepare articles on Soul Science so that regular lecture sessions could be held. The lectures that follow are the result. All these lectures were given in open session and are to be considered as Soul Science work, though in entire harmony with the teachings of the Rose Cross Order.

The work of the Rose Cross Order as given to its students can never be published. It is a secret, sacred work between teacher and student. It is a Soul Training, an *inner* Initiation, and such work continues until the student has reached Initiation, after which he is called upon to attend a Convocation, and at which time the degree work is conferred upon him, but the *inner* work *always* precedes the outer work, as the outer work is only a bond, binding together the Brotherhood.

Thus a word in explanation. Many, having heard of the Great Order and its work, and actually knowing nothing of its inner work, have, ignorantly or with fraudulent intent, established so-called Rose Cross bodies, and these bodies, knowing nothing of the true work of the Rose Cross, have nothing but a Ritualistic initiatory rite or degree work.

We would refer all seekers to authorities on the Rose Cross and on Initiation, and they will then find that the TRUE Rose Cross is actually a School of Spirituality, with a degree ceremonial Initiation as the climax.

By the Hierophant of the Order.

PREFACE

Early in the summer, instructions were received from the Hierarchies to call the Inner Circle of the Rose Cross Order into session, and thus to fitly celebrate the 68th year of the Rose Cross Order in America.

Orders were immediately issued to those who have the privilege of attending this Convocation, and on June the 1st the Convocation was called to order, and the preliminary lectures were started.

At this Convocation all delegates were instructed to prepare and to deliver articles which should have a bearing on the conditions of the present day and which should be the means of helping humanity.

However, because of the limited amount of time at the disposal of those who could attend, only a few were enabled to prepare such lectures, with the result that there were not as many lectures delivered as might have been had the delegates had more time at their disposal.

But even so, there were from two to three lectures each day, and most of these lectures will be found in this present volume, though many of the lectures cannot be given in book form, as they were only delivered as from teacher to those of the Inner Circle.

From the beginning of the month until the day of the thirteenth there were lectures in the Assembly Hall which had been built in 1910 for the express purpose of holding these yearly Convocations, but on the thirteenth, there were no lectures, as all of the day was required for making the preparations necessary in order that the Ancient Mysteries might be given to the delegates in a form of Symbolism, consisting of three degrees.

I can do no better than to give the article prepared by Grace K. Morey, of Buffalo, N. Y., the Secretary of the Rose Cross Sacred College, for the Buffalo, N. Y., papers, and which appeared in the "Buffalo Express" July 16th, 1916.

ANCIENT MYSTERIES OF EGYPT GIVEN IN AN INITIATION OF THREE DEGREES

Under the authority of the Rose Cross Order founded in America in 1858 prominent delegates of the Order were gathered in the most remarkable conclave held during the last 5000 years, the publication of whose records now opens to the world, the connection of Egypt in her ages of true religion, power and glory, with the Mystic Seal of the United States, whose Heraldric symbolism declaring the mighty destiny of America, has, until now only been known to a limited number.

At "Beverly Hall" in the beautiful Tohickon valley about four miles from the town of Quakertown, men and women of all ranks of life, and from all parts of the world, high Masons, and members of the Eastern Star, physicians, teachers, authors, and members of all denominations inclusive of the Hebrew, all these assembled at the call of the Grand Master of the Rose Cross Order for the sixty-eighth Convocation.

Some years ago R. Swinburne Clymer, author of the Philosophy of Fire, Ancient Mystic Oriental Masonry, The Rosicrucians; Their Teachings, Mysteries of Osiris, Soul Science and Immortality, and over thirty other works, bought a mountainous tract of land, and on this was built "Beverly Hall," an Assembly Hall, press rooms and libraries, and chemical laboratory which, surrounded by orchards, vineyards and rose gardens, set in terraced lawns, presents with its Collie kennels and poultry plants, a splendid combination of the beautiful and the practical.

To this has been added the Mystic, for in a secluded and wooded tract of fifty acres of this land, an artificial lake was made from a mountain stream, a throne room erected and other improvements made which would be needed for the Initiation of Neophytes in the Egyptian Mysteries.

The Convocation was called to order on June first in the Assembly Hall, built over five years ago for that purpose, and the delivery of a series of lectures upon practical as well as Mystical subjects began and continued until the close of the Convocation. The delegates and teachers presented the lectures, which were followed by discussions upon the subjects of Eugenics, Scientific Motherhood, Code of Ethics for the Schools and home, Spiritual Christianity, Personal Hygiene, Diet and Health, Sin, Authority and Individuality, Jacob's Ladder, Initiation, Reincarnation, Soul Development, The Second Coming of the Christ, and the Mystic Significance of the seal of the United States,

In the time of Solomon as in the time of the Egyptian Priesthood, no ceremony was ever held, unless the circle of Solomon, commonly called the Sacred Seal of Solomon, had been previously prepared, but since the fall of Egypt and of the Temple of Solomon, this seal has been practically unknown, except to a limited number of students of ancient religions and mysteries.

During the first week in June, in the grove especially prepared for the dramatization of the Ancient Mysteries of Osiris, the Seal of Solomon, often called the Magic Circle, was especially built, and on June 11 the dedication of the Magic Circle took place in the presence of the delegates of the Rose Cross Order, some of whom were natives of Germany, England and Russia. This was in accordance with the system as practiced by the ancient Priests of Egypt and the Sanhedrin of the Temple of Solomon.

On the night of June 13th the first section of the class, including those of the Order taking part in the Initiation, assembled in the grove of Osiris, which was illuminated by electricity from a central power house especially prepared for the purpose, and the Initiation of the Ancient Mysteries of Egypt in three Degrees and six scenes.

All students of the Ancient Mysteries and religions know that in the Temple of Solomon there were three Courts, the outer Court for the people being composed of seven hundred selected teachers and leaders. These were members of the First Degree, Illuminati, called also, seekers, travellers or soldiers. The middle Court, or members of the second Degree were seventy in number, and were supposed to be in the Hall of Meditation, and acted as mediators between the people and the inner Sanctuary. Above all was the Inner Court, or circle of the Seven Priests and the Master or High Priest, who were the teachers between God and man, mediators between the seen and Unseen.

In the Egyptian Mysteries, the first Court was made up of the Royal youth of Egypt, and such students from foreign countries as desired to enter the Temple and Priesthood, and these, during probation, were often known as the "Soldiers of the Priesthood," as it was their duty while undergoing the preliminary training and tests to guard the Priesthood and its work even to the death.

The second class corresponding to a Second Degree were those who had passed this test and who were in the Hall of Meditation, and purification, in preparation for the first vows, and the dedication of the body, mind, soul and spirit to God and the service of mankind.

The third class called The Third Degree were those who had passed with credit the tests of the first degree, the purification of the second, as well as the various stages of development required of all students in the Halls of Meditation.

In the Royal Third Degree, which took place in the Temple the Neophyte received the final instruction. After this came the final test in the beautiful ceremony of the death of the old life, the giving up of the body and its temptations and the raising of the slain Orisis or Spiritual body, by his faithful spouse Isis, the Soul, with the final Illumination.

On the fifteenth of June, the first section of the representatives left "Beverly Hall," for their respective homes and the second section began to arrive for the preparatory lectures, and on the nineteenth of June the ceremonies were repeated so that all might witness the Initiation and take part in it so as to become members.

So far as can be learned either through travel or history never before since the fall of Egypt and its Priesthood and the fall of the Temple of Solomon, has there ever been a grove, a lake to represent the Nile, a Magic Circle, or a Temple prepared, nor is it believed that anywhere in the world does there today exist such a Circle.

Nearest to this, however, is Stone-henge of the Druids of Britain, to which their descendants travel each year at a certain time to greet the Sun, and renew their vows.

This is the first time, therefore, in 5000 years that any Order has attempted to build up this Sacred emblem under the stately oak, so that people of modern civilization might witness the beauties of the life and religion of the ancient people, whose teachings of individual soul development, made the glory of Egypt, the lost dreams of all Israel, the teachings of the Magi of Persia, all that was true in India, the splendid philosophy of Greece, the magnificence of the early Romans, the basis of pre-Christian Ireland's great schools, as well as the familiar Holy Grail legends of Briton, Celt and Gaul. In this light of Brotherhood of man and Fatherhood of God was founded this great Republic foretold by Virgil, upon whose seal is set the Egyptian Pyramid, completed by the White stone of Spiritual purification as the crown of the ages.

The American Constellation of thirteen stars set in the form of a double triangle was foretold by Merlin of King Arthur's Court, and the Philosophy of the Holy Grail and of

Egypt's glory and Solomon's Temple, has been the Day star of every great American Statesman from Washington to Abraham Lincoln.

After the ceremonies in the grove, there was given in the dining room of "Beverly Hall" at midnight a "Feast of the Gods" at which neither meat nor spices formed part of the menu, but only fruits, nuts and other products of sun kissed foods.

The conclusion of the rites was held at sunrise in the grove with a musical communion service, in which Nectar of roses, distilled from the thirty thousand roses blooming each June upon the lawns at "Beverly Hall," was served as emblematic of the wine of the Soul, and for this service the rose bushes were planted several years ago.

I wish that all the readers of this book might have been present at the preparation, at the building, and at the Dedication of this Ancient Magic Circle. Or, I wish that I might be able to give a detailed description of these sublime ceremonies in this book. However, I cannot do this here, though I hope that in some future work I will be able to do so. Sufficient be it to say, that when the stone, made out of cement by one of the Brothers, was nearly finished, the Dedication took place, and the emblems placed in the stone itself before it was completed, were:

The American Beauty Rose in full bloom. This as a representation, or symbol of the Soul that has reached full Illumination.

The Mystic ring. This was a solid gold ring, belonging to one of the members present, upon which had been engraved the Cross and Pentagram. All members of the Magi will know what this symbol stands for. The ring itself, as is known to the Magi, is a protecting agent against all evil or malignant influences when worn during any ceremonial or developing work.

The True Magic Mirror. This is an emblem of the Soul, which when fully developed will act as a mirror to the universe wherein may be wisdom and truth.

Lastly, a complete copy of the private text book, "Ritualistic Occultism," which contains the ceremonies as made use of by the Magi, and four of these ceremonials were made use of by four of the Magi, in the dedication of the Magic Circle.

When all of this had taken place, the stone was completed and then later in the day the characters were engraved upon the stone by the Brother who had completed the stone.

Of the midnight "Feast to the Gods" and of the morning services which took place in the grove it is not lawful for me to speak at this time, but it is my sincere prayer that all who are enrolled in the Sacred Schools may some day be present with us and witness these sublime ceremonies, especially as they are conferred in the Spring of the year.

Arrangements were made by the delegates present, through voluntary contributions, to either buy another large grove, or if that is found impracticable, to build a much larger Hall in the "Grove of Osiris" so that advanced ceremonies may be held the coming Spring at the 69th Convocation of the Rose Cross Order.

CONCERNING THE LECTURES

As before stated, many of the lectures were only for those of the Inner Circle who were present, and these were all delivered by the Master of the Sacred College, of Buffalo, N. Y.

Mr. Charles C. Brown the Order considers as one of its most untiring workers, one who has labored in his native city for many years and through untiring efforts it has been possible to organize four large classes in that one city, classes which meet on different days of the week and which meet the requirements of students in different stages of development.

Within the near future, it is proposed to open some of these classes, under authority of the Sacred College, to the people of the city so that Eugenics, Scientific Child Culture, and other important subjects of like nature may be taught to the people at large. All of this work in Buffalo will be under the supervision of Mr. Brown and his able assistant, Mrs. Charles K. Morey.

Of the Kansas City College and its able Master, A. W. Witt, and his Assistant, Mrs. A. W. Witt, not much need be said as they had charge of the lectures and their lectures, given in the present work, speak for themselves.

One of the lectures delivered and which is of great importance, not alone to Occult students, or students of the Mystic, but to all true Americans, is that concerning the Great Seal of the United States, and its Mystic indications, for, just as soon as these things come to pass, then shall the Eagle soar over all things, and America will be the Mistress of the world, though she will not rule through either arms or politics, but by love and wisdom.

The other article by the same author, is the "Code of Ethics," which is given in full.

All true educators have come to understand that if the Public School system is to be retained in the United States, then it will be absolutely necessary for a complete Code of Ethics to be taught to all scholars and the Illuminati is the first great school of thought that has ever attempted to formulate such a Code of Ethics.

Naturally, the code as given is but a bare outline of the work, but it is sufficient to give an idea to all mankind as to what the Illuminati is attempting to do for young America, and it will not stop in merely suggesting the teaching of such Ethics, but it will fight for the adoption of such a Code in the schools. Aye, the Illuminati will give mind and body, the last drop of blood, in their fight for a better educational system, a greater care of the children so that these children shall not continue to become the victims of that class of humanity which comes to near utter depravity. The slogan of the Illuminati shall be, "Save the children of our glorious country, give them wisdom so that they may be able to look after their own protection." Cannot all true men and women in our country say "Amen" to this?

The Second article, which was given by Mrs. A. W. Witt is that on sin, and has to do with the conception of sin, or wrong doing as we of the Secret Schools understand it.

The Third article, prepared by Dr. Ira L. Kepperling,, with the help of Mr. Charles Wolf, of Kansas City, Mo., is on Reincarnation, and is a subject of supreme importance to all people. Once this law is understood, much of sin and wrong will pass away, and right doing take the place of wrong doing.

The Third paper on Evolution, by the same authors, is also of extreme importance, for it is through Evolution, reinforced by conscious Development, that the race must be quickly improved. I venture to say, that if the last few pages of this lecture were heeded by all men, the world would become a Paradise within a few generations.

The article on Initiation by Mr. A. W. Witt is of extreme importance just at this time because it clearly states and explains what true and REAL Initiation is.

This is of utmost importance just at this time, when we find that no less than five different Orders, calling themselves Rosicrucian, have sprung up within the last few years, and not one of these five has a shred of the true Rosicrucian teachings.

Some of them are deliberate frauds, claiming to be what they are not, while others are clearly under the guidance of members of the Black Brotherhood and their doctrines are absolutely destructive in that they uphold practices which are too abominable to even mention.

One of these orders, claiming to be Rosicrucian, admits that it has no teachings, that it is all ceremonies, when history tells us clearly that the Rose Cross Order was founded with the idea of leading men to their higher selves. In other words, while the Rose Cross has its ceremonial Initiation, its foundation is upon a training school for souls and its ceremonies are but secondary.

The lecture on the Second Coming of the Christ is also of great importance at a time when many false Christs are put forth for people to kneel down before, when in fact, most of these are not only false Christs, but are of the lower grade of humanity in as far as either Evolution or Development is concerned. Mr. Witt clearly points out what that Christ is and how He must come to all of us individually if he is to come at all.

Authority versus Individuality by Mr. Witt is also of great importance though it must NOT be understood that the Rose Cross school is against authority such as is held by church, state or institutions, for we clearly uphold the idea and doctrine, that so long as society exists it must be governed by those who are chosen to govern it and we do not in any sense desire to destroy authority, but rather to uphold it, however, we are also a school of Individualists and believe that the personality of the individual should be changed, transmuted, developed into an absolute Conscious Individuality. Thus the community would be a community of conscious Individuals, but ruled by one supreme head who also had become a Conscious Individual. Egypt in its glory, is an example of this state of Society and Government for at that time none could be ruler over Egypt except an Initiate who had also been crowned as King or Ruler.

Reincarnation, by Mrs. Witt, considers this extremely interesting and important subject from another standpoint than that considered by Dr. Kepperling and Mr. Wolf and this standpoint is as important as that taken or considered, by the Brothers.

Prayer is a subject thought to be so well known that no consideration is ever given it. But is it an understood subject? I think not, for I believe that the masses are totally ignorant of the meaning of true prayer, or what is the power of true prayer. This subject is therefore a timely one in an age when there is no longer any faith in the efficiency of prayer.

The article on "Body, Mind, Spirit and Soul" was one of the last lectures to be delivered. This paper became necessary about a year ago, when we found that but very few of even the advanced students understood the difference between Spirit and Soul, using the terms interchangeably. We hope that in this article the difference is made clear and that by referring to the article "A Soul Science Primer" and "The Great Seal of the United States" this subject will be fully understood.

"Invocation of the Hierarchies," by the same author, as the last article mentioned, might well be called "The Higher Form of Prayer," since it is really prayer as understood by the Masters but little understood by the vast multitude of those who consider themeslves students of the Mysteries. It deserves careful consideration. In fact, is receiving careful consideration, as we find that many of the Inner Students who are building their own homes are setting aside a room in the house and are modeling it for this very purpose. This article, therefore, deserves the most careful consideration as it is of the utmost importance to every sincere student.

The lecture, "The Fraternity Sons of Osiris," deserves more than passing attention.

It was prepared in 1906 by H .O. A. Under instructions of the Masters and was then but a prophecy. In 1908 it was printed in booklet form and copyrighted under title of "Immortality or External Death." That was the second step.

The third and highest step, for there are always three steps in everything that shall continue to live, was when the Degrees of the First Temple were conferred upon the delegates in the "Grove of Osiris" which had been especially prepared for this very purpose, and which is the first and only grove of its kind in the world at this time.

We are especially pleased of the happy culmination of this work at this time, for the reason that all its work had been kept secret, so secret in fact, that no one thought enough of it to steal the titles as used by the orders, and this had been in the minds of those who had the work in hand, knowing well that if they made the work as prominent as they had made the work of the Rose Cross Orders, members of the Black Brotherhood would as deliberately steal the name and palm off something which had not the slightest right to the title, under that name.

But now, after the successful issue of the work, after men from many parts of the world had taken part in the Sacred Ceremonies, we fell at liberty to proclaim the work to the world.

Before this volume will be ready for delivery another Convocation will be in session, as the work of the Black Orders has made this necessary so that we might protect the true work, and in due time a complete record of this second Convocation, will be ready for those deeply enough interested to desire it.

Before closing this Preface, I will comply with the request of several who had not the pleasure of being with us, and give an outline of

A DAY AT "BEVERLY HALL"

Those in the Hall are at liberty to arise at any hour they

desire, avoiding however, disturbing those who desire to rest.

As nearly every student has been taught the desirability of taking the morning cup of hot water in order to cleanse the system of impurities, and for the purpose of building healthy functions, hot water is served in the large sitting room at exactly seven o'clock.

Between this service and breakfast there is one hour, as breakfast is called at eight o'clock. No student in the Hall is supposed to enter either the dining room or the kitchen, any more than those in the kitchen are supposed to enter the private bedroom of a student unless especially invited to do so.

Breakfast for the student is a very simple matter, as we hold that breakfast does man but little good, but much harm. Usually breakfast for the student consists of either a weak tea, without the tannin, and dry toast, or weak cocoa and dry toast. Every student present is supposed to obey the rule of the house. They can, if they wish, ask for other food, but their marks of grade progress, record of which is held by the Master, is according to the manner in which they harmonize themselves with the rules of the Order. Nothing being forbidden the student, nothing refused him, but his or her marks being made according to the harmony as expressed by his or her acts.

After breakfast an hour of rest when social chats may be held, notes compared, walks taken.

At ten o'clock lectures are called and all are supposed to be present, and must be present, unless there is some good excuse for not being present.

After the lecture there is another hour of rest, the noon meal being called at twelve o'clock.

No meat is ever used at the Hall during Convocation time, and a noon meal may therefore consist of:

Whole wheat muffins and butter,

Asparagus with cream dressing,

Tomatoes, usually sliced with a wine-vinegar dressing,

Baked potatoes.

Simplicity rules here. The master of the Hall orders all meals and these are in absolutely correct proportion to assure strength to the body and mind, and purity to the blood, as well as the necessary material for the building of a healthy mind and an Illuminated Soul.

We hold, with many of the highest medical authorities in the world, that more people die from starvation because of overfeeding, than do from underfeeding. We aim at the Hall to have sufficient, but not too much. We find that many people are weak, ill-nourished, underfed, weakminded, neurathenics, because of eating too much food, this we try to correct, and demand that students obey the rules of the house. If we find that some one present is not in harmony with the Laws then he or she is given the liberty of bidding good-bye to the rest of the guests.

In the afternoon there is another session at which one or more lectures are given, following that, there is time for a walk before dinner and when fair it is found that all students desire this walk.

Dinner is a simple affair, possibly consisting of:

Soup

Egg plants—these being the meats of the vegetable kingdom,

Salads

Some kind of pulse.

No drink of whatever kind is allowed at either the noon or the evening meal as we hold that it tends to destroy perfect digestion. No deserts.

After the evening meal there is an hour of rest, after which the master of the house may take charge and answer questions or explain some of the Divine Laws. Arguments are not allowed, because of the fact that the student who asks a question is naturally not supposed to know the answer, and is supposed to accept the solution of the question, such solution being always in harmony with the Divine Law as taught by the Secret Schools.

Time for retiring is at nine o'clock, as we hold to the old law that man gets his most perfect sleep before midnight, while the best time to arise in the morning is with the sun.

All students are supposed to obey the rules of the house absolutely. If they are unable to do this for the short space of one, two or four weeks, the teacher certainly cannot have faith in them that they will obey the rules and teachings of the sacred instructions for the time they are away.

Moreover, the rating of the student will be according to his obedience while at the Hall, and his advancement will be in accordance with his obedience and the spirit shown in his obedience.

"Thou hast been faithful in a few things, I will make thee master over many," has direct bearing in this work.

Moreover, the student in the Mystic holds himself somewhat above the average person, but is he above the average person if he has not learned to obey the Divine Law in spite of what his own little personality might desire or wish him to do or to receive.

Oh yes, admittedly, we find some who wish to be catered to, who desire special notice, and who, not receiving it, feel deeply grieved, but these are in the minority, and these are of

THE SELF

It seems that the very hardest thing to overcome, the greatest enemy the student has is his little *self*.

Thus we find that out of every ten students who come to the Hall there are two or three whose bug-bear is this same self.

And how do we know this? Because these students watch every move of those in charge, and if they think that one student is receiving just a little more attention than they, they are hurt to the quick.

What these students cannot be forced to comprehend, is, that these things are within themselves. They cannot be made to understand that it is the little self within which wants attention, and the more conscious this self is, the more attention it wants, the *smaller* is the *true* man or woman within.

With the true student it is different. The true student has learned to forget the self, to him or her extra attention is UNDESIRABLE for he or she feels that others might be hurt by it. Such want only the truth, they listen attentively to what the teacher has to say and even if the teacher were to forget to serve them they would take it as a test, as a lesson, and would not feel hurt by it because it is only the *little* self that is ever hurt and not the true man.

It is these students who have forgotten the self and who come to the Hall, NOT for personal attention, but for what they can learn, who make the Masters. It is these who are willing to accept the crust of bread, the glass of water, and the hard bed, who are the Teachers of the people of the future, while those who must be constantly catered to are the slaves to themselves and *will continue to be slaves to others as long as they live.* The Hall does not desire these and they receive only the attention that littleness deserves, and in this way they can often be awakened.

From this it must not be understood that the student body at "Beverly Hall" moves about with long faces. The contrary is true, you cannot find a more contented, or more happy or more harmonious assembly of people anywhere in the world than you find at the Hall during Convocation time, nor are innocent amusements forbidden, but are rather encouraged, since we believe in the Masonic Rule:

Eight hours for work,
Eight hours for study and recreation,
Eight hours for rest.

On the other hand, students do not, and should not, come here because they think they will be catered to, because they imagine there is feasting, because they have the services of maids or valets, for if they do they will be sadly disappointed. They should come and meet with us because of the feast of knowledge, the good things of the Soul, and obtaining these things often means the denials of the pleasant things of the material for these can be had at home more easily than at the Hall.

INTRODUCTION TO THE GREAT SEAL

It is rather a strange and an unknown thing for one to write an introduction to a single chapter appearing in a book, but the conditions are so unusual as to warrant it.

More than a year ago, Grace K. Morey, the author of the article, "The Great Seal of the United States and Its Mystic Significance," prepared a sketch for a short primer of the Illuminati teachings, and in this sketch, as will be shown by the drawings, it was brought out that man is not only a threefold being, but that he is actually a four-fold being as well. In short, that when he has succeeded in reaching Soul Illumination, he is the completed Pyramid or true Triangle.

If the student will give serious study to the article on the Seal of the United States, he will find that on the reverse side of the seal which is as yet uncut, there is to be found the Pyramid, but with the capstone as yet not placed, and thus he will see that the Philosophy of the Illuminati is the absolute and undeniable Philosophy upon which these United States are founded as is clearly indicated by our four-fold philosophy, by the drawings representing our Philosophy, and by the drawings of the reverse side of the United States seal.

And thus it would appear that the Unseen Hierarchies which shaped the foundation of the great Republic which must some day rule the world, are the same Hierarchies which gave us the Soul Science Philosophy as taught by the Illuminati.

And now let us look into the future, not far, but just beyond the line. We find that scholars condemn the design of the reverse side of the United States Seal, that it has never been cut but has remained hidden as though it were something to be ashamed of.

However, though this appears the truth, it is not the truth. The reason why it has never been cut is because the time is not yet as the cap-stone has not yet been set.

And what is this cap-stone? My reader, prepare for a shock.

When Atlantis ruled the word, that which is now America was connected with Egypt by what is now Mexico, and in Mexico, in the territory of Yucatan, there is a Pyramid in which the Fire Philosophers worshipped God as Divine Fire and Life in like manner as did the Initiates of Egypt, for the two *were then one.*

America is not complete, and will not be complete, cannot be complete, until Mexico is *again* part of America as she was in the long ago, and when Mexico is once again a part of the United States, then will the cap-stone have been set on the Pyramid and the reverse side of the United States seal will be cut.

Thus you will see that the Soul Science Primer with its drawings, is but the beginning of the article concerning the Seal of the United States, while the article on "Body, Mind, Spirit and Soul" is the finale thereof.

May it not be long until the Holy Pyramid shall be completed and may it be completed without the shedding of blood.

Lovingly given,

R. SWINBURNE CLYMER.

"Beverly Hall," Quakertown, Pa., July 6th, 1916.

MYSTIC CHRISTIANITY

ORDER OF THE ILLUMINATI
SOUL SCIENCE PRIMER

"That you might have life, and have it more abundantly."

As there is an outer meaning in the teachings of Christianity, so is there an Inner or Mystic sense. Only those who live the life are able to find this Mystic sense and to understand the Christic teachings as they should be understood. Therefore, he who reaches Illumination must have passed through three degrees. These are:

First Degree: Purification.

Second Degree: Illumination.

Third Degree: Mastership.

"Seek and ye shall find, knock and the door shall be opened, ask and ye shall receive."

Were the Bible written in only one sense, and were it to be taken literally, then this admonition would not have been given by a Master teacher. It therefore follows that our contention is correct, and that there is both an inner and an outer meaning to the Scriptures.—Isaiah 29-11.

This Inner meaning is never taught openly. In fact, it was not so taught by Jesus, for did he not say: "Seek and ye shall find, knock and the door shall be opened, ask and it shall be given." Truly it was his desire that all men should SEEK for the truth, that they should so live as to be able to KNOW, not to merely believe as they now do.

Is there any more proof that there was an inner knowledge, a wisdom not given to all? Listen to what the Bible has to say.

Why speak ye to them in parables?

That is the question that was asked of Jesus after teaching the multitudes in parable instead of in plain language. Why, if he wanted the people to have the whole truth, did he teach them in parable? Did he not want them to seek for the truth and therefore to KNOW, instead of merely believing what some one taught them, which is belief but not knowledge?

To his disciples he said:

"To you it is given to know the kingdom of heaven, to them it is not given."

In this he shows clearly that though he worked for humanity, nevertheless he fully understood that the truth could not be given to all men, but that instead, the truth had to be given to the vast numbers in hidden language, in parable, while the mysteries might be given only to the few, and in this he followed his own teachers who taught that there was both an inner and an outer circle. That the few might belong to the inner while the masses belonged to the outer.

And this will effectively answer our enemies who accuse the Illuminati of being unjust and ungodly, because we hold that all truth cannot be given to all men, moreover, it proves that those who hold that the mysteries are for all men, have not themeslves yet found any part of this great truth, nor have they found the mysteries or been admitted to them.

Where is the kingdom of heaven? "The kingdom of heaven is within you."

Here Jesus taught the same doctrine that the Illuminati holds, namely, that heaven is not in some far off sphere, but that heaven is found within man, but that no man can find this heaven unless he reaches Illumination and finds the Christ within. This, then, is Soul Illumination and is taught by the Illuminati as a goal for which all mankind should strive.

"Except ye be as little children ye shall in no wise enter the kingdom of heaven."

To be as little children is to have faith. The child always has faith in those to whom it goes for help or instruction. The man or woman who awakens to the fact that there is something greater and deeper in life than the things that are apparent, should have the faith to follow the instructions of those to whom he or she goes for help and instruction.

Thus, if you appeal to the Illuminati for instruction along the lines of Soul Culture and higher development, have the faith, the manhood, to follow such instructions to the letter and if you do, then will you reach Soul Illumination, which is the kingdom of heaven within you.

It is the work of the Illuminati in its Soul Science instructions, to help all true seekers to find the Christ within, and all who faithfully obey will find this Great Within. If any one tells you that there are none to teach you, then call them anti-Christ, the mockers of God, for they then condemn the very things which Jesus taught while on earth.

"Art thou a master of Israel and know not these things?"—John 3-10.

In this day we find teachers of many kinds, some who call themselves New Thoughters, Divine Scientists, Christian Scientists, Meta Physicians and even some who call themselves of the Illuminati and the Rose Cross, but who say that no man has more spiritual knowledge than another. These are the true Anti-Christ, they are the Black Magicians, they are those who teach the negative philosophy which sends men and women to destruction. Beware of those who wear the Sacred Triagle with the two points up, because it means that the Spirit of God, the Soul, has been steeped into the earth, the material, and that thus degeneration, instead of regeneration, has taken place, it is perversion of that which is Sacred and Holy.

"Whoso readeth, let him understand."

It is not hard for men to read the letter and to understand the letter, but it is very hard to read the letter and understand, or *find,* the Spirit of the letter. Moreover, we of Illuminati hold, that none can find the mystery of the parable unless such have lived the life, obeyed the Law, and found Illumination, and until all men have reached this state of Illumination, the Illuminated must teach those who have not yet reached Illumination.

But there is a deeper meaning in this for us, namely, if there were not a spiritual meaning, besides the literal meaning, then Jesus would *never* have told his hearers that "whoso readeth, let him understand" and when we once come to understand that there is a spirit in the Sacred teachings, besides the mere letter, then we are well on the way to understanding.

"To them that are perfect."

This statement gives us the proof of two things: First, that some may be perfect. Second, that *not* all are perfect. If there were none perfect then Jesus would not have mentioned this at all, if all were perfect, then again there would have been no reason to make such a statement, therefore, common sense tells us that there are some who have reached perfection and it is given these to do great things and to teach great truths. No one man, it is freely admitted, has a monopoly on truth, but according to the statements made by Jesus throughout his entire ministry and according to the statements of every other great Master, there are those who have more of the truth than others and it is these who are to teach.

He who says that one man may not know more than another, thereby convicts himself of being in ignorance, and the Illuminati is not called upon to refute the foolish statements made by such. Moreover, by making the statement that no one can know more than another, then they themselves *claim superior judgment and knowledge for themselves,* since they claim to know that one man cannot know more than another man. That in itself is a great judgment.

"Ye Masters in Israel."

To be a master in Israel one had first to be master of his own interior Israel, just as to be a Master in this day, means that we must first gain mastery over our lower selves, and in this we find both the Great Work and the First Work. It is a work that may well stagger any man.

The companion command to "a Master in Israel" is: "Man, know Thyself." To know oneself is a gigantic task, and it is only when we begin to know a few things about ourselves that we begin to understand how little we really know of ourselves and of others. Be a master in Israel, for then you will be a master of yourself, and you will then know where the kingdom of heaven is.

"Straight is the gate and narrow is the way, and few there be who find it," Matthew.

This simply means the same as when Jesus told his hearers to be of *one mind.* To be of one mind is to take up some work and follow that work to the *exclusion of all else.* When we do that we are then living the *concentrated life,* and to live the concentrated life will gradually bring us to the Great Center, then we have found the Soul, man has become the Son of God.

Straight and narrow is the way. We cannot follow every ism, every doctrine, every dogma and every practice and reach the Center. That is diffusion. Diffusion *always* and *forever* ends in death. But if we follow the narrow Path, then we will follow but *one only* thing to the exclusion of all else. That is

Concentration. Concentration is Life and ends in Immortality.

In this day men are no longer masters, they are dabblers. They are not satisfied to concentrate, they must follow every ism, every creed, every cult and the result is that where you find one master. you will find a million dabblers. "Straight and narrow is the way, and it is only through *one* gate that you can reach Illumination, or find the kingdom of heaven.

"For now we see through a glass darkly, but then face to face."

The man of the flesh, the man of the world, the dabbler, can see only through a glass darkly. He has not concentrated, he has *not blazed the way,* therefore the glass is still dark, the material substance still hides the Fires within and everything is dark.

But as he gradually begins to *live the life,* as he burns up the dross of the material and thus cleanses the Soul *fires* within, the cloud upon the glass will gradually clear away; and when Illumination or Soul Consciousness takes place, then he sees face to face and he knows the Soul and all its beauties and he stands face to face with the *fires of God, which burn brightly upon the altar,* he becomes a Philosopher of the Sacred Fire.

"For a veil lieth over their hearts until the time of the Gentiles be fulfilled."

This veil is materialism. Materialism and unbelief, even a disbelief in the very existence of God has become so great that there is in man no longer any faith whatever. He believes in nothing, not even in himself and thus he sails over the ocean of life as does a ship on the seas without a rudder.

But the time of the Gentile is passed. Men are awakening. They are becoming conscious of the fact that there are deeper things in life than they knew, and it is the Illuminati that is helping the thousands to this greater awakening and showing them the way to real knowledge and a more sublime and exalted life.

Are you weary of death, tired of sickness and doubt, and do you wish to enter the straight gate to life more abundantly? Then here is the Way, Now is the time, and we are here to help you to the Way, the Life, and to the Haven of Peace. Let the Trinity of God, the Triangle with its point towards God and His heaven, point out the way to you.

Historically, too, the veil lay over the minds of "Lost Israel," the Christian nations, so they knew not their identity.

THE TRINITY

God	The Father
The Holy Ghost	The Mother side
The Son	The Christ Principle
Body	Physical Manifestation

MAN A TRINITY

Mind	The Builder
Spirit	The Life or Breath
Soul	The Christ Within
Body	The Base or Foundation

THE BIRTH

My little children of whom I travail in birth again until Christ be formed in you."—Gal. 5-19.

If as churchism claims, the Christ is an exterior being, a being who lived centuries ago and now is seated on the throne in heaven, what then of this Christ of which Paul taught that he had to be born within us? All things point to the one great fact that Jesus came here as a worker and teacher, that he lived, suffered and died in order to show mankind the way. "I travail in birth until the Christ *be formed within you.*" Surely nothing could be plainer than this. All who desire to understand may easily comprehend and thus the more readily come to find the way.

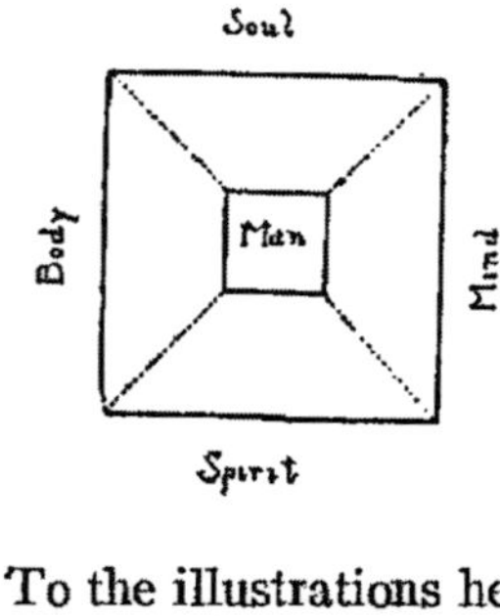

Man an Incomplete Temple

To the illustrations here given we can come to understand the threefold being, for here we are clearly shown the Trinity, but that man must be *four-square* before the Trinity can manifest in, and through him. The Jewish altar was four-square (Ex. 30:2) symbolizing a perfect manhood and typical of Christ the altar of his people, as our example of the shrine within each.

In order that the seeker after truth may the more easily and more clearly understand these symbols, he should carefully study the article on "Body, Mind, Spirit and Soul" appearing in the present volume, for with these symbols and the above mentioned article, he will have a complete and sane philosophy whereon to build his Immortal structure.

MAN IS A HOLY TEMPLE

Man, which is to say, Mind, Spirit and Soul, is the dweller in a house not made with hands which, if he will, may become eternal in the heavens.

"Ye are the temples of the *living* God." Thus said the great Master some thousands of years ago, but he simply repeated the statements made by other Masters centuries before him. Nor did he claim to have given this philosophy for the first time, for he was but a reconstructor of older philosophies as we are reconstructors of the newer Philosophies.

"Ye are the temples of the *Living* God," but see to it that you keep these temples in the condition of purity and holiness, for unless you do, God cannot dwell therein and other gods, who are not desirable will take possession of the building which should be dedicated to the one God.

The temple of God is the physical body, that which we call the man, for God and the Soul can manifest only through the physical, as the physical is the vehicle of God, just as our material houses are the structures in which we live.

We can Glorify God in body and in spirit when we keep the body clean and when we use the life of the body only in a constructive and true sense.

Jesus said: "Therefore glorify God in body and in your spirit which are God's." The body we all understand, but few know that the Spirit is the Life Principle, it is from God and is, in truth, God, and returns again to God.

We glorify God in our body when we keep the body clean and undefiled, when we do not use the body or any power of the body for the ignoble purposes and we bless and thank God, we glorify him *when we use the body and the powers of the body in doing some good work.* It is then we also glorify God in the Spirit, and we fulfill the Law according to Cor. 6:20 when we refuse to use either body or the *life principle* for anything ignoble, but use it for some good and noble purpose.

"The body is not one member but many."—I Cor. 12-27.

There are many members or powers of the body. That this is true, is proven by the fact that the different members of the body can be used for different purposes. Thus, the speech can be employed in defiling God and man, while other members of the body may be used in destroying the very Principles of Life which are within us and which would cause death to body and Soul.

"The Lord is in his Holy Temple, let all the earth keep silent before him."

All the earth is the material man, for the body of man is of the earth and belongs to the earth. But the Soul of man, the Christ when the Soul is finally awakened, is the Lord or God and it is He who is within His Temple. Then let the earth *obey the Lord its God* and man becomes in truth the Son of the Living God.

"Know ye not that your body is the Temple of the Holy Ghost which is in you, which ye have of God, and ye are not your own."—I Cor. 6:19.

Does man need any more positive statement than this to prove to him that when God speaks of the Temple, he actually means the body of man, and that this Temple holds within itself the Holy Ghost, which is the Love or Soul Fire from God Himself?

It is this mighty truth, mighty when once understood, that the Illuminati is trying to teach mankind, for we know, that once we can get man to really understand that he is in truth "The Temple of the Living God" he will no longer defile that temple but will gradually begin to hold it sacred because of that which dwells within it.

"If any man defile the temple of God, him shall God destroy, for the temple of God is holy which temple ye are."

This the Illuminati has been trying to impress upon the mind of mankind ever since its foundation just as the parent of the Illuminati, the Rose Cross, has been trying to impress on the mind of man for the past centuries. But it is only now that man is awakening to the truth of the statements made by Jesus two thousand years ago.

And still there are those calling themselves leaders and teachers, who say that man cannot be destroyed. That man cannot destroy himself, while Jesus and all other great Master-teachers have taught that if man defiles the temple he *thereby destroys himself.*

"Ye are the temples of the living God, as God hath said, I will dwell in them and walk in them."—Cor. 6-16.

IS YOUR TEMPLE HOLY?

Ask yourself this question time and again. Live the clean, the Exalted, the Constructive life, and ye shall know God and walk with him as did the men of old.

THE MIND

Mind is the builder of the Immortal Soul.

If mind be not built with Soul, then mind dies with the body.

Soul is subject to mind in earth life, because mind is the thinker, the builder, the constructor or the destroyer.

Mind builds the Soul, Mind builds the body perfect. But the mind which awakens to the truth, and then builds both body and Soul perfect, builds that which is Immortal and Eternal.

"Wherefore gird up the loins of your mind, be sober and hope to the end for the grace that is to be brought unto you at the revelation of Jesus Christ."

In this command we have the old, old statement, so often made:

"As a man thinketh in his heart so is he."

That which a man thinks in *his heart* he is apt to be guided by. Thus, if we believe in our heart, that a certain church is the right one, we will join that church in spite of everything, aye, even die at the stake for it as thousands have done. In like manner, if we believe in our heart that a certain system of living is the right one we will live accordingly and it is for this reason that the Illuminati is trying to teach a right system of living, an Exalted Constructive life, knowing that when it awakens man to the fact that the body is the Temple of God, and that a certain life is the true life, and when man truly believes this, then will he live accordingly, and as he lives, so will he grow, until at last he becomes the *son of the living God.*

Mind is but the builder of our immortality. At the death, there is no more use for the mind, because then the Conscious, Illuminated Soul takes charge of itself and there is use for neither the mind nor the body.

Both the body and the Soul are subject to the mind in the earth life, both mind and body disintegrate at death, leaving the spirit and soul to meet the consequences of the life lived, and happy is the man whose mind became awakened during his life on earth and thus was enabled to build the Immortal Soul.

Will your master mind, or let it master and mislead you to your destruction?

THE SOUL

The Soul is not yours but belongs to God. God gave you, as a part from himself, so that you might develop into an Individuality, a God like himself, and thus, in His likeness and imagery glorify him. If you obey the divine dictates, then you will thus develop, but if you do not obey the Divine Law, then gradually you must return to the God-head, only to be sent out again, but as an entirely new entity from which all the personality of your present unworthy self has been burned away through the searing fires of the Godhead. This is the eternal death spoken of in the Bible.

The Soul is a Divine White Fire. It is a flame within the body of each individual. In some very large and burning as a flame of white intensity, in others but a tiny Spark which is almost totally submerged with the material being.

It is not an individual entity unless you make it so. If you awaken to the truth that man is something more than skin and bones, a machine to make money through the ruination of others, and if you attempt to live the true life, thus fanning the spark into a flame, you may become a Conscious individual, and thus become Immortal.

But if you live the life as has been lived by man these many thousands of years, then you live only in the personality, the

Divine Spark is not at all awakened and you die as you have lived, ignorant of your Divine power and heritage, and this Divine Spark returns to the Godhead, enters the universal melting pot, and comes out a Spark from God to again undergo another pilgrimage, but without any personality at all. All of you is dead and buried because your life was not worthy of leaving an impress on the Divine Spark.

You had been given a talent by God, but you buried it and when the time of accounting came, even this one talent was taken from you. Will you awaken to the better life or are you willing to live and to die and to be forgotten even by God Himself?

Is your own personal Christ ever to be in crucifixion upon the black cross of the material life, the life of the earth? Are you willing to believe that Jesus was willing to die in order to save your unworthy soul, while you do not make a single effort to free the Christ within you and elevate Him upon the Throne? This is a question for you to decide and upon the decision hangs your Immortality or your Eternal death.

"The Soul that sinneth it shall die."—Ezek. 18.

That has been the Divine decree. It was the fiat cast by God the Father when He created Souls, and neither He nor anyone human power, nor any power in creation can set aside that fiat.

You cannot plead ignorance. You have the power of choice. God has said that He dwells within the temple, but only if you purify it. If you do not make it a fit dwelling place then God cannot dwell therein and if He cannot dwell therein, then it follows as a certainty that the Soul has sinned, and is sinning, and the Soul that sinneth it shall die. Thus speaks God in thundering tones to be heard by all.

"What doth it profit a man if he gain the whole world and lose his own soul."—Matt. 16.

Here again we have the same statement, clearly indicating that we may so develop the mind, the powers of the mind, and physical efficiency as to control the whole world, but that even though we thus develop body and mind, we will still lose our own Soul unless we develop that Soul also, and here is answered those self-constituted teachers, who, fearful of losing a following if they teach the truth, deny that the soul can be lost.

There shall be many teachers in these last days, but most

of them are false prophets who come not to lead man from destruction, but, who, in order to gain their ends, lead man to destruction, and many of these even go so far as to clothe themselves in the clothing of true teachers in order that they may deceive the masses and thus the more easily lead the masses estray and to their destruction.

"The Soul that sinneth, it shall die." That is the Divine Fiat, but there is no necessity to meet with this destruction as it is not so very difficult to find the *right* way and to live the *true* life.

All those who seek and who will but obey the teachings of the Illuminati can find this way and will quickly came to understand the Law which will lead them to Life and Immortality.

"And the Lord God formed man out of the dust of the earth and breathed into his nostrils the breath of life and man became a living soul."

The soul is not given to man at the time that conception takes place, but at the time of birth.

The body is formed by the mother, through the seed planted by the father. The mother fashions the body as she wills, and at birth, when the first breath is drawn in by the child, then it is that the Divine Fire is also drawn in.

While the body is fashioned the mother in her secret laboratory can do much towards the perfection of the body, and towards the preparation of that body for the influx of a great Soul, but it is at the moment of birth, just before, and during, the time of actual birth that she can, holding a Divine Mantram, a Great Soul Desire, draw into the body of her child, a mighty Soul. Here is the secret of genius, the secret of THE RECONSTRUCTION OF HUMANITY. It is this mighty secret that the Illuminati would teach to all humanity and thus people the earth with mighty souls instead of with ghouls and vampires.

"Hear and your soul shall live."—Is. 5-3.

Herein again is indicated the great fact that the soul which will not hear, which refuses to obey the Divine dictates, shall not live. In these words we have repeated the Divine Fiat, "The Soul that sinneth it shall die."

The sense is a little different, in that it indicates clearly the possibility of eternal life to all souls who will heed the command and live the life, for such souls shall live, and when God says they shall live it means that Eternal Life—Immortality shall be its reward.

Have you a Soul? Can you answer that question? It is easy to believe that you possess a Soul, but do you *know* that you have one?

Ay yes, we well know that many teachers will tell you that man cannot know absolutely whether he has a Soul or not, but these speak not from knowledge, but from ignorance. They are the false teachers and prophets which abound in these days and will lead you to the endless death if you listen to them.

THE SPIRIT

Spirit is the unseen form of man, the breath of his life.

When the child is born, and when it takes in the first breath, it is the Life Principle, the Spirit of God, that it draws in. This Life Principle it continues to draw in all during its life. It breathes in, it breathes out. Always, like the tree and the flower, it draws in the breath of God.

At the end of life on the earth plane, when the lungs no longer take in any air, then the rest of the life principle leaves the body, and as this is truly the spirit of the father, the link which holds Body and Soul together, it, the Spirit returns to God, while the Soul, if it has become awakened, goes to the next plane of existense, but if unawakened, it also, like the Spirit, returns to God, there to be revivified and again sent out to try for Conscious expression and Individualization.

In God it is the Holy Ghost, or Mother side, and in the universe it is the flowing floor of the worlds, the sustainer, for without it no life could exist.

Mind and Spirit, (breath) united, build the Soul, for without mind there could be no building, while without Spirit or Life there could be no Mind.

God is a Spirit in that He is the very principle of Life, the Life-Giver. It is God which gives Life to all things, because God Himself is Life.

"The Spirit of man is the candle of the Lord."—Prov. 20-27.

A candle is usually a light giver, thus we have it that the Spirit is the Light giver. For instance, without air we cannot have fire, because there could be no combustion, in like manner, without the breath, which is the life, man could have no Light as the Soul could not exist without the body, while the body cannot exist without the life-principle.

"He that ruleth his own spirit is greater than he that taketh a city.—Prov. 32.

This is an actual truth. Health, strength and power depend entirely upon the amount of the life principle we take in and use. In the Higher Knowledge this is called the AEth. If man so trains himself that he continually takes in enough of the *active* principle of life then he will have health, strength and all power, and this may become so great that he needs but little food, say one full meal a day while he can do for days and nights in succession without sleep and still retain his full strength. He, therefore, who can rule his spirit, that is, take in sufficient of the life giver to sustain himself in health, strength and power, is greater than he who taketh a city, because he who taketh a city might not be able to take enough power to sustain himself in health and strength, and what does the possession of a city amount to, with him who has neither health or strength with which to enjoy his possession?

"Take not thy holy spirit from me."—Ps. ii.

In all times the truly wise have recognized the desirability and necessity of possessing a healthy body and a strong mind, and thus it was that they constantly prayed to God for more of His sustaining and life-giving power. But we of the Great Schools not only Invoke the Father for such Life-giving power, but we have learned to draw in this Holy Spirit, or AEth power as we need it.

"The letter killeth but the spirit maketh alive."

In all things it is recognized that it is the Spirit, the life-giver which is most desirable. We now recognize that in the Sacred writings there is an inner meaning, the spirit, which is of greater importance to both ourselves and humanity than the mere letter, however, important that letter may be, and the Illuminati is attempting to teach mankind the spirit as well as the doctrine.

Has mankind not read the Bible by the letter long enough? Consider the state of mankind, universal conditions as they now exist, and you will find the answer as to whether mankind has profitted much by living according to the letter.

A TRULY MYSTIC SEAL

THE GREAT SEAL OF THE UNITED STATES AND ITS MYSTIC SIGNIFICANCE

Most Americans have a dim idea that the Great Seal of their country shows an eagle, a constellation of stars, an olive branch signifying peace, and a set of thirteen arrows which probably means war in case of necessity, but few have ever seen the reverse side of the seal or even suspected its existence.

Nor has the reverse side ever been cut, a strangely restraining hand having seemingly been laid upon every attempt to bring it before the public. When the large painting of the reverse side which was ordered made together with the familiar obverse, for the government display at the Chicago World's Fair, was to be hung, those in charge exclaimed: "What a peculiar design: Why were we given this inartistic symbol?" and once more the white stone was rejected, the painting was turned face to the wall and only the obverse side displayed.

But the time has now come when the full knowledge of her seal shall be made known to her people, for America must henceforth stand before the world as its teacher, leader and the promulgator of a new and perfect system of ethics, religious leadership, a citizenship that is efficient and free, a just industrial democracy, and a justice and generosity to other nations that shall emphasize the brotherhood of man and the Fatherland of God.

Late in the afternoon of July 4th, 1776, the new Continental Congress "Resolved, that Dr. Franklin, Mr. J. Adams and Mr. Jefferson be a committee to prepare a device for the Seal of the United States of America." That committee was identical save for the omission of Robert Livingston and Roger Sherman with that which had drawn up the Declaration of Independence. The Declaration had been signed about 2 o'clock in the afternoon, and Congress desired to at once complete the evidences of the independence of the United States by formally adopting an official sign of sovereignty and a national coat of arms.

The arms of England, the mother country, expressed the union of Judah's lion, with the unicorn of "Lost Israel" in accordance with the Science of Heraldry, but the young republic had finished with thrones and crowns and must blaze a new path through the forest of liberty, which should express her descent from all christian nations and hold open a door for all other races which should seek help and shelter upon her shores.

A knowledge of heraldy was considered a part of an education in the early colonial days, and it was through William Barton son of the rector of St. James Episcopal church of Philadelphia, learned in heraldry, and through Baron Prestwich, of England, that the designs expressive of American destiny were given and drawn. Yet other dabblers in heraldry failed utterly to understand the mystic meaning of the seals. Professor Charles Elliott Norton, of Harvard, regretted its lack of art, and complained it could never be other than a dull masonic emblem, while a Mr. Wilson, considered a great historical scholar, declared the reverse side "in very bad taste, unintelligent and commonplace, and if it can be laid away and kept in the dark why not keep it so!" Even the constellation of thirteen stars came in for criticism, as "very bad heraldically."

Again and again the pyramid with the white cope stone and the glory, were rejected, until in 1916 members of the Rose Cross Order, Illuminati, and others of the six pointed star of the seal, hung it officially in their class rooms and declared it as expressive of their philosophy-religion; the Bible wisdom of the common people rather than of the collegian.

In the two sides of our seal are expressed in heraldry countless ages of the evolution of man, from the time of his so-called fall, through his progress in Egypt (eagleland), where for a time a wondrous race incarnated to build astounding monuments, receding, but returning again as the Hebraic Confederation to receive the knowledge of ancient Atlantis in the shade of its ancient altar, the Great Pyramid, uniting in a blaze of glory in the building of Solomon's Temple, parting, the northern tribes to leaven, though lost to history, all Europe, Judah and part of Benjamen and Levi, returning to hold Jerusalem until the Master Jesus should be born, journey down into Egypt to the ancient altar and receive light yet left in that land of darkness.

"In that day shalt there be an altar to the Lord a pillar in the midst of Egypt, upon the borders thereof, and it shall be for a sign and a witness unto the Lord," said Isaiah. It is needless for learned historians to tell us, who hold the records, that the Great Pyramid is but six thousand years old, for we know it to have been built when the morning stars sang together and the "Sons of God" shouted for joy, in that far Edenic period, when Atlantis the mighty stood in her purity, where in part America now stands. Built at the center of the earth, as a temple of the highest initiation, symbolic of a perfect man, foursquare in body, mind, soul and spirit, with its white copestone, symbol of complete immortality, it represents the measure of the earth, as well as that of the universe, and the evolution of man through those countless ages of reincarnation now drawing to a close.

Thither the Atlantians went for instruction in its galleries and rooms at the hands of mighty priests of the Priests of Melchisidek* and Osirian Brotherhoods, and throughout the succeeding ages those who would attain self mastery have turned their footsteps toward the ancient centers.

"The last Cumaen Song now comes," wrote Virgil, who prophesied that a race should arise which would be offspring of all races and bring to an end the ages of iron (war) and usher in the Golden Age. Hence it was fitting that the mottos upon the reverse side of our seal above and below the pyramid should be taken from Virgil, "Annuit Coeptis," "Prosper us in our daring," and "Novus ordo seclorum," "a new and select order," which many of us have now the honor to have entered, and whose door we hold open to all who will accomplish the spiritual work necessary.

"The day of freedom dawned upon the earth."

---

*As this book is being printed, we received information of two Associations using the title "Order of Melchizadek," or like it. One is a Spiritualistic body and the other a pure fraud. Neither body has the right to the title as this belongs to the Magi, who has used it for unknown years. Any body of men claiming, or using, this title does so without any authority and they are *not* members of any Order of Melchizadek. "Given by order of the Royal Fraternity Association, Incorporated."

And the infinite cycle of Atlantis was begun anew," wrote a poet, of the American Republic. In Central America there yet stands a companion pyramid, key to the connection of Atlantis, Egypt, and now American Atlantis rising again upon the great cycle. Hence Arcane and Magian learning which is the source of the Bible, could give no other symbolism to the young republic, than that of the ancient pyramid, its copestone and glory, significant of the descent of the New Jerusalem, for the one side, and the eagle, and the ever repeating thirteen of Mansasseh, thirteenth tribe of Israel and the son of Joseph (the Britons) who was separated from his brethren in Egypt, in the parting asunder of northern Israel from southern Judah, and first to cross Europe in search of the "isles afar off," to re-establish the ancient throne of Israel at Tava in Ireland.

Turning the hitherto rejected reverse side of our seal to face the people of these United States, we remind them that they are called to a Great Work as offspring of all races, a mighty Mannasseh, whose history began in Genesis and culimantes in America, and by whose stripes the whole world must be healed. Joseph, our father, married a daughter of a priest of the Temple of On, in Egypt, we are told, and today one pillar of that ancient Temple stands in London, while its mate stands in New York. These are reminders of our connection with Egypt, with all Europe, and with our father, Joseph, as an Anglo Saxon culmination of all Israel, and that through our union, between those pillars must all the world pass into Ephraim, or Shiloh, the Millenium to which Ishael alone of all nations looked forward and by the measure of whose twelve tribes the whole earth was apportioned.

"The whole Bible is written in the stars, both the law and the gospel, while estorically the entire story of man is set forth upon the sea of Manasseh. The obverse side is Israel in the Old Testament, the Reverse is the offspring of all Israel under the New Covenant, as the hope and outcome of Christianity. The two sides reflect each other and cannot be separated being the Bible in its most condensed form, summing up all old world history in twelve tribed Israel," says Professor Totten.

Long ages before the discovery of America, Merlin of King Arthur's court wrote of our constellation of thirteen stars:

"When the cock (France) shall woo the Dove (America)
Mother and child shall cease to love (Rebellion of colonies)
When the cock (France) shall guard the eagle's nest (France's aid)
The stars (our constellation of 13) shall rise all in the west
Then seven and six shall make but one (E Pluribus Unum)
The Lion's might shall be undone."

The stars upon our seal are set in the form of a six pointed star or a double triangle. This was anciently called Solomon's Seal and was embroidered upon the curtain of the Temple, which hung before the Holy of Holies. At each point of the star was placed the symbol of an Order which set forth Arcane wisdom, and no man might pass into the Holy of Holies save he had mastered the learning of these Orders with safety to himself, because of the Presence upon the altar within.

Today in America we have the restoration of this knowledge in these six Orders, the Order of Illuminati, Order of Rose Cross, Ancient Order of Alchemists, Fraternity of Osiris, The Magi and AEth Priesthood.

The especial symbol of America, aside from the pyramid and eagle, is the white rose, identical in meaning with the white stone. The constellation of thirteen stars was in early drawings set in a wreath of white roses, showing that the early designers knew the future of American individual spiritual development. It is now drawn set in white clouds, but the white rose is ever the symbol of the American Rose Cross Order, and stands for spiritual attainment.

Solomon's Temple was the Temple of a perfect man, and the Bible tells us of a three cornered cope stone which was rejected, but later became the headstone of the corner. We hear too in Genesis of Joseph, the keeper of the "stone of Israel," and it was with the Magian or Holy Grail teachings that the Britons crossed Europe to Arsareth, Land of Betrothal (Esdras 11-13 Chap.) in search of a land where they might keep God's worship pure and undefiled. Hence through Joseph, who was separated from his brethren, we inherit the white stone of all Israel, cope stone of the pyramid, and of Solomon's Temple, that rock upon which Jesus reminded Peter, he should build His church, the rock of spiritual unfoldment within each individual, that the gates of hell (death) should not prevail against it. My little children of whom I travail in birth again until Christ be formed in you.—Gal. IV-19.

Thus it was in keeping that an Englishman, Master of Heraldry, should give to the young republic, in the midst of its struggles to separate from the mother country, the design for the Great Seal, which should express the whole future of its work as a world teacher and exponent of the Christic teachings of the Holy Grail.

The All Seeing Eye, looks down upon the ancient pyramid, which too symbolizes America and all she must mean to the world, out of a glory, sign of the descent of the New Jerusalem. This emblem, the eye, is as old as man's appearance upon earth, being found upon ancient Chaldean monuments, Egyptian and Greek, while the Arabians looking upon it named the Highest and Holiest name of God with hushed voices and whispered, "I am that I am." The triangle about the eye, stood from the most arcane times as the emblem of the Trinity, of Osiris, Isis and Horus, Father, Holy Ghost and Son, as they stand today with us, and in which is sealed the law of the eternal three of the universe and of men as its highest product. "I will guide thee with mine eye.—Psa. 32-8.

Although writing is as old as Atlantis, and Adam, the only legend set in the Great Pyramid is esoteric, in numbers, measures, and weights, and in them may be read the ages just completed, and the prophesy of those yet to come. Of these great ages each with its leader as set forth in the application of the legend to the "Stone Kingdom cut out without hands," the greatest of all was the Master Initiate Jesus, who became the Christ, who descended into the grave and rising ascended Master over death, into heaven before the eyes of His disciples. Him especially and the return of the Christ Age, does the white cope stone represent, and after Him America as exponent of His teaching and life. America now prepares to become the headstone of all the world's ages when God in the Christ shall descend to crown the edifice of human liberty and immortality completed, and once more the morning stars shall sing together and the "Sons of God" shout for joy."

Architecture, mystic numbers, heraldry and the heavens themselves are telling the great race in America of their destiny and responsibility. As the head, body and limbs of the great image, made of different metals represented each Messianic age, a new truth, and an empire directly relating to some manifestation of that truth, so must America represent the white stone, a nation fashioning itself until it shall have obtained the *Messiahship* over all nations, overshadowing all that has preceded it. This cannot be accomplished until each citizen shall throw aside the veil which lieth over his face, shall no longer see through the glass darkly, but face to face, when Judah shall no longer vex Israel nor Israel envy Judah, but prepare to come together into that land which the Lord has given them for an inheritance forever.

The time has come spoken of by Isaiah, the prophet, when though the learned cannot read the book because it is sealed, nor the unlearned because he is unlettered, yet shall the book be unsealed, for the ancient wisdom applies to the individual and his following of the Christ in his quest of the Holy Grail, in the drinking of the cup of unselfishness, of his love for his neighbor and the stranger within the gates of our own Ellis Island, that the stranger may grow to the light of this republic, or carry its torch to other lands.

Each fortunate heir of this glorious inheritance must seek the white stone which crowns the pyramid, within himself, in body, mind and soul, the Holy Trinity of each Son of God. Then may America realize her destiny as a city set upon a hill, a star that shall never go down, and the world ruler that shall call down the light of the New Jerusalem upon the battle scarred earth, the Christ to rule for a thousand years.

Go ye therefore and teach all nations.—Matt. 28-19.

OUR CODE OF ETHICS

FOUNDATION FOR A CODE OF ETHICS FOR HOME AND SCHOOL

TEACHER AND PARENT

"The worst possible waste of time and money," said Emerson, "is to spend them off the line of your career."

There can be no greater work than God's work of moulding souls for a better life here, and a life of immortality hereafter, and there can be no better opportunity for undertaking that work than that found in teaching and parenthood, while to slight this all important work, or to turn aside from it when once trained for it or having entered parenthood, is to write failure across your life's fair page, to lose your own life lesson. Teaching and parenthood, may not be confined to merely the schoolroom or family for the true worker applies the trade learned to all children wherever encountered.

REVERENCE FOR THE CHILD

A child is a soul enrolled in God's school of life. The dull, defective, or criminal and immoral, born under unfortunate conditions, fighting blindly upward toward a far gleam of light, hampered by poverty, squalor, and unfortunate environment, are as precious in His sight as the daintily cared for darling of welcomed birth and refined surroundings, for Heaven cannot be perfect until all have reached it.

Recognize each child as of God, for of such are the kingdom of heaven. See the Divine Spark as the light that is hidden within, and realize that it will not fail to flash out when kindled from the love and purity in the heart of the teacher or parent. Look for the spark and wait patiently for the flash for as you measure out love so shall it be returned to you. Love can be firm but just, compelling respect and obedience, but eventually all will be love, the necessity for the sterner qualities retiring to the reserve force in the background.

Prizing as jewels the innate qualities of love and teachableness in the faces looking up to us, we shall, as teachers, cultivate within ourselves reverence for each small personality as expressing the sacredness and value of a gift from God to us and the nation, as well as of the gift of life to the child from God.

The child is not a chattel, nor merely one of a mass to the true teacher, but is an individual, and heir to a glorious republic, life and immortality. Therefore, teacher and parent will appeal to the child's higher sense and spiritual self, with confidence that he will respond to the appeal as one on the same plane, and with the same sense of honor and understanding.

The beautiful things of life such as poetry, or the necessary things in study, such as mathematics, will never be given the child in punishment, for that is the negative method of teaching, but the giving of these to learn for the love of them and in the sense of doing a loving act for the teacher or parent will unfailingly arouse the love of the child for these studies, inculcating a sense of the beautiful and the exact.

Love is the Throne of the Universe, and the ethical guide of all its movements, as it sweeps on to a far off event. Our own inner light is lighted from the altar before that Throne, and it behooves us to keep it shining and pure, illuminating our faces, if we would find instant response from the newly born souls, which look up to us for guidance in daily tasks.

Warnings of the strongest nature have hedged in the parent and teacher regarding our care of these little ones. Commands that we despise not these in our charge, nor is it the will of the Heavenly Father that one of these perish spiritually, yet we are commanded not to spare the rod when all else fails, lest the child lose its way, but remember to temper justice with mercy. The sense of justice is strong in a child's inner life and will practically never fail to respond to an appeal.

We are exhorted also by holy writ, that wanton leading astray of one of these little ones, should bring upon adult heads a punishment so severe that it were better a millstone were hung about his neck and he were cast into the sea. "For their angels do always behold the face of the Father."

HIGHER IDEALS IN TEACHERS

A continually increasing demand for teachers of higher ideals is noted by observers of the trend of public thought. The life of a man or woman leads outside his or her own schoolroom is becoming of more and more importance to the taxpayer.

His religion has little to do with the life of a teacher as a rule, the separation of religion and ethics having been made many centuries ago, but the ethical and moral standards of the teaching body is coming rightly into the limelight of public opinion. Teachers who are in the profession for the money there is in it, or because it affords them a refined method of earning a wage, or because they have been forced to earn a livelihood in some way, will soon be relegated to the background, for they invariably lack the love for the child, and the patriotism required for the best needs of the nation.

Moreover the life of the teaching force led outside their work is to become of more interest to the taxpayer in future. If a teacher is daily instructing students in a clean and righteous habit, is he living up to the standard of his instruction? Is he lecturing to or punishing boys for the cigarette habit, and indulging in a quiet smoke himself when the building is out of sight? Are women teachers preaching simplicity in dress and themselves appearing at school functions in garb suitable for an evening reception? Are they teaching the evils of slang, gossip, and the misuse of the English language and indulging in these misdeeds themselves when off duty?

The educational system is sacred to the United States, and its strong foundation stone, therefore the educational staff is dedicated to a holy work and will more and more be required to live up to the ethics of that work.

Nor will the parent fail to regard the school building as sacred to the coming generation in their use of it as a neighborhood center. His conduct when in the building, the language he uses while near it, his tone in speaking of it before the child makes part of his citizenship. Teacher and parent must work together in upholding this bulwark of the nation, the public school. All schools should be public. No greater menace faces this country than that of a class educated apart from the ideals of the republic.

NEIGHBORHOOD CENTRES

The organization of neighborhood centres, Parent-Teachers' Associations and Mothers' Clubs, should be of inestimable value to the work, as it brings the people together having the same interests, gives backing to the educational staff, brings the staff and parent together, and induces co-operation and neighborhood education in cities, as well as in the country districts.

Under this head might come the "Little Mothers' " classes held after school where girls are trained by a nurse or physician in the care of younger children. This is especially recommended in crowded districts in cities, where poverty makes little mothers a necessity, and the instruction should include correct bathing, dressing and general care of infants, diet and the serving of meals, cleanliness, hygiene, study of food values and combinations for young children. Here also should the warning against giving young children coffee or strong tea be sounded, as well as instruction against the eating of heavy meats, and the knowledge of nerve value to the healthy child, and its destruction by the cigarette habit be thoroughly inculcated.

Classes after school in which courtesy and good breeding is taught and illustrated should be held by either the teachers or some mother appointed from some of the neighborhood organizations. Here the child should be trained to meet the awkward age which often leads to much embarrassment and suffering. To pass the child through this period with its attendant evils and with its plastic, formative era, by drill in gentleness of speech, and mannerism, courtesy to elders and ladies, is to serve both the child and nation in the most practical way, for it gives the public a graceful and attractive boy or girl whose gentle breeding wins half the battle in finding employment.

Here should be discussed the cigarette habit, gum chewing, slang, evil report, slander, vulgar tongue, and debasing thought in firm but gentle leadership, drawing out opinions from the children as far as possible. When a child once expresses himself along right lines he is apt to struggle to live up to it before his mates.

A thorough handling of the cigarette habit, and its destruction to the nerves, as well as to self mastery, and the danger of thereby setting the various diseases upon the system, or opening a way for numerous ailments should have a prominent place in these classes in courtesy.

Emphasize the teaching of the Holy Temple, and its clear windows the eyes, as the shrine of the Day-Star, from on High, the soul, and the fact that we are always angel guarded and are never alone, under the constant watch of the angel presence, a child who knows of this guide will be twice on guard, where not knowing he will be careless and slip into temptations.

Thus the soul is twice guarded in the child's mind, and he assumes a personal responsibility for his own share in the work, for the unseen is very much closer to the child than to the adult who has allowed the mind to overwhelm the spiritual things of every day life.

The careful teacher will steadily hold the students to the lessons learned in the classes in courtesy, in the matter of opening doors, offering seats, handing books or other objects with grace, lifting the hat, allowing a lady to pass, or the acknowledgement of the lifted hat on the part of the girls.

Practice in the above as well as in table manners, church and public etiquette, should be held in these classes, and will prove a delight to be looked forward to as well as an instruction. A play written and enacted bringing in these courtesies is recommended.

EUGENICAL INSTRUCTION

Much discussion pro and con has been indulged in as to the advisability of giving this instruction in public schools. No satisfactory arrangement has so far been reached, and there still remains the child whose home environment is such that no instruction can be received, who attends no church where spiritual education might be given and who becomes a menace to his mates.

These should be under the instruction of a mother or father chosen from the Parent-Teachers' Association for that purpose, one in whom the Association has full confidence. Failing to secure such the instruction should be by the principal or a teacher according to the sex of the student. The surest way and most effective method of eradicating disease is strong and sane instruction along these lines while the child is young and impressionable.

PERSONAL RESPONSIBILITY

Personal responsibility is the keynote to strength and true manhood and womanhood. Coercion, however, along these lines will develop antagonism and a non-interest in right living. Hence the subject must be presented to each pupil as though he were a rational human being, thus appealing to his pride and subjective self and innate sense of being, varying the language to suit the age of the student. All the years from the cradle to adolescence are of supreme importance in setting the habits of thought and character. During these years the child must be made to understand that he is here for a purpose, and that life is a glorious opportunity to grow toward God and that all thinking and acting along right lines will develop a power which is to be used only for good. To be positive for all that is pure and good and not half hearted in attitude, will bring greater trusts given into his hands. He cannot be trusted with great responsibilities until he has demonstrated that he has been faithful in small things. Each individual is a free agent to build for himself a strong, fine character, but he must realize that no one may build it for him, although they may show him the way. In his own hands he holds a glorious future, to make or to mar, for life here and hereafter, transforming himself from weakness and inefficiency into strength and self-mastery. It is the way of the cross, with many stumblings along the path, and many backslidings, with heavy burdens, which are to be made light, but the goal is ever above us, and though the cross be heavy we shall find that a crown of self-respect, responsibility and the friendship of our fellow travellers goes with it. The student must be reminded that man is but little lower than the angels, and he is set a lesson here in which to conquer life problems, for a reward of angelhood in an existence to come.

Choosing the cross we gain the crown.

CLEANLINESS

"Cleanliness is next to godliness," is a familiar saying, and to be clean in body, live in the cleanest way possible, and upon the cleanest diet, and to think the cleanest thoughts is a part of the building of an immortal soul.

It requires concentration of mind, observation, application, determination and will power to maintain cleanliness within and without in the daily habits of life, but the result is health, and success in place of sickness, poverty and failure, for these are first stepping stones to a successful life.

The outside world judges us at a glance by our neatness in dress, precision in small details of bathing, cleanliness of the hands and fingernails and condemns or approves without waiting to look into the inner life.

But we must regard the body as a holy temple in which we are living for awhile, never forgetting that life has been given us as a blessing and an opportunity to grow toward God, and that heavenly home whence we came. Hence we will keep this body, or temple, clear of rubbish and dirt, healthy and pure by frequent bathing outwardly, and by pure thoughts inwardly, for we owe this in account with our souls, the precious trust given us.

Beautiful well kept houses are never surrounded by rubbish, straggling hedges and tumbledown fences. The condition of the window panes, the front door and the neatness of the children who issue forth from a house, set the seal of neatness or slovenliness upon the mother of the family. So is it set upon the personality of the student in his daily dress and habit of neatness. Neatness is not overdress or display, nor is it rags and carelessly made garments, but simplicity and perfection of the whole.

A clean, wholesome and pleasant habitation is absolutely necessary to the environment of that precious gift of God, our soul, hence we will beware of our outward appearance lest it indicate a decrepit inward condition.

SIMPLICITY

Plain living and high thinking was the rule of the Pilgrims from many lands who formed our educational system, and upon which the safety of this republic rests. Forced to live in an unpretentious manner, there sprang from them some of the greatest statesmen of the world, who have helped found this mighty democracy. Lincoln was a rail splitter, and Grant the driver of canal horses, Franklin came a penniless lad, and Washington enjoyed the simple country life of his Mount Vernon farm.

Let us jealously guard each rising generation that it may

not drift away from simple habits, which pave the only way to true happiness, health and a well spent life.

Late hours, heavy foods, show in dress and entertainment, lead but to mental, moral and physical breakdown. To surround ourselves with useless bricabrac, expensive today, and valueless tomorrow, to load oneself with flashy jewelry whether it be costly or cheap, to crowd our homes with expensive furniture of doubtful taste, and to entertain lavishly and showily either within or beyond our means is by no means the ideal set for the citizens of this glorious country which is the climax of the ages.

Laughter and play and innocent amusements are a part of true development. More joy may be found in amusements which draw out the wit, tact, alertness, courtesy and originality of the child than in the very questionable forms of entertainment, to such as the growing child is now frequently subjected. Heaven is all about us if we will but throw off the earthly trammels and look for it. It is in the simple white dress of the girl graduate, made by her own hands, in the neat suit her brother earned in which to stand beside her, in the pride of the father and mother, who realize the early lesson learned of self-dependence and in the hearts of the teachers who see the school doors close in June behind a class well fitted for the work of the world.

The sensible and patriotic mother will aid the educational staff of the schools in holding the children to these high ideals of one standard for all, poor and rich alike. That will mean no select parties will be given to which some class mates are not invited, and which promote jealousy and ill feeling. It will mean that the wealthy parents will not display in any way upon graduation night, with a profusion of flowers or gifts, which may cause heartburnings among the less fortunate.

In some schools a middy blouse and plain white skirt make up the dress of the class for the girls, and the calling of autos for the students or the use of them in bringing the students is discouraged. Walking is healthy, and heartburnings are unhealthy, but no more so for the good of the nation than the effect upon the child of daily habits of indolence and inaction in regard to outdoor life.

Presents and collections for principles and teachers is to be discouraged at commencement time, because the tax upon the less fortunate at that time is in many cases at the highest point, and here again the pride of the family and heart aches of the children offset any good the gift might accomplish.

Let simplicity be the keynote of every educational institution, and more especially of those select and private schools to which are sent the children of the rich. Upon these fundamental principles of brotherhood and equality rests the safety of the nation, as well as the work she must complete for the rest of the world.

THE DIGNITY OF LABOR

Each star in the universe has its appointed place and work. Each tree and flower, each animal and bird, each ant and bee labors in its way and in keeping with its sphere. Then there can be no drones in the human family in God's School of the soul; brain and hands must be occupied, for the brain worker needs manual labor to balance the strain upon his nervous system. Let none expect to live in idleness upon the work of others, nor think he has the right to eat unless he has earned it in a legitimate way.

"Labor is a fire of purification through which all must pass," said Carlyle, "and in which mental and physical poisons are consumed." Satan is ever busy finding mischief for idle hands, and the sooner all are trained to some profession or trade, and the knowledge of the value of the trade the sooner will Satan lose his oldtime occupation.

Let each man and woman go into training for some definite purpose or work that shall be of benefit to the race and earn a livelihood for themselves. The day laborer if he give honest work for honest wage is as important to the country as the millionaire who works at his desk early and late that great industries may furnish honest labor for the workman or safe investment for the capitalist. The laborer is worthy of his hire and he has a God given right to live comfortably. Brain and brawn combined may move mountains but the two must labor together for the good of both and the well being of the nations. Something for nothing cannot be the basis of well-being in this or any other country, but the workman must earn his wage, and know his trade.

Patience and persistence in small tasks bring a reward of greater trusts. Work regulates the world, creating order out of chaos. Do not expect happiness except through tasks well done. Work never hurts us, but the worry of an unsettled and fretful mind, combined with hard labor is the serpent in Eden. We must be proud and glad each night that we sink into a delicious sleep brought about by a day of faithful and honest labor, that has entitled us to an honest wage. "Do with thy might what thy hand findeth to do."

At "Beverly Hall," even during the sessions of the Sacred College, the dignity of labor is recognized.

You will find the master of the Hall, even though all the responsibility of maintaining harmony amongst the units, giving his attention to the various departments of the place just as if no strangers were present. You will find him, early in the morning, on the chicken farm, overseeing and actually working, so that every fowl and every chick may be well cared for. You will find him, even before breakfast, looking after the welfare of the beautiful collies in the kennels.

But more than this, you will find him giving personal attention to every personal letter that comes in so that every student in the field will have personal attention, during the time of the sessions, just as at all other times.

Further than this, he believes that no man or woman should be a drone, a parasite on society in general, and, very often, there are no servants at the Hall but he selects such of the delegates as he knows have reached a stage of true development where they can understand that, in order to serve they must first serve, and these he selects to look after the Hall, the dining room, even the kitchen, and, while these give good service, for they do their work in love, nevertheless, there are often, as one can well imagine, some amusing incidents connected with this Love service.

Labor done in Love brings a bigger and quicker reward than the human parasite could obtain by following the highest Invocations for an eternity.

When men and women, boys and girls, are taught that there may be real pleasure even in hard physical labor, then will one of the problems which have thrown former great civilizations in choas, be solved.

IMAGINATION

Imagination is mind at play, builder and destroyer of all form in the realm of mind. We go to sleep reveling in it, and waken to at once take it up. That it may be working an injury we never consider, hence, unless reason and a determined will control it it drifts at will among the shoals and rocks of fear, pride, grief, disease, accident, the worst forms of evil and degenerate thought, bringing death to the soul and body.

The student must be impressed with the danger of allowing the imagination to drift idly, on negative or evil lines, and aroused to the necessity of being master of this most important adjunct of youth.

From the earliest days of childhood to the age of twenty-one, this faculty must be guarded with a strong hand, for these are the important formative years.

The student must be taught that there is no time in the short years allotted us to let the mind drift at will, but trained to hold it under control every moment in beautiful, pure and holy images, or those of strength and uplift.

Let him understand himself as a complete immortal spirit, in dominion of mind and a glorious birthright, bound to control at will his thoughts and image-making.

"The thoughts of youth are long, long thoughts," their dreams are far reaching and have a lasting influence upon the whole after life, because the delicate tissues are plastic. Beware then of the sort of imagery for which the mind is used, for by it a man or woman may be made or ruined. Death or invalidism, poverty and failure may be wrought by this faculty, or glorious achievements, mighty orations, splendid possibilities or dreams come true.

Be masters of imagination and not mastered by it, thus becoming a blessing to all mankind, inspired and using powerfully, for good, this gift of God. Every achievement of man was first brought forth in his imagination before he wrought it in reality. God has given in every soul His own image, therefore imagination must be considered a holy thing, and of mighty soul building power.

FAITH

It has been said that with faith we may remove mountains.

To become what we desire to become we must have faith in ourselves and in our priceless heritage of free will to become a son of God and all it implies.

Every great scientific discovery, or invention, every building, painting or piece of sculpture was produced by faith in the ability to accomplish. Faith is the substance of things hoped for, the evidence of things not seen. It is by faith we create the visible out of the invisible, and by it we overcome selfishness and subdue all bad passions. By faith are we brought in touch with purity and love, lifting us upon firm ground above the temptations of our appetites and passions.

Faith in our at-one-ment with God, in our sonship of the Father, builds the soul into the image of the Divine Father, kindling the fire of His love in our hearts toward our fellow students and associates in every day life.

Faith in ourselves, gives us faith, too, in the homeless, heedless, friendless and outcast, for by faith in ourselves we realize that these too are sons of the same Divine Father as we ourselves. It leads us, too, to search for the Divine Spark in the unfortunate, to see that the light yet burns and to attempt to fan it to a greater brightness through kindness, sympathy and faith in the forlorn, thus instilling faith in themselves, and an ambition to rise again for another trial of life's opportunities and responsibilities.

APPLICATION

Be faithful every moment with all the power that is in you to the duty that lies next at hand. "Do with thy might that which thy hand findeth to do," is an ancient precept.

It is an impossibility to live earnestly, work faithfully and live continually with one object in view without gathering power for yourself. Every victory gained is that much stored up energy and personal force conserved for use in the future. Resist every temptation to omit your faithfulness to the duty at hand, work, study or play, and undreamed of strength will be yours.

MEMORY

Be masters of memory, using it when you desire and as you think is for your good, and never allowing yourself to sink down under unpleasant thoughts. The art of forgetting is one to cultivate, when it aids in removing depression. Change unpleasant thoughts and memories for pleasant ones of other times, thus changing your mental condition from despondency to happiness. Bird songs, happy days in the open, pleasant happenings, substituted for nagging cares soon bring you into a cheerful frame of mind. Concentrate all your will power upon memory exercises, for building habits of mastery in study, work and leisure hours. Retain memory's treasures, and reject all that harms, depresses and injures the mind, for eventually they will build the soul and character.

All have memories, unpleasant, pleasant and of indifferent value. Most dangerous, however, are those of impure stories, words and deeds. The sensitive mind of youth struggles often in vain to be relieved of them, and devils thus retained are steps downward. Face such with determination, and put them behind you, by substitution of pure and holy remembrances, and gradually the brain cells will respond and cease to repeat them. Beware of receiving new ones into the brain, of this character, Be master of memory and not allow it to master you!

HONOR

"To thine own self be true. Thou canst not then be false to any man." Honor and self-respect are inseparable and a part of the soul itself, a part of the personality. Our word once given, must be kept, a promise to perform, an act must be made good, and a controlling sense of what is right, just and true, be an integral part of ones dignity.

The finest sense of honor is constituted in care in performing acts for the neglect of which we would not be punished, or the neglect of which would arouse little or no criticism. Such care is a most important asset in character building. A character so built attracts high consideration and respect from all beholders, because of its chivalry, and knighthood, high-mindedness and nobility.

Stealing, lying, deceit, have no place in the makeup of the honorable man and woman, boy and girl. Each little lie, each small infringement of the code of truth, leaves a gate open by which greater error may enter, and sets a hard look upon the face, and a shifting expression in the eyes, the soul's windows, that he who runs may read.

Take care that one can steadfastly gaze back into the questioning eyes of parent, teacher and friend, and never be compelled to drop the eyelids because of some inward unworthy thought or memory.

Let us keep ever in remembrance that our mission here on earth is to build for immortality, and that the Soul intrusted to our care for building is the most precious possession we have, and honor is the soul itself, its defense and shield. To violate ones word of honor, or pledge of integrity is a deep disgrace which will bring us a bitter reaping in years to come, by opening the way to greater violation of all that is sacred and holy in our personal temple.

COURTESY

Hand in hand with honor goes courtesy. Good breeding is expressed by the courteous recognition of the rights of others. Whether our courtesy is appreciated by a smile or thanks from those to whom we offer it or is passed carelessly by without recognition, does not concern us. Our duty is to ourselves, for our own character and its building concerns us far more than lack of appreciation from those with whom we come in contact.

Nor will we criticise those who thus fail in courtesy to us, remembering God judges them and us. It is ourselves alone we must look out for.

It is the little things of every day life that count most in character building, and good breeding. The hat removed in the elevator, or in the presence of ladies, and older persons is obligatory upon the builder of a fine presence and personality.

To remain seated in the presence of ladies or older persons, to fail to offer seats in street cars, the churches, or other public places, to selfishly fill the air about us with tobacco smoke, offensive to the average woman, to eat peanuts and throw the shells around in public, to chew gum in the face of the inoffensive and innocent fellow passenger on a street car, or other public vehicle, to talk loudly, use slang, boast, whistle and sing, expectorate or eat lunches in an offensive manner injures the perpetrator of the unmannerly offense far more than it does the silent endurer of it, for it leaves an indelible mark upon our courteous habit of life hard to eradicate.

Here must we be absolutely selfish and look out for the future of our whole life, lest we later present an awkward, ungainly appearance and person much to be dreaded by all well bred society.

The girl who fails to thank the gentleman for the seat tendered, door opened or acknowledges the little courtesies of hat lifting or favors offered fails in her duty to herself far more than the boy, guilty of discourteousness for woman is the finer of the human race, and with her the race falls or rises. She has twice the responsibility, and dignity of position in the case.

HABIT

Be master of your habits and not mastered by them. Watch jealously each creeping thought or act that it be healthy and of good report lest an evil habit crystalize itself upon you. Character is completed habit, and you will fail or succed in the same ratio as you master thought habits first, and then put into physical habit. Aimless, careless thinking is degenerating to both body and mind, while a lax irresponsible mind will imagine itself to be the victim of circumstances which it created and for which it must suffer the consequences.

Carelessly leave some gate in your mind ajar, and your most valued forces will pass out, which you may need at a crucial moment. Habits of allowing opportunities to slip away will finally prevent any more coming your way. Force your mind by daily thought to build right habits. Mind is all powerful, but it is but a machine by which we grow habits. It is but the boy's mind which leads him to take up the detestible weed, tobacco, which wreaks a first terrible vengeance upon him, and then by his persistence, conquers his physical resistance, and settles itself upon him as a habit which wrecks his nervous system, and his self mastery.

The nerves are the electric wiring of the body, subject to every play of thought. Tobacco drugs them into insensibility, and later opens the way to every disease. More deadly as a habit than alcohol, because more insidious, it fastens upon the child through her mind. Right habits of thought inculcated in the perilous days of adolesence and before, form a wall of resistence when under temptation all through life. Never say you cannot control a thought, forget an injury, avoid interruption in necessary duties, that a good thing is an impossibility or that you cannot accomplish a task set before you or break off a bad habit you find you are forming.

Mind is a machine, given us to build a perfect life and an immortal soul. Let us see to it we are masters of that machine, and not allow it to master us. Let us be transformed by renewal of our minds.

THE MIND

Man is possessed of a soul, spirit, body and a mind which ordinarily rules over him in his personal kingdom. Mind must not be allowed to thus usurp man's throne, for while we are to regard mind as important, and its training as necessary, we are by no means to bow down blindly before mentality as a god. Overmental development is a dangerous thing leading to crime, unbalanced judgment, self conceit, insanity and an undeveloped soul in the life to come.

Ancient philosophers likened mind to water, because it was never at rest, therefore mind must be subjected to our will, and guided and held firm for good, lest it run away with us through our imagination and the senses which are ever at play upon it.

Concentration along stated lines of study is the best method of controlling mind, and making it subject to the will of the owner.

THE WILL

Each student should realize that he is possessed by a Divine will and also has a will of his own. His own will must be in harmony with the Divine will, guiding him through trust in the over ruling Divine will, but his own will must dominate his impulses, desires and imagination in order to keep him in tune with the Divine will.

A weak will does not exist, but a will may be obstructed and damned up by fear, desire, grief and selfishness. Convincing the child of this obstruction allows his will to flow into the will-stream of the Universal will, and is the sure way to accomplishing all good, while keeping the will strong.

Aggressive, forceful brute will, never wins in the end, but the deep, calm, steady flowing will, wins eventually. Apart from God our wills are powerless for good, but will and interest united to God redeems the world and works miracles of Divine power. Let teacher, parent and student determine to be at one with the Divine will, and there will be no such word as "fail."

Consider each obstacle merely a test, putting all your mind power behind your will, saying ever I will, and not "I hope to."

CONSCIENCE AND THE SOUL

There is a still small voice within each of us, which speaks to us when we do wrong. It is the voice of intuition or the voice of the soul, and it is more than that for it is the voice of God speaking within us to warn us of our Divine origin, our subjection to the treacheries of a carnal mind and our pilgrimage through earth life in quest of the completion of immortality.

We cannot hide from the voice of conscience, for the soul is the living, immortal part of us, but we can stifle it, deny it, and refuse to listen until it grows weaker and weaker, and its light dies out of our eyes. If we persist to the bitter end the Divine Spark, which was given us from God, will die out and return to Him from whence it came, leaving us little above the animal kingdom.

Soul or conscience has been called subjective mind, indurance to the strong, objective mind of the brain. To each of us it is the Christ crucified within ourselves upon the cross of the daily temptations of life. It is the most priceless gift of God, and daily we abuse, and subject it to indignity.

But if we steadily learn to listen to the little voice it will grow stronger until it controls our lives, and we become more and more like God. We must think of it as a pure white flame burning upon our inner altar. We may feed it with pure and holy thoughts, and it rewards us with untold happiness. All the powers of the body center at this white shrine within us, which sends out the warning when we do wrong. Will, imagination, anger, fear, hate, love, evil thoughts, unhappy memories, spiritual laziness, play upon the mind which builds or tears down this holy flame, the soul. The soul and conscience are all love, for God is love, hence the little voice is one of love, God's own daily protection over us, speaking directly down to us from His mighty throne.

Conscience is the voice of the angel of the shrine of the soul within us. We will guard that angel that it may never leave us until we follow it to the gates of heaven itself.

JUDGE NOT

Judge not, for through the workings of the Great Law God takes this task upon Himself. We cannot know what individual weakness may cause our brother to stumble and fall, nor is it for us to decide when unfortunate inheritances or physical weaknesses bring suffering upon ourselves through another, what especial form of punishment shall be meted out to the offender, that is God's work, and we wisely assume the attitude of a spectator, knowing the Great Law of compensation never fails to act.

Each must reap his sowing, and although we may help or advise, or protest in a kindly way, we must remain silent as to pronouncing judgment, and refrain from the carrying out of revenge. If one seemingly more fortunate in worldly position or wealth, reviles and scorns us, attempting to push us from the path of progress or attainment, forget not the spectator's attitude of calmly looking on, but return good for evil, remembering that we ourselves may have committed the same fault toward another, and this is but our reaping, while as for this offender, the Law never fails.

Each victory won, over self in such a trying time, builds strength for us and makes the next trial easier. Revile not, either those who offend you or those who prove false to all that is holy, for tomorrow may see you lying in the same ditch of wrong doing as the fellow traveller who so offends.

In His own good time God judges, and in His own way he meets out justice with the same measure we have measured it to our fellows.

AS YE SOW

God is a God of love and not of hate, although He has been called a God of hate, because by the breaking of His laws by man, the inevitable punishment descended upon the human race.

God cannot be bought, and neither can He be hired to forgive. He punishes no one, but He does not prevent the working out of the laws which we set in motion the moment we commit an evil act toward another or toward ourselves.

The Great Law of "As ye sow so shall ye reap," acts in several ways. For example: ordinarily we must pay the penalty for a wrong done another, but there are wrongs we may commit which we find it impossible to right. To offset these we may instead perform some act of kindness for another, thus lessening the penalty of our reaping for the evil we were unable to make right. If we give a note for borrowed money, the day will surely come when that money will be required of us, but in life's lessons we may pay out the note by faithful work, in this way offsetting the debt of wrong doing when it becomes due. Thus we gradually learn to guard our tongues from evil and mischievous speaking, our minds from evil thoughts, our eyes from evil sights, and our souls from harm. This is the foundation of the technique for self mastery, patiently to be acquired in daily life. God's lessons are given each hour to learn. Master them patiently and bravely, and as we cheerfully work out each wrong done another or forgive those done us we grow daily stronger. As we progress each good act performed for the wrong we have committed is passed to our credit by the Recording Angel who watches over us all. It is worse than useless to waste time in censure and bitterness toward others, but rather let us reflect and determine if we had not earned the reprisal received for some act committed thoughtlessly against a fellow being. The law never teaches "An Eye for an Eye," but rather "overcome evil with good."

GOD'S LITTLE ONES

The animals, birds, flowers and vegetations are God's little ones who devoid of power of speech and subject to man, and of another plane of existence climb the ladder of evolution below us.

To man they look up as to an elder brother, and on man they depend for their well being and very existence. Man has been so untrue to his trust that the birds of the air fly in terror before him and the innocent brute creation regards him as an enemy. This is because he has needlessly maimed, hurt and destroyed them. Thou shalt not kill, applies to the animal creation as well as to the human race, for man has little need of animal food, nor does he gain by useless experiments upon the helpless bodies of his fellow creatures. For every deed committed against the denizens of the lower kingdom, wantonly, cruelly, and idly we pay the price in a mark set upon our faces, minds and soul.

HELPING OTHERS

Because the Great Law of "As ye sow" is absolute, and just, and because all men reap only that which is due them, should not prevent us from helping others when in need or when requested to help them.

Our full sympathy must go out to that fellow traveller upon the path with ourselves, whose ignorant sowing or unfortunate mistakes have brought a bitter reaping. All help given to others is that much credit passed to our account with God, thus paying some of our own debts which otherwise we might not be able to pay save by supreme suffering and loss.

Often it may be that the best help we can extend to our neighbor, is to help him to help himself. To think for him, find him work, or to see that his self respect and personal responsibility is not injured by our assistance. A kind word and a sympathetic glance often go much farther than actual physical assistance. At no other time will the inner Spirit so plead with you if you but listen to it, than when you are confronted, with opportunities to assist those in your intimate surroundings, who are struggling with the dibilities, of mistakes, sickness, poverty, humiliation, sins or lack of will power to help themselves.

To listen to the inner voice of conscience, to act upon the good advice it gives, is to become one with God, and to know God's law. Every instance in which we conscientiously do this, enables us next time to meet the case with surer judgment, with less self questioning and embarrassment.

> "Who gives himself with his alms feeds three
> Himself, his suffering neighbor and Me."
>
> —Brotherhood in Charity.

ADOLESCENCE

A new light in the eyes, a fresher bloom to the cheek, unknown delights and dangers, awkwardness and self consciousness in the boy, with moods and tempers in the girl. Dreams and imagination, lack of vim in study and work, mark the entrance into the danger zone of sex consciousness.

But at no time will instruction concerning the soul and all it stands for be so well received and be so necessary as at this age.

God cannot send souls into the world without the help of both men and women. Men must become industrious, clean lived and pure to become good fathers. Women must be patient, self controlled and chaste to become good mothers, and the greatest, most sublime work men and women can engage in and the work which brings them nearest to God and makes them His co-worker, is that which brings them together in holy love, and which rears around them a sacred home, shelter for the little children which they bring up in His name.

The love between man and woman is holy, and on no account will we listen to play, story or speech which drags that holy love in the dust, neither will we look upon any picture or book, which belittles or betrays holy and pure love, for to do so would be a danger to ourselves and a disrespect to those parents to whom we owe obedience, and who have in love built our earthly temples and kept them so faithfully in sickness and health, a lack of respect for ourselves.

The soul is the shrine of love, within the temple of the body, it is of God, and the Christ within ourselves, and can only reach perfection through keeping the body in the highest state of purity and cleanliness through obedience to God's law.

Each morning looking in our mirror we may tell, by the soul-light in our eyes, whether we are keeping the shrine pure, and each evening we may review the day, and note whether the mind has kept guard over its temptations. Woman's whole life is bound up in love, she is its custodian and keeper of its shrine for the whole human race. She is man's equal in every respect save strength of body, but she is his superior in the spiritual qualities that guard the home, the race, and the soul. She is supreme in her own sphere.

GIRLS AND BOYS

In the girl's hands rests the most important part of the nation's future. At the earliest age possible this responsibility should be impressed upon her.

Her dignity, the gentle whiteness of the soul she has been given to guard and keep, must be taught her.

In the pairing off and foolish mating ideas which begin to appear by the eighth year, experience shows the girl is much more to blame than the boy. She early forgets the simple comradeship of school life, and becomes the temptress.

The teacher and parent will take the matter strongly in hand at the first appearance, reprove any silly conversation going on among the elders, or joking on this most serious subject. Plays and entertainments that lead in this direction must be avoided by the child, and her mind kept fully occupied by study, play of healthy nature and work .

The average very young girl has too little to do. She must begin some form of helpful manual labor at the earliest possible age, and all tendency to avoid steady occupation and responsibility for some part of the household machinery be combated steadily by the parent.

Neatness, daintiness, thoroughness and purity, self respect and self reliance are fundamentals of girl character.

That she is the finer side of the human race must not be forgotten, and that she owes herself, dignity and respect in order to expect it at the hands of her boy playmates. Hence she will doubly guard her lips and thoughts that no taint may come upon her girl's purity and self respect. To lower herself in the eyes of boy companions is to inflict upon them an injury, and upon her sex a disgrace. Woman's importance begins with the earliest years, for no nation ever rose higher than its women. She is the race barometer, and with her purity, and cultivation along right lines nations stand or fall.

BOYS AND GIRLS

Teacher and parent will combat insensible efforts made to pair off the children by foolish friends and classmates, keeping ever the comradeship, and brother and sister idea and influence in the foreground.

Sweethearts naturally are attracted to each other by the time the students have reached the age adolescence or shortly before. Any undue attention called to mating, or undue forcing of this subject upon the attention of the children must be met with strength and determined opposition, for the healthy child mind must be kept clear of this subject until well formed, and the habit of clean thoughts and right action be well set.

Guarding the mind from evil stories, and words, the memory from the impression of evils recorded, must be impressed upon the child in these years before adolesence, that a firm foundation may be laid for this trying time of unknown and little understood temptation.

The holiness of the body, as a temple of the soul, the free will of the owner to make or mar its purity must be strongly set forth by the parent or teacher. Personal responsibility for the white soul entrusted to the child's keeping, will be readily understood by the child, and it will see at once the need to preserve this shrine from vulgar words and acts, or evil influences by which it may be surrounded.

The boy will see that the delicate girl comrade is to be reverenced by the stronger playmate. She is to be protected, helped over rough places, shielded from evil words and acts, by him as a guardian of all that is good and pure. Mentally she will meet him on his own ground, but physically he must realize his strength and never use it against her, but only for her protection.

All natural and healthy childish amusements which bring out the originality and self development should be encouraged especially before the age of adolescence, in preparation for the new consciousness of sex difference which arise about that time. Speaking and spelling contests, games which give pleasure and teach strength of character, and healthy rivalry should be planned. Keep the mind occupied, when not engaged in study, thus Satan will find less occupation.

SWEETHEARTS

The time of happiness and dreams, jealousies and self distrust, must be met firmly, and the whole attention of the student held as far as possible to his own personal responsibility and development for a life work quite regardless of the ripples of friendships, and their attendant pleasures and pains.

Discussion with them in private classes or individually, of the bases of all cosmic force, and its God-like purity, its dangers, and their own free will in the matter to make or mar their own lives. Plain talks upon the wonderful privilege of a home of their own, barred and banded from the outer world in holy love, must be given, emphasis being put upon the fact that where love is not, there can be no lasting foundation, and that to marry without love is to drag the holiest gift in the mire, hence each girl should be taught to train for an independent self supporting life, that she may never be tempted to marry for support alone, for convenience, or for wealth.

The dignity of woman, and her importance to the world, her duties as a mother or assistant to some other mother, is vital. That she insist upon her dignity and self respect when with boy companions, in a sensible manner is the surest way to win esteem from the opposite sex, as well as to teach them the spiritual superiority of woman.

Boys will never attempt familiarity with such a girl, or to smoke cigarettes in her presence, be rude, or careless in language, invite her to a questionable place or play, if the girl stands steadfastly for her own dignity as a habit. This does not mean a stiff, and stately demeanor, calculated to freeze all life and gaiety, but rather a protecting inner shell built about the person which shall shield through all fun and recreation, any approach to the debasement of the love force and holiest shrine within each student.

Through these lessons we prepare them for the time of motherhood and fatherhood, its responsibilities and pleasures, and by which they become co-workers with God, in the rearing of immortal souls for His kingdom in heaven.

"For have I not a right to be as wholesome and as pure as she,
Who thro the years so glad and free, moves gently onward to meet me."

—True Knight of the 20th Century.

THE BROTHERHOOD OF MAN

We have been pilgrims of the night, but we may make our way a path of light. Brothers and sisters, children of the one Father, we climb together the ladder upward to Him who gave us the glorious opportunity of life.

There is no other way to reach God and Heaven save by individual effort, and the building of an immortal soul by daily self conquest. In God's sight one child is the same as another, and He loves all alike. If we are on different rounds of the ladder it is because of our own weakness. There are as many mansions in Heaven as there are conditions of men on earth. We are our brother's keeper in every sense of the word, for his well being is bound up with ours, his sorrows prevent our complete happiness. If he is sick, poor, out of work, or suffering from his bad habits it is our duty to assist him with a remedy as far as in us lies, or as far as his self respect allow.

Each of us is a citizen in a glorious country, destined to lead the world to freedom, truth and light, but that leadership cannot be attained if a part of the country's populace is poverty stricken and ignorant, or lacking in the self respect which makes for true manhood. All nations are represented in our public schools. Their representatives are here by God's decree to learn the most wonderful lessons given any nation. Revile not the stranger for God has sent him to us, and he is not only our brother, but the stranger within our gates. Therefore he is doubly sacred and in need of our aid and patience. America stands for the coming in of the Christ age, and by the stars and stripes of our flag shall all the nations be healed, through the teaching of the brotherhood of man and the Fatherhood of God. We must learn brotherhood in the strongest sense of the word, sharing with the stranger his every triumph over the difficulties with which he is hampered.

"Love one another as I have loved you."

CITIZENSHIP

"Humanity with all its fears
With all the hopes of future years
Hangs breathless on thy fate."

America is the dream of the ages, foretold by all great prophets, sages, poets and philosophers as the Shiloh of rest to war worn nations, the Manasseh of Israel who should prepare the way for Ephraim, the Perfect One, the Golden Age.

Our pilgrim fathers fled from a despotic government to brave the savage and the untried wilderness in quest of a land of liberty, and here they established a Plymouth Rock of religious freedom and moral culture. They have been followed by millions of the down trodden and oppressed from every nation under the sun seeking also liberty, light, education and a better life. Ellis Island is the coming Plymouth Rock of America.

The whole world now turns to America as the leader in commerce, mental achievement, democracy and the one nation alone fitted to give the much needed religious leadership. But before she can guide the waiting nations to a just industrial democracy, to respect for science and expert knowledge, to an art that is beautiful without danger of decadence, to free citizenship that is also efficient, to a system of internal dealing that is just and generous and to a firm understanding of ethics and religion that shall be lasting we must first demonstrate our self accomplishment and mastery of these much desired qualities, and that can only be accomplished through a perfect educational system that shall include individual spiritual development beginning with the home, the parents, the teacher, and above all, the child.

Where other nations have attempted to force their culture upon the world by war and conquest, America must first demonstrate that she herself has acquired one worthy of imitation and before she can convince the world that the unhappy religious question of all ages is capable of a happy solution she must stand a living example.

Each of us bears upon his shoulders this responsibility, and each child is a foundation stone in the temple we rear, and of unexampled importance. If America fails, the world declines into darkness, for she is the light of the world. If we fail in our duty to ourselves in the building of strong personality and Christic character, we fail in our duty to our country and she suffers accordingly, and we fail again if we neglect the foreign brother and sister and his offspring within our confines.

Each must accept the situation as a holy trust from the God of the nations and each be ready to establish a strength and clearness of sight within himself that shall enable him to lift the burden and carry forward to completion the principles of justice and equality for all, which the fathers planted at the founding of this republic, and which was emphasized by the mystic seal in its pyramid and copestone, its eagle symbol of freedom, and its constellation of thirteen stars, the statue of liberty in New York harbor, and that other figure, standing upon the capitol at Washington, which, with drawn sword, faces the east, whence anciently came all that wisdom which shall henceforth be the peculiar property of America.

America is divinely appointed of God to teach the world the meaning of the white stone, or the spiritual kingdom within each man and woman, which shall be the healing of the nations, and which makes for true brotherhood under the law of the Divine Fatherhood the equality of man and woman and the recognition of woman as the highest spiritual human representative.

God gave us the privilege of being born in this glorious land or of having adopted her as our mother-land. To be unfaithful to her and the principles upon which she is founded is to be unfaithful to all that is high and holy within ourselves and to God.

Let us reverence then, as sacred, her stripes which shall heal the nations, her stars that shall lead them upward to God, her patriots that have suffered for her principles, and tread in their footsteps by conducting ourselves with the dignity befitting a citizen and voter of the mightiest nation the ages have yet seen.

Fathers and mothers that now are, and mothers and fathers yet to be, each bears in his forehead the mark of personal responsibility for this country of light and hope, that shall bring the world to a knowledge of God and His laws, and the immortality of the soul, the Christ within, and peace.

"We are heirs of all the ages
Foremost in the ranks of time."

Go ye therefore and teach all nations.—Matthew 28-19.

SIN

The student who is earnestly seeking first principles and fundamentals is confronted with great confusion of thought in the religious and philosophical world of today. In addition to the principle religious institutions, there are hundreds of sects, cults and religious societies, every one claiming to teach truth, and yet every one using terms differently; so that the student is bewildered by the multiplicity of conflicting opinions and interpretations. All this confusion may be traced to lack of proper understanding of Divine law and to the fact that most of the misconceptions are based on theory and not on real knowledge.

The question of sin is an all absorbing and important matter for the reason that every individual every minute of the day and every day of his life is confronted with it. From the cradle to the grave we are called upon to make correct decisions as to our conduct; and as conduct is inseparably bound up with the true understanding of sin, we will be better prepared to cope with the problems of life, if we first grasp the fundamental meaning of sin.

What is sin? We will understand this question better if we arrive at a better grasp of our relationship to God and his laws. As Man is an integral part of the universe in which he lives, and since the universe is the image held in the mind of God, Man lives, moves and has his being in the mind of God. God is love, *the all,* life and law. We know God through the love that is in us and by the visible manifestations of harmony, law and order which governs the universe. We cannot conceive of the universe without associating with the thought—law, harmony and order. If law and harmony did not exist, chaos would prevail. From the study of nature, the consideration of planetary systems, and our observations of life from the simplest to the most complex forms, we arrive at the conclusion that law and harmony is the fundamental basis of creation. In reality there is but one law. God is one and *the all,* and there is one law that prevails in the universe. It is the law of love. All other laws are but restatements of this one law of Love. Every phase of life manifests this law. We speak of the attraction of atoms for each other. This is the expression of this law on the lowest plane of life. There is one God, and there is one law. And God and the law are the same. God is the law, or God is love.

We speak of the ten commandments of God. But in reality these laws resolve themselves back to one law, the law of Love. For, if we love, we cannot hate, we cannot steal, we cannot lie, we cannot defraud and we cannot commit adultery. To love, or to live in accordance with the great law of love is to fulfill all other laws. God is love, and love is life. Therefore to love is to live and grow.

All rules of conduct are merely the different aspects of this one law of love. Therefore our problems become simplified if we measure every thought and every act by the one great law of love. Love is the standard of the universe. All thoughts and acts of man that conform with the law of love are desirable and in harmony with the Divine Intelligence, and all thoughts and acts that are contrary to the law of love are undesirable and inharmonious. Therefore all thoughts and acts that are contrary to the law of love constitute sin. Our one great law is love. If we think and act in accordance with love, sin will have no place in our being. But whatever we think and do that does not measure up to the law of love results in sin.

When one loves, he will not kill, he will not harm others, he will not hate, he will not be angry with his brother, he will not be envious or covetous. How helpful then is the understanding of this great law in the solution of right thinking and right doing. We cannot go wrong and commit error or sin if we love.

Sin may be considered from another aspect. All thoughts and deeds are either constructive or destructive, positive or negative, up-building or down-tearing. Love is positive, constructive and up-building. Therefore, any act or thought which does not conform to love is of a destructive and negative character and constitutes sin.

The question of sin is based on the understanding of Divine law and not on man-made law. It is possible to break man-made law (if not based on Divine law of love) and still not be committing sin. Thus if priestly custom forbade the healing of the sick on the Sabbath, if one violated this law, one would not be committing sin, for the reason that the act was not contrary to the Divine law of love. On the contrary, if one would obey this man-made law and omit to render service to a brother in distress, he would be committing sin by breaking a Divine law. And this latter case proves that one may live in harmony with man-made law and yet be committing sin against Divine law. Therefore, this gives us to understand that Divine law precedes man-made law and is the higher law that should govern the conduct of man.

In the consideration of this subject we must recognize the fact that it is of prime importance to distinguish between sin as it is popularly conceived and which is based on customs and theological dogmas, which may or may not be founded on Divine law, and sin which is the result of breaking the Divine and universal law of love. In the former case, we have to consider that most of the rules governing the conduct of Man have been given us by priestcraft, who have not always interpreted the Bible correctly, and who for the most part have instituted customs to be observed by the people, so as to give the priesthood more authority over the masses. For, in the dependence of the masses upon the priesthood for their religious guidance, and not upon the law of Love, lies most of their misconceptions as to the true meaning of sin. History shows us the record of creeds, dogmas and rules for the guidance of conduct, which were given the people by priesthoods at various times, and which were adhered to strictly in their day only to be discarded to the scrap heap later. For instance, at one time it was considered a sin according to theological dogma to pluck and eat corn on the Sabbath. But the Master Jesus proved the fallacy of such a thought. There is a sect that considers it a sin to shave the beard, but we cannot see how the act of shaving is contrary to the Divine law of love. The regulations of pleasures, recreations, observances as to dress and conduct on the Sabbath as well as on all other days that have been instituted by priesthoods, in all times, to govern the lives of the people, have not always been based on Divine law. So that the act of going contrary to forms, customs, ceremonies, creeds and dogmas, for the most part, does not constitute sin.

Divine law is universal. It not only governs man, but

worlds and universes. It is eternal, it was, it is and it will ever be. While man-made law is temporal and changeable.

The greatest crimes in the world's history have been committed in the name of God and religion. For instance, the Spanish inquisition, the Crusades and the various Massacres in almost every land, were instigated and approved by the authoritative churches of their day. It was considered holy and Godly to kill in order to save souls. While, we, today, reflect with horror upon reading the pages of history smeared with blood. It was not considered a sin to kill in the name of religion, while we today consider killing a violation of the law of love.

Mankind has been taught falsely to regard traditions, customs and formal observances as constituting religion; so that the people think that if they live up to these traditions, customs and formal observances they are truly religious and Godly; while if they break these customs and traditions they consider themselves as sinning. They pay little or no attention to the desires of the heart and their thoughts, overlooking the fact that the quality of their desires and thoughts determines whether they sin or not. At the time of Jesus, the Pharisees considered it a sin for an individual to eat with unwashed hands. To them Jesus said, "For out of the heart proceed all evil thoughts, murders, adulteries, fornication, thefts, false witness, blasphemies; these are the things which defile a man, but to eat with unwashen hands defileth not a man."

How important it is for man to guard the desires of his heart and his thoughts far more so than living up to religious customs! For the quality of the desires and thoughts determines whether a man sins or not. Thoughts are either constructive, positive and up-building or destructive, negative and downtearing. If our thoughts conform to the law of love, they are constructive and positive; for God is love and love is growth. But the harboring of destructive thoughts is what constitutes sin.

The mind of man is his builder and creator, and it is with the mind that man must begin; and his first step to live a Godly life is to cleanse his heart of evil or sinning desires and his mind of destructive or sinning thoughts. Here undoubtedly we are confronted with man's most troubles. For in thinking thoughts that cause injury to himself and others does he sin.

For, here, too, the standard of measure of our thoughts and desires must be Love. If our thoughts and desires are loving, we are free from sin; but if they are not loving, then we are truly sinning. Thus, envy, greed, malice, jealousy, worry, hate and similar destructive thoughts are sinful, and cause injury not only to ourselves but to others.

Thought precedes the act. A wrong thought is as evil as a wrong deed. To think contrary to Divine law is just as much sin as to commit a wrong. Jesus said, "Whosoever looketh on a woman to lust after her hath committed adultery with her already in his heart." The worldly world stops at deeds, but never give much consideration to the tremendous power for good or evil and their desires and thoughts have.

Man of all creation was given a mind with which to build and to create. He uses mental power or force to accomplish definite results. Mental power or energy in itself is neutral, but the direction or use to which this power or force is given determines good or evil. And as Man is a free moral agent, it is his option to choose his mental powers for good or evil. But man chooses to use his mental powers for the accomplishment of selfish and destructive desires which results in sin.

Thought radiates in vibrations, and these thought vibrations are either constructive or destructive in character. And as these vibrations first pass through the individual, they affect him first, and will be for his health and up-building or for his ill and down-tearing. For disease and sin are one. Here we see how important it is to hold the mind in the proper attitude of thinking constructive and loving thoughts. We all know how destructive thoughts bring about physical disturbances in the body. Disease is the result of sinning through the mind.

Just as unloving thoughts constitute sin, so improper care of the body leading to disease means sin. Man is endowed with a body to sustain him. It was of no use to his mind and soul, there would have been no necessity for its existence. The body is the foundation of Man's being, and the prop on which he leans. The mind and the soul depend for its strength and growth on the condition of the body. How important, therefore, is it to give the body proper care? A knowledge of hygienic and dietary laws should be well understood and practiced. To treat the body carelessly, to feed it with improper food and drink, and to overtax its strength, constitutes sin. For, in as much as the body is the handiwork of God, who out of His love for Man, gave him an earthly temple, it becomes imperative for Man not to neglect his body. Thus we see that, by breaking the law of love in not caring for the body properly, does Man sin.

The greatest sin that Man commits is sin against his soul, for the soul is his real and Divine self. The Bible tells us that "The soul that sinneth it shall die." When Man uses the fires of his soul for lust and when he wastes his soul and energy for sensual gratification, in time he dissipates his soul fires, and he ceases to be an individualized being. This means "the wages of sin is death." The meaning of life is individualization and the accumulation of soul fire. He builds his soul through overcoming and transmuting base passion into pure gold of love. For love, God, soul and fire are one. It is therefore Man's duty to transmute his sensuous desires into higher love; for such desires if directed towards lust and base passion, tend to dissipate some of the fires of the soul, and in time totally destroys the soul. Man must do as Moses did. "As Moses lifted the serpent in the wilderness, even so must the Son of man be lifted up."

We have defined the meaning of sin and what constitutes sin. Every individual of the race of Man is the result of past and present deeds and misdeeds against his body, mind and soul. Sin is the effect of a cause or causes, the result of violating the Divine law of love, and every individual is reaping what he has sown in sin. To the man who has sinned, it is of most vital importance to know how he can atone. Can he atone by faith and blind beliefs alone, as some authoritative churches teach or must he atone through a living life in conformity with the Divine law of Love?

We quote from Dr. Clymer's book on true spiritualism, "As to justification by faith, just think of all your friends adhering to the above belief. It makes men vegetables or machines, while its twin dogma makes devils under the garb of saints. I boldly make the claim that nearly all the crimes known to mankind, are really caused by this foul and unjust doctrine, it gives man the opportunity to commit any crime, no matter how terrible, with the privilege that he recant, as it were, and simply pray for forgiveness, His victim may have suffered all the pangs of hell, and continue to suffer, but he, simply saying a few prayers, will be forgiven and need not suffer for his crime. This doctrine is so utterly unjust, that it seems utterly impossible it should be believed by any rational mind, and, yet, through superstition, there are thousands that believe this to be a true faith, not knowing that the Christ, whom they believe they are following, never taught such a doctrine, but that He did teach the law of Karma, as taught by all true Mystics and Occultists, namely, 'As thou soweth, so shalt thou reap.' If a man commits a wrong, he must suffer for it, and there is no law in heaven or earth, through which he can escape his just punishment."

Since Man, in the possession of his free-will and free-choice, wills and chooses to go contrary to the law of Love, and commits error and sin, so through the same God-given powers, by and through the law of love, he can regenerate himself and free himself from past errors. The law of justice is impersonal, ever operative and ever just. No man can commit sin without suffering the penalty therefor. Faith is good, but faith alone can never free man from past misdeeds. If a man through untold crimes has brought suffering to others, it would be unfair to free the wrong-doer from his crimes through blind belief alone. The law of love is just and merciful in that it allows wrong-doers through salvation and regeneration to square themselves with the law of justice.

If man has sinned he can atone for his misdeeds. To atone is to become at one with God. No man can become one with God until he has paid the uttermost farthing and has purified himself. In the beginning the soul of man was one with God, but in descending into flesh, through his own thoughts and desires, he has wandered away from God; and to attain at-one-ment, he must become reconciled to God, he must become purified and perfect.

"He must be reborn, must make himself an image and likeness of goodness and truth." To become born again is to enter into new understanding, to free the body of impurities and disease, to cleanse the heart of all evil desires and to train the mind into thinking loving and constructive thoughts. Salvation and purification is a long process. It means the paying of the uttermost farthing for past misdeeds; it means returning good for evil.

Regeneration is within the grasp of every man. It means

the living of a life of love and of unselfish service to mankind, and not merely believing in some religious creed. No mere belief in any creed ever saved anyone from paying the penalty of their past misdeeds. Life is action and salvation implies living and not mere believing.

Regeneration is the transformation of sinful, senuous, soul-undeveloped man into a pure and soul conscious being. It is to be accomplished through living a Christly life and through training in soul building as taught by Soul Science.

In Romans we read, "For the wages of sin is death; but the gift of God is eternal life through Jesus Christ our Lord."

To live a life contrary to the law of love, or a sinful life, brings disease, sorrow, suffering and in the end death. All sin finally ends in death of the body, mind and soul. Death is the extinction of our individuality which deprives us of remaining a seperate entity and of becoming the Christ soul. But the gift of God is eternal life and immortality of soul and can be had only through developing a Christ soul, as Jesus the Master did. Just as Jesus overcame all evil through love and developed within himself the Christ soul or the master soul, so, too, by living a life in conformity with his teachings and through training in soul building as taught by Soul Science, can we become illuminated or Christ souls. Faith in Jesus, the man, cannot save us. But that faith in his teachings, which enables us to recognize that Jesus came to teach the world soul building, will save us.

Thus we see that there is one law in the universe and for man, and that it is Love; that going contrary to the law of love constitutes sin; that man sinks into materiality and suffering because he loves evil and not good; and that he can rise into purity and immortality of soul only through love of truth and goodness. Love is the golden route to "the way, the truth and the life." There is no other route.

REINCARNATION

Ever since man was, there have been thousands of problems which have confronted him, and have absorbed his attention. He has at all periods wrestled mentally with the solution of some of the mysteries which he has encountered in his every-day life. What is sleep; what is a dream; what is breath; what is life?—these and countless others have caused him to rack his brain in his efforts to comprehend them. But these propositions have mostly been for those who have been the thinkers of the ages; those who have stopped in the busy work-a-day world, and have pondered upon the why of existence. The common mass of men have either had no time to study about these things, or else have taken them as a matter of fact—as so many things about us are taken—and have been content to eke out their existence and take things as they come to them, not knowing why, or caring how or whence they came.

There are, however, two phases of human existence which thrust themselves pre-eminently upon each individual that is born into the world, no matter in what clime, no matter whether that man be what the rest of his fellows calls high or low, rich or poor, ignorant or philosopher; whether he be white, black, red, or yellow—at some time he must come face to face with this two-fold problem—Birth and Death. At some period in the life of every soul on earth, these two opposite poles of the proposition of life have forced themselves upon it for consideration. Either must the individual have met them in his own mind, or have been brought face to face with the reality, in a practical way. There is, and has been no escape from the proposition, until it is solved, and the solving of the mystery of these two extremities of human endeavor has been the bent and aim of men for all times.

Birth is one of the greatest mysteries of existence. It is something no one has been able to explain to the masses. The ordinary man has been wont to look upon birth as a matter of fact; he does not try to explain it, except superstitiously, perhaps, and he takes it as one of the things which must be, and which is, and further than that, he is willing to accept it as a matter of course, and gives it no concern.

Death, however, is one of those mysteries with which he is brought sharply face to face. He can not see in this mystery the growing child, the unfolding body, like a rose spreading its petals; he can not see the breath raise the bosom and develop the form; he can not hear the sweet child's voice learn to lisp his name, and call him "Papa;" but rather, he sees an absence, a depletion of all things; a form lacking in everything which he has known in that loved one, and barren of all the faculties which he himself has. There remains nothing, apparently, but a piece of clay, without any other properties which formerly animated that body. And this sight has struck terror into his heart, for he know not whether this last manifestation upon which he gazed, spelled the end of all for that one, or whether there was something unknown beyond. The uncertainty of the proposition brought it sharply and unmistakably before him, and he has been for all time trying to find the solution, the antidote against death, because he has not wanted to die; he has considered it unnecessary to do so; he does not want to leave all these things which he has met, grown to love, and possessed. He can not understand why, if he was placed here at all, if there was the least purpose in his coming, he should have to be torn away, against his will, to go whither he knows not, into a problematical future state. There seems to be some foundation for the questions which man has asked about existence: If I came here, why should I go away? If I was not meant to live here, why should I have come? And the one who has thought even deeper, propounds the further question: If I can live seventy years (the limitation of three score and ten which man has set for his sojourn on this earth); if I can live even thirty years, or five years, yea, even for a day, why is it not possible for the very functions which sustain my life for that period, to carry it on forever? Is there any cessation of Life? Isn't life under a definite law, capable of being appropriated in the building and uplifting of the individual? Is not Life universal, eternal? Why, then should there be so many changes of manifestation? Why should not life manifest its eternality, and build one perfect form after its image and likeness, immortal, indestructible.

Science has discovered that the human body absolutely renews itself every seven months; that not one atom or cell of the human body of seven months ago remains in the present one. And man naturally wonders why, if this renewing process goes on, he can not go on forever; why should he be called upon to lay down that body, and change his estate or habitation?

And in his extremity, man has through the centuries, made religion take care of this phase of existence after death, for he has believed that there must be a hereafter somewhere, somehow. Religion has given him hope that after he has been forced by some unknown power to lay down the body, he would still exist, and not be resolved into nothingness, into total oblivion. He has reasoned that this life could not be the end of the soul, and that the soul or the individuality of man, has always, and will always live.

But notwithstanding the hope of religion, man has been in constant rebellion against taking up his abode in the perfect bliss which his religion has promised; he has devoted his every effort against the encroachment of death. Unlike the phase of existence called birth, man has not been willing to accept death as a matter of fact, as inevitable, and there let the problem rest. Evermore the thoughts portrayed in Hamlet's soliloquy:

"To die, to sleep; to sleep, perchance to dream,
Ah, there's the rub! For in that sleep of death,
What dreams might come, when we have shuffled off this mortal
coil, must give us pause,"

have rung in the ears of mortals, and in their oppressiveness, in the desperation of avoiding the final enemy, men have sought fountains of eternal youth, chemicals, the aids of known Science, and various other ways of prolonging, even for a short time, the existence which they held so dear. Fundamentally, the solution of eternal life has been the end and aim of all man's efforts. Man accumulates a fortune, in the hope of enjoying it; he gains knowledge for the purpose of enjoying it, either in teaching his fellows, or for the plaudits of men. And so, out of this effort for longivity, out of the desire to solve the riddle of the universe, all peoples have evolved their sages and wise men, who have delved into spiritual things, and have endeavored to give the light of their understanding and illumination and wisdom to the masses. But the retarding influence of superstition and stubbornness, the adherence to preconceived beliefs, and the engrossment in their every day activities, have precluded the common mass from accepting the higher ideals, and the knowledge of the working of laws which would make the very thing which they sought a living reality. But there have been souls which have been able to look beyond the appearance of things, and discover the laws upon which creation is based. They have found that the same laws apply in the mental and spiritual realms as apply to the material. All law is based upon cause and effect. The one great Law of the Universe is the law of Karma, the decree that like produces like; cause produces definite unerring results, and here, in this wonderful edict of the universe, like at once the hope of the spiritually awakened to use this law for construction, and the blasting of the hopes of him who does not know or follow that Law .

But in this every-day world, in the physical plane of manifestation, man has discovered the law of the conservation of energy, that is, that every particle of matter which has ever existed, still exists, only perhaps in a changed form. Nothing is lost; nothing can be lost, and there is only one intent and purpose of creation—to build, better, more beautiful, more useful forms of existence. The impulse of all Nature is upward and onward. Nature does not favor devolution or "backward progress." One need not look afar to see the evidences of this truth. The old tree which does not bring forth fruit, rots, and is resolved back to the original elements. Whenever anything ceases to grow, to expand, to evolve, to go onward and upward, Nature says, "I have no more use for you; you must give place to that which will manifest my exuberance, my spontaneity, my youth, my beauty, the thrill of my Life, the Love of my heart, the ideal of my perfection, and make for the new creation through which I may express the highest in me, that which will manifest the newest and highest impulses; that which wishes to grow and become the embodiment of the highest concept of its kind." And nature takes the substance of the old tree, which it has refined through its Alchemy, and gives it to the new plant, and the wonder of youth is again manifested in the growing creation thus brought forth.

Can the conclusion be escaped that if these things work thus in the creation of the plant, the animal, the rock, why not in the greatest of all creations, Man? Is God going to neglect and fail to take care and provide for him who is made in God's own image and likeness? Will God allow to be destroyed the only creation in all the Universe which has a Soul? The only creation in all the Universe which may so become the instrument of God that God can consciously think through him, express his desires through him, and thus finally, through this faculty of man, Intuition, direct and control the entire activity of the Universe? If the tree and plant continually take up the substance which formerly formed the old, and which, through the working of Nature can be again appropriated to form the new, why does nature thus continually bring back the same creations, under the law of Like Produces Like? If there is not the desire of Nature to reproduce things after their kind, why would not one existence of an oak, a stalk of wheat, or an animal, end that existence forever? Does this not forever explode the theory that if there is any creation or reproduction at all, there can be no cessation of reproduction on all planes of existence, meaning the mineral, plant, animal, and the highest form, Man? What once was, can be, and must be. God works under Law, and to interfere with that law would be to throw all things into confusion, chaos, destruction. God could no more interefere with one of his laws than he could destroy himself, for to interfere with a single law of the Universe would be to destroy everything. Law is the order of the Universe, and God is under that law; he is that Law.

And so, out of these natural phenomena, which man sees all about him, and out of the teachings of the Masters who have gone before and demonstrated the possibility of immortality, he gets his hope and assurance of the return, the reincarnation of all things, especially himself.

Birth and death are the two opposite poles of man's earth existence. Between them is contained all the Hope, and all the discouragement; all the Faith, and all the Doubt; all the Love and all the hate; all the Success, and all the failures; all the conjectures, all the theories, all the religions, all the efforts of men for all time. Between these two opposites is contained all the research, all the endeavors of men, everywhere, at all times. And still, to the mass of men, the solution of Whence came I, and whither do I go, is still as remote as if it had never been suggested.

But thinking man looks upon the planting of the grain of wheat in the ground; he sees it disintegrate, and apparently die. The old form vanishes, and is apparently resolved into the original elements; but lo! out of the old body comes the tender shoot. He sees it, through the appropriation of sunshine and air through the nourishment of the rich soil, take on form and beauty; he sees its fruition in the ear, and the reproduction of itself an hundred times. In this every-day experience he gains a two-fold lesson: First, he sees that everything must develop, must evolve. Nature says to all "Grow or die; evolve or deteriorate; produce, or pass on into oblivion, so far as your individual form is concerned. You can not remain neutral; you can not be purposeless, vapid, stationary." And then the heart urge in everything: "Let me express myself through you, and I shall make you great." Secondly, he sees the lesson of the continual reproduction; the fact that what once was, can continue to be. In other words, if a grain of wheat once was, and returns, reproduces itself, then the law of nature, the desire of nature must be for reproduction; that nature is unwilling to let any of its creattions fall into naught. And the hope springs up in the heart of man, that if nature rebuilds, reproduces even the smallest grain, how much more must nature desire man, the highest type of creation, to return, go through the process of reincarnation, until the perfection which is Nature's ideal for man, has been reached. As the evolution of things becomes higher, we pass from the tiny perennial stalk of wheat to the great Oak, which is almost the symbol of eternality, and we see as intelligence manifests itself, the possibility of individual initiative in development becomes greater, and the contemplation of the higher forms of creation has filled man's heart full of the joy of living. He has been able to look out upon the wonderful creation which nature has placed around him, and inbreathe the very hope and inspiration of the Almighty in the attaining of his ideal.

And man has had brought before him one of the greatest examples of the returning life which is manifest in the world. He has seen the caterpillar spin his cucoon, and fix it to the branch of the tree, and remain dormant through the long winter months, covered with snow and sleet, perhaps, until the flowing of the sap in the Spring, when the stir and the thrill of the life within called it forth . The worm possibly has no concept of what is before it. It follows blind instinct in the weaving of the cucoon, and gives no thought to the future, if indeed it can think. But as the warm days come, there emerges from out of that seemingly lifeless mass of leaves, the soul of the caterpillar, the wondrous butterfly, the delight of all lovers of beauty, as it flits here and there in the garden, exemplifying life itself in its scintillating movements. Is it possible that one can fail to draw the lesson of the perpetuity of life from this manifestation? Is it possible to doubt that if the caterpillar can evolve into such a beautiful embodiment as this, can again return to the worm, through another medium, and reincarnate over and over into the beauty of the moth, that this life, which is the same in one manifestation as the other, is not an embryotic example of the existence of man, and that man too has at least the same opportunity as the lower forms of creation?

And passing on to the great mystery of birth, man sees from a single drop of protoplasm, the development, the unfoldment of the beautiful child, with a mind to think and create, and a soul to love. Can man doubt the pereptuity of recreation in such an example? Is there anyone foolish enough to think that through the marriage relationship, man can create a mind and a soul? Man produces man—form man—under the law of the universe, but man is only the receptacle, and the crucible wherein that wonderful artistry takes place; he is but the laboratory for the performing of the miracle which he does not understand. But can he say he is the producer of that manifestation? Can he explain why the children in a family are so totally different, one from the other; why some are thin, some fleshy; some blue-eyed, some gray-eyed; some large and dark; some small and light, partaking not of the natures of either father or mother?

So, at this juncture, we are brought face to face with the problem of reincarnation, and we are made to ponder the problem of whence came they, and whither do they go? As we heretofore suggested, all laws work the same; they are coincidently exact. The Spiritual Law is, like the mental, a counterpart, on its plane of manifestation, of what takes place in the material universe. One is naturally confronted with the problem, that if all the human beings were living who have ever lived, the whole earth would be covered seven deep, and the question would naturally arise: Where could these souls all exist?" There is only one solution, and Reincarnation offers that by readily showing that only a certain number of souls exist, and that these return again and again until they have gained perfection, at which time will be the millenium on earth, the Paradise which the Bible teaches. But the Orthodox man and women will not accept this explanation of existence, because it is suggested that one must be converted in order to gain heaven. Knowing, as we do, that not one in an hundred thousand out of all the millions who have ever lived became converted to Christianity, even in the ordinary sense, it follows that those who were not so converted, among which are numbered our brothers, sisters, fathers, mothers, sweethearts, would be among the lost. Hence the church people do not wish to accept the doctrine of Reincarnation—which would give these "lost souls" another chance to come back and again live the earth life in a higher form—because "they would not meet loved ones." This idea, of course, is preposterous, because under this Law we do meet again all that we have met before, and instead of meeting loved ones, only to see them damned before the judgment, as we do the criminal in Court, we see them given the helping, guiding influence, the lifting impulse, the encouragement, the freedom from the body whose senses pulled down that soul, and these are given another chance, in another body, under posibly different environment, to express that higher impulse that urge which is within each soul from the beginning of eternity.

Is it possible, then, to cease thinking about the purpose for which we were placed upon this earth; can one be satisfied with living for a few short years, and again pass on into uncertainty?

And man, as he ponders over the problem of existence, sees in the natural world about him the counterpart of which he himself is expected to do; he hears the one great command from the Creator of the Universe for Development. He recognizes that his very existence is dependent upon growth; that he must unfold and develop in order to produce, and production in man's world means evolution, progress. He gleans the lesson from the development of the caterpillar that life is continuous, and eternal; that neither the idea which produces the plant or animal, nor the soul of man can die; that these are eternal and can not be destroyed. That reincarnation is but the effort of the great God of the universe to cause man to help man to inspire man to bring forth the perfect creation, and that perfect creation—if the soul of man is indestructible, and lives forever—includes the building of an eternal, everlasting body. Reincarnation, in the ordinary sense conveys the idea of putting back into a body which rather leaves the impression of putting the soul back into the same old body, at least the same material. We have seen how, in nature, in the plant world, the old is resolved back into the original elements, and transmitted into the new, the young, the growing, and it is not therefore strange that this idea has grown apace with the strengthening of the belief in Reincarnation. One can readily comprehend, under the law of conservation of energy, how, in a sense, the soul, in its reincarnation, uses the refined old body, for the building of a new structure.

And so, Reincarnation is the great opportunity of man to start to build where construction ceased at death. After death, the soul is powerless to develop. It is then in the resting stage, much as the caterpillar was in the cucoon. It can then act only through the law of attraction, and is waiting to be attracted to those of the same vibration or power of attraction in the flesh, who will again give it the opportunity to take up another body, and start its new constructive process. You will remember in the story of creation, the allegory is given that "There was no man to till the soil?" The soul has no power to develop while in the soul world. It must develop through the instrumentality of the mind, which only takes its seat of authority when the child inbreathes its first breath. The Soul receives its impressions through the five senses of the body and it must have a body and a mind in order to develop itself, as well as to in turn "till the ground" (body, material) so that body may be raised to the highest, through the refining fires of the soul. And at birth, the period of development starts. Man is given that governor, that guide, that director, which has the power to use or discard all the forces of the universe in his ongoing. And that Director is the Mind. There can be no building without an ideal, a plan, and that plan, that ideal must be held by the mind. The mind thinks, and it sets to work all the great substances, the ethers of the universe toward the accomplishment of its purpose, whether that purpose be toward construction or destruction. Without the mind, man would be but as inert, inanimate piece of clay, without the power to create, or even move. The Mind is the governor, the constructor, the tool which shapes the destiny of man towards everlasting life, or toward the destruction of the body, in which latter event the soul must again go through the process of reincarnation in order to again have the opportunity which in its last incarnation rejected. And in this opportunity which is given man, he is placed, as is everything else in the universe, plant, planet, animal, God, under the law of cause and effect. God has endowed man with the greatest of all natural faculties, the Mind. As a man thinks, he creates, and he has the power and opportunity to create that which he wills. If he, through the knowledge of this law, and the love and ideal in his heart, should miss the mark of perfection, he, through the law of Reincarnation, will be of such high vibration that he will be attracted in his next reincarnation to parents who will give his soul every opportunity to express, in the highest environment, that which his soul craves. Do you remember how clearly the Bible states this, when Jesus asks his disciples "Whom do men say that I am?" And the answer is given that some said he was Elisha, and various of the other spiritually developed men who had lived before him. But when he asks his disciples, his faculties who he really believed himself to be, the answer, came, "Thou are the Christ, the son of the living God;" the goal, the ideal was thus established in his mind, and the building continued for its attainment.

Friends, this question is one which every individual soul must himself work out. Suggestions may be offered, but primarily, it is a matter of individual unfoldment and satisfaction. No one can think your thoughts for you; no one can develop you, but others may point out what the ideal, the ultimate is and must be, and from their suggestions, you may be able to build a new building, from which you may receive the inspiration and hope which your soul has long craved.

No one wishes to die. Everyone desires to live and to live forever! If it were not intended that we should inhabit this earth, what would be the purpose of coming here at all? But all men have not understood the process of living. They have not understood the wonderful law under which eternal life may be constructively established. They have not known that any destructive thought towards another results in bodily destruction for the thinker. And so they have gone on blindly, as has the animal, and the law of Reincarnation has been forced to take care of them in order to give them another opportunity to express that which it was meant for them to express. And this process must of necessity go on until the individual realizes the attainment, the purpose of creation, of existence—what he himself is and must be. This may take centuries. God knows no time, and eventually the problem will be worked out.

But there is no need for delay, in the perfecting of the body and the doing away with this continual endless reincarnation. The soul which knows, need not cease its growth, need not go through the sorrow of the passing out, and the derangement of the change of environment; it may remain and build as God has intended it to develop and build. It may use that wonderful builder, the Mind, and create, fashion, shape its body into the picture, the ideal, the plan which it holds in mind. And this is the lesson, the practical every-day lesson which all must get out of the contemplation, the knowledge of the laws under which all things manifest.

The plant returns, rebuilds; the caterpillar changes its form, involuntarily, and because of the urge of creation within it; fruit, flower, and tree produce under the law of "Like produces like," and the process is involuntary, because they are not given individual initiative. The animal falls under the same law, and produces after its kind, without the opportunity, the faculty to build any more than an animal of itself, because the possibility of conscious Divinity, the Soul, was not emplanted in it at creation. But Man, Man the image and likeness of the Creator, has both the Soul and the Mind. He has both the God-embroy, and the Architect himself. God has said to him, through his reason and through his Intuition: "Son all that I have is thine; thou in me, and I in thee, and if thou wilt recognize me, follow my laws, these things and greater shall ye do; nothing is impossible to you." And the great masters of all times have shown man the possibility of the God-hood; the body has been perfected, made indestructible by these who have in times past followed the Intuition within their hearts, and have consciously, slowly, step by step, thought upon thought, builded a God-mind, a Christ Soul, an Imperishable Body, through the observance of the one great law of "Cause and Effect"—"as a man thinketh in his heart, so is he"—and the listening of the

God Voice within the Soul, for the guidance, the direction, the hope, the inspiration of the Almighty. And so, man is put under the higher law. He is given volition and freedom to accept, to use, to appropriate these wonderful forces and powers of the Universe, or reject and cast out of his mind and heart the desire for the uplift the guidance of the Great love, for man's perfection.

Then what is the true lesson of Reincarnation? Is it necessary for us to die in order to be given another opportunity to build the ideal which should be in every heart? Does God wish us to die? Can God die? If not, why should the Son of God die? Friends, true Reincarnation is the conscious, unceasing, unfaltering building into the mind and body, the ideal of the illumined Soul, and through the bringing forth of the illumined Soul, the Christ, the becoming of the Son of God, the unchangeable, the imperishable image and likeness of God himself, that which is through all times, and has all of the properties and powers of God himself. Reincarnation to the student of the Soul, is the transmuting of the baser desires, the baser ideals, the baser metal, into that fine, high, pure, beautiful entrancing ideal, and the conscious, loving, all-engrossing desire of the mind and heart to build that ideal here and now. Then there will be no more need to return and perfect that which before had been a failure; then will all the things be under the dominion and control, the management and subject to the disposition of the soul which has attained. Then will the work have been finished, and sorrow and distress will have been banished from out of the life of such an one.

God's ideal of you is Perfection. God does not mean that you shall have sorrow, sickness, death. God wishes you to have joy, peace, and the happiness that comes only from a true relationship with the All-happiness. Look about you, and behold the beauty of the unfolding rose; take its lesson of quiet, calm, trusting unfoldment, with only the one thought in its heart, only the one ideal before it, that of the expression of the perfect flower.

Can we not all, in our on going, emulate the example of this blossom, by steadfastly, unfalteringly, undoubtingly, holding, moment by moment, the ideal which God has set before us; opening ourselves to the Great Sunlight of Wisdom which is continually shining within the Soul; warmed by the heat of a love which will burn out all dross; guided by an unfaltering loving hand and the voice of Intuition within the Heart; sustained by the great Strength which is ever at our call, until we are finally brought into that dream of the ages, that hope, that ultimate Ideal, where the last enemy will slink out of our lives, because we have set up the standard of the Perfect man, the Christ, the Son of the Living God?

EVOLUTION

We look about us in our every-day activities, and we see the rocks, the flowers, the trees, the fruits, the animals, and other men and women like ourselves. We gaze out of our windows, and see the rivers, the lakes, and the mountains. On the balmy Summer evening, we see the magnificent planets, the stars rivaling the diamond in their brilliance, and here and there we see on the horizon, the little fluffy clouds floating in the azure spaces like down puffed out of the hand of some mighty being. We see the moon moving majestically along the pathway of the heavens; and the sun by day, in its wondrous brilliance, shedding heat and light upon mother earth. We look, and lo, everything on our planet gazes heavenward. The flowers lift their heads toward the sun; the grass springs up in all its luxuriousness, stretching its blades upward towards the light; and as we behold the beauties about us, we feel a lifting, an exuberance as if something wished to soar into etherial heights. The Soul entranced by the wonder of creation, rises above the commonplace and sordid things which sometimes occupy our thoughts, and refuses to be trammeled in the expression of its ideals, in the glory of its freedom.

And the question arises in the mind of the thinker and student of life and living things: Whence came this creation; why is it? And, seeking, reaching back as far as the human mind can conceive towards original cause, one is confronted inevitably with the proposition: If all these things came from One Source, why are they all different? Why are they not manifested in the same way; why is not all creation a succession of trees, or flowers, or rocks, or animals, instead of the entrancingly diffuse and varied forms among which we are?

These are questions which have confronted humanity ever since man has been a thinking entity; and in the consideration of these problems, and as a means of offering an explanation for them, there have arisen two great schools of thought and research. In times gone by, these were diametrically opposed to each other in their teachings; but gradually as each discovered certain laws on its plane of research, they have been converging in their thought, and coinciding in their opinions, until in our day the expression "Science proves Religion" has become almost axiomatic. One is the great materialistic school, or Science; the other is Religion—a Religion not as based upon some dead, orthodox belief, but a Religion of growth, of expansion, a living vital Religion, which recognizes man's return to his Creator, and realizes the laws under which he may become the shaper, the moulder of his own destiny, and bring himself into Immortality. Every individual in the Universe has belonged, consciously or unconsciously to one of these great institutions. There is no half-way point in the declaration of one's intentions and beliefs. Either the man has believed himself a "worm of the dust," a materialist to whom Nature says: Everything in the manifest universe must follow my law of disintegration and oblivion," or else he has believed that somehow, somewhere, through the Great Creative Forces and Substances of the universe, there was the possibility, the opportunity for unfoldment, development, which would turn back the natural tide of the dissolution of things into the elements and make toward that perfection which knows no change.

And thus, we have these two seemingly opposed schools of thought, which seek to offer the explanation of why these things are, and what they may be.

Man is fundamentally a materialistic being. He has, ever since birth, given most of his attention to the satiation of his feelings, his desires, his appetites, and thus, in most instances, he has been content to go on satisfying these faculties and senses, taking the materialistic basis as the real, and explaining every phenomenom which presents itself, through deduction from his starting point. He has gradually discovered laws through which he is able to arrive at different conclusions, and these laws seem to be definitely established, notwithstanding the fact that the text book of Chemistry of fifteen years ago is practically worthless in the present-day field of scientific research. And such has been the experience with practically all the investigatory efforts of man. But among all the Sciences, Chemistry is the one upon which the materialist basis his ultimate hopes of solving the riddle of existence. It is the chief among the physical branches of knowledge. It is the key that unlocks to him the door to that which he knows of nature, and reveals its beauty to him. This Science, although young in years, is a giant in knowledge of materialistic things. It seeks to tell us what matter is; shows us its different grades and qualities, and teaches us its composition and nature, leading us back to the primary invisible inert condition, and shows us its primary unity and simplicity. Chemistry, aided by the other sciences, teaches us all we know about matter. By its aid we can resolve matter back to its primary elements, to its original gases.

Chemists claim may divisions of matter, four of which they call the "principal gases," the heaviest of which is carbon, the lightest hydrogen, which is fifteen times lighter than air, and beyond which they have not been able to investigate, claiming that the next step in deduction would result in nothing. But the Chemist realizes that as these lightest gases cannot be reduced lower, nor destroyed, this form of matter always was.

And right at this point, in steps the Religionist, as we will call him, the follower of Religion as the means of attaining his ideal, and says that the conclusion of the Chemist is a natural one; that the Chemist, the materialist is dealing with material things, with the effect side of the proposition, and that the cause, the real, lies beyond the discovery of the mind, the microscopes, the reason of man, and that Spiritual Things can only be spiritually discerned; that back of all manifestations is the one Great Creative Substance; that this is Spirit; that only the development of the heart, the illumination of the Soul of man, can finally bring him to an understanding of things as he sees them, and offer man the satisfaction which he seeks in the problem of life.

So, again, the whole proposition is resolved into an individual search for satisfaction. Each Soul must for itself find the solution in and of itself. No other entity can map out the path of development and produce development, without the acquiescence of the one for whom this growth, this expansion is desired.

So, for the purpose of this lecture, we desire to offer some of the salient points which have been brought forth in the researches of men in the past, not only what has been discovered by Scientists, but also that which has been attained and taught by the spiritual masters and adepts who have gone before us.

Primarily, regardless of how refined it may be, matter is always inert, and cannot move itself. Evolution is growth, and if matter takes on new forms, grows, as we term it, there must be some moving force which takes hold of the particles, and forms them, molds them into shapes, changing, renewing, constructing and making them continually over some new pattern; and that process must be towards some definite end or purpose, because we can not conceive of this being done at random, haphazardly, or in accordance with no law or purpose. It follows, then, that if matter is inert, and can not of itself have motion, this moving Force, which prompts and guides the formation and the reformation of matter, must be a definite, though seemingly intangible force, exercising Intelligence in its activities. We, through Physics and Chemistry, know something of the properties of Light and Electricity. We know that these two forces work under definite, unerring laws, and have discovered some of the laws under which they work. We know also, that these forces or properties are subject to the direction of the laws under which they work, and that they, of themselves, inherently, are not creative in their nature and do not exercise primary initiative, that is, are not thinking, directing forces. We can not, then, escape the conclusion that there is something more than mere force as the primal cause of the things we see about us, for force, like matter, is inert, non-creative, and without direction, can not be set in motion, or become productive. Hence, we see that there must be intelligence manifest before there can be development, or even growth.

Material Science has not learned what Electricity and Light are. It has been able to learn somewhat of the effect of light upon certain elements, and organisms; to measure its velocity, its penetration, and ascertain certain phases of its vibration; it has learned what electrification is, and to a certain extent, has discovered in what manner it operates, and some of the laws governing its action. But, as heretofore suggested, the cause of these manifestations is still unknown.

Transcending the material evidences of electricity and light, we see visible manifestations of a superior intelligence in the creations about us. There is demonstrated attraction and repulsion, sensation, instinct, reason and intelligence, and the

Religionist again offers the explanation that these things are the result of the manifestation of what he calls Spirit. One can not doubt that these faculties and propensities are inherently the result of the activity of matter, because matter of itself has no action. It also follows that if this guiding intelligence, which we call spirit, were removed from matter, matter would be devoid of its forming intelligence, its holding-together, adhesive power, and would of necessity decay, or lose its forming power and shape.

The conclusion can not be escaped, that if there is a principle, or Spirit which is the basis of material manifestation, that Spirit can not be weighed by any known scales, however delicately constructed, nor does it occupy exclusive space; nor is it inert like matter. In other words, it is in no sense like matter, because, as a matter of logic, if it were, it would be matter.

Matter furnishes material to form physical bodies, but can not, by reason of its inertia, furnish either life or intelligence. Spirit, then, of necessity furnishes principle to produce sensation, instinct, reason, intelligence, and, according to the Religionist, Immortality. And at this point, the Religious adherent almost maliciously injects the query: "What is matter, anyway?" But whatever it is, the fact remains, that if Spirit is removed from ever so perfect a material body, all life is gone, and we have the primal elements.

Spirit, like matter, is of many grades of fineness and manifestation, according to the amount of spirit and development of the form in which it functions. Spirit being in everything, in proportion to the fineness of matter and perfection of form, we see it manifesting according to the certain laws, in the magnetic iron; the charming serpent; the fascinating woman; the magnetic man. It flashes in the air; sparkles in the mineral; blooms in the vegetable; feels in the worm; thinks in the animal; reasons in the human; shines resplendant in the soul, full of love and wisdom, radiant with immortality and eternal life, the highest Intelligence in the universe.

We have tried to contrast in a brief manner, the bases upon which the two great schools of thought are founded. We have suggested the properties of matter and Spirit; we have tried to show their relationship in a manner that would harmonize with the great laws which we only dimly comprehend, realizing, however, that all laws work identically on the different places of their manifestation—always does cause produce effect, no matter what the field of operation of that law may be. But let us go a little further.

We find matter diffused through space, and principally concentrated in certain locations, as in planets, for example, and the world we inhabit. If matter is thus concentrated, is it not reasonable to suppose that Spirit also has its center of activity, its Source? Reason tells us that if we could find any planet or sphere which is different from matter, or is not matter, it would be the other principle, which we call Spirit. The question arises: How do we know planets are matter? The answer is suggested by our material senses. We know they are matter, because they have the qualities of matter; they are heavy, solid, opaque, do not radiate heat or light, and can not either move themselves or other planets.

Let us consider then, if there is any known orb or sphere which has none of these qualities, but has qualities directly opposed to those of matter, and exactly like the qualities of what we call Spirit? We look up into the heavens on a bright hot day, and we are confronted with the possible solution of our question: Embodied matter is planet. Could not embodied Spirit be the sun? We have here the two phases of the proposition, showing the relationship between them. Matter concentrated into spheres makes worlds; Spirit concentrated in spheres, makes suns. Planets, having the properties of matter, can do nothing of themselves. Their motion and light is given them from the Sun. The sun, true to Spirit moves and lights, and gives life to all worlds.

Let us closely follow the explanation of the Religionist, in his effort to prove to us that the sun (with the assistance of matter) does all that is known that Spirit can do. It is known that the sun acts electrically, and attracts and repels, moves, and controls all planets. Electricity is a manifestation of Spirit. The suns light up all worlds, and all space where they shine. Light is not matter; light passes through matter, like other grades of spirit do. Spirit light shines on particles of matter, and illuminates them, making them reflect light to us. But light is clearly and grandly a spirit manifestation.

The Sun throws out its heating power, and acting on, and through matter, warms all matter, and passes through matter, as matter can not do, therefore clearly proving that heat is not matter, and must, therefore, be Spirit, and comes from the sun, the only source of Spirit.

The sun throws out its spirit electric power, and magnetizes atoms, minerals, vegetables, insects, animals, and humans, and all these throw out their received magnetism in proportion to the amount received, and their will and ability to so radiate.

Spirit from the Sun, acting through its suitable manifestations of heat, light, electricity and magnetism, acts upon invisible, primary matter, attracting, heating, illuminating and condensing it by its own laws of Spirit power, thus concentrating primary matter into atoms; atoms into nebula; nebula into comets; comets into spheres; spheres into planets; planets into worlds. Spirit acts upon gaseous matter, and converts it into water, the most negative of all matter, thus making itself, as we are told, a proper mate, for, it is reasoned, it is not good that even the Sun should be alone.

Gradually, as this cooling orb gave the hardening crust, almost imperceptibly came life. At this point, leaving the abstract, life becomes more intelligent. The Spirit, Sun, shone upon the moistened matter earth, converting the surface of the hard sterile rock into living soil; and out of this same living soil, by the power of spirit fructifying the vitalized matter, sprang into growth the lower forms of vegetable life, scarcely in degree above the mineral. And the same fructifying generating process of spirit went on vitalizing and refining matter, and thus gradually produced higher, and yet a higher and more perfect form of vegetable life, until the perfect tree, with its glistening leaves, scented flowers, and luscious fruit proclaimed the perfection of the vegetable kingdom. There was life, perfect vegetable life, in all its magnificence and grandeur; there was life and growth and perfection. Still there was yet no intelligence in all the boundless realm of nature, because there was as yet no organization competent to produce or employ intelligence. The organism which could transmit or embody that Intelligence had not yet evolved. But nature went on with its creative process of Spirit Power and unchanging law.

From the highest vegetable to the lowest animal life, there is no more stretch of power or change of progressive law than there was from rock to soil, or from soil to vegetable—all are but parts of the same creative process and manifestation of Spirit Power. Then, from the lowest to the highest type of animal life, the process is analogous to the production of the higher vegetables from the lower. All Nature is a process of evolution. As all vegetable life develops from the lower, to the higher, so does all animal life evolve, through the working of the same natural law, by the same unchanging, illimitable and exhaustless power of Spirit. All came in harmony with Law, and in proper order. There was no "missing link" in this chain of creation, nor can there be a disturbing of the natural sequence of unfoldment, for if there were, it would be contrary to the law of evolution, growth, and one can see without much study that if the law of creation were not absolute and unchangeable, the whole order of the universe would be disturbed, and nothing would be certain. For instance, in such a state of uncertainty, the planting of a peach seed might produce a lion; or the fruition of the acorn be a crop of snakes or Hottentots.

We can thus plainly see the growth, development, and variety of vegetable life, as it is produced by cultivation, circumstances, climate and soil, and that the great varieties of species, with their degrees of perfection, come from the one or at most the few original stocks, low down in the vegetable scale, as in comparatively modern time, we find that all varieties of apples, apricots, pears, quinces, and other fruits, came from the one original rose-bush, and that all cherries, plums, peaches and similar varieties came from one little insignificant poisonous plum-peach of Persia. Thus, the growth, development, variety, and perfection of all vegetable life, foreshadows, prepares, and proclaims the growth, development, evolvement, and ultimate perfection of animal life—Man.

Animal life began without intelligence, and through the law of positive spirit acting through negative matter, evolved into or up to Intelligence. Commencing with the lowest form of life, and developing through the progressive grades of animal growth, up to sensation, instinct, reason and intelligence, the hope of humanity, of those who pin their faith upon the possibilities of conscious evolution, is that the ultimate, the climax of all human endeavor, of all evolution, may be attained—Immortality.

Tracing animal life in its development from the quadrupeds, to quadrumana and duomana, up to humana, there is a gradual ascent, and plainly marked line of lineage; an unbroken chain, not as Darwin, Huxley and Spencer have suggested, a "missing link." There can no unbridged chasm be found. Nature is complete in all her works. From the lowest animal, to dog, ape, baboon, monkey, orang, gorilla, chimpanzee, up to the Terra del Fuegians, who are entirely without civilization, or improvement, who apparently have not even the intelligence to procure themselves the necessities of life, and are naturally most beastial in their habits. They are so low in the scale of human development, that scientific explorers have not as yet been able to classify them, whether with man or beast. The next links in the chain of development of man are the digger Indians, the Bushmen, and the Andaman Islanders; then successively, the Guinea Negroes, the higher grades of Africans, the Indian, the Malay, the Mongol, the different grades of Circassians, and then from the lowest Britton. who was a wild, warlike person when Julius Caesar, one-half century before Christ, landed a settlement of Roman soldiers in Great Britain, to the highest American—one vast chain of evolutionary progress.

Thus have we set forth briefly the contentions of the Materialistic and the Religious schools of thought. As we before said, all development is a matter of individual concern and endeavor. But we would fall short of our purpose if, after taking the subject to this point, we did not draw some conclusions which would be of benefit in the development of those who are desirous of carrying forward to yet greater and higher attainment, this possibility of the ultimate evolution of which man has always dreamed, and to that end, we desire to sum up, in a few brief remarks some suggestions as to how this may be accomplished.

We have to-day the greatest civilization which the world has seen for ages. There is at the present stage of human development the acutest awakening of the intellect, and the greatest research into occult things which the world has ever known. But can we say that humanity has evolved to the highest attainable goal? Reason tells us that the present high standard of humanity is the evolvement of the lowest form of life, through the successive stages of perhaps plant, animal, and human development, and that this development, in the first stages at least, went forward without the faculty of individual intelligence; in other words, that there was no individual initiative of intelligence or reason. What, then, are the possibilities of a Soul endowed with that precious jewel of reason, the Mind, of attaining heights beyond man's wildest dreams and fondest hopes? Is the step any greater from the present day man or woman to the Christ, than it was from the lowest forms of animal life or the most primitive mortal to the man of to-day? No thinking man or woman can gainsay this proposition. Added to this, we have the assurance, the promise of those who have gone before us, that it shall be; and it does not really matter how long the journey may be, the ultimate attainment is as inevitable as is the existence of God himself.

Everywhere we see the evidences, the earmarks, the indications of development. Things of fifteen years ago are called "old-fashioned," because they no longer meet the needs of present day civilization, and are no longer up to the standard set by the human race in even that short space of time. Thought is far more advanced along all lines than it was even five years ago, and the stride of civilization has been rapidly forward.

Looking back over the development of the plant and the vegetable kingdoms, we find that the progress in times past was slow. Thousands of years were required to even add a petal to the rose. In the animal kingdom, it took thousands of years to lengthen the neck of the desert antelope so that it could eat the foliage from the tall trees, and develop into what we call the Giraffe. But in all these evolutions we see that the main principle of true development was absent, that of Intelligence. As soon as that faculty was added, growth became rapid. Now, in our civilization of to-day, with the highest degree of intelligence ever manifested by the human race, changes take place so rapidly that things become "out of style" or "old-fashioned" over night.

This advancement, this standard of thought pertains to all fields of industry and all branches of human knowledge. Through the application of the brain of man, we see the ordinary sand plum transformed into the luscious nectarine. By a series of interminglings of breeds, horses, dogs, and our domestic and wild animals are almost rendered unrecognizable as springing from their original species. And the mind must pause in its contemplation of things, and wonder, if such results are obtainable, perceptibly, consciously, by the application of the intelligence of the human brain to the lower forms of life—the plant, vegetable and animal kingdoms—what possibilities may lie dormant within the human soul, which, through the application, the concentration, the lifting power of the human mind, might be manifested, and raise the whole being into immortality.

If the grain of wheat and the flower seed can go into the soil and then grow and reproduce after their kind, without the initiative of a guiding intelligence of their own, but only through outward conditions, and the Divine impulse within their hearts, can any reasoning human being gainsay the possibilities of at least a proportionate development for man? The flower seed can only produce after its kind; it can not make or change its growth, except through outside conditions and influences. It has no individual initiative. The soil may stunt its development, or make it grow luxuriantly, but, without these outside influences, it will always be the same kind of a flower. But the moment there is intelligence added, in the form of a Burbank, a variety is obtained which does not, as it were, recognize itself. It changes from a seeded variety to a seedless fruit; it evolves from the most common to the rarest variety of which we can conceive. And through what? Through the outside influence of a guiding intelligence, a brain; a brain which can take the forces of nature, and through the laws which nature decrees, mould the substances of the universe into that which it wishes to bring forth.

What a lesson man may derive from this! The key-note of all creation is development, evolution. The impulse of all the forces of the universe is onward, ever onward and upward to higher, finer, newer manifestations, and forms of life which will express and show forth the highest expressions and possibilities of the Creative Force back of them. And to man are given the wonderful advantages of Intelligence, combined with Soul, express and show forth the highest expressions and possibilities to express the ideal which God holds in his mind of him. Man has the greatest opportunity of all creation for his development. He has that wonderful shaper, that maker, that guider, that governor, the Mind. The Mind is the master builder that takes the substance of the universe, and if it will listen to the guidance of the soul, it may build an eternal habitation. It has the opportunity, and the authority to take the Divine Essences, and like the sculptor, mould out of the substance of the universe the ideal which it holds in mind; to make an imperishable body, to construct a Divine Mind, and build an Illuminated Soul.

And from whence is it given this authority; from whence comes this power? Always from within. All development or unfoldment, all evolution is from within out. Nothing develops from the outer inwardly. Nature is an unfoldment, not a surface growth. Everything must come from the idea, the root, the heart. Heart development is soul development. Mind development must eventually gradually give place to the heart guidance, and without any guidance, nothing can be accomplished. And with these wonderful faculties of mind and soul, man has the most glorious opportunity that can be afforded anything in the universe. His mind permits him to comprehend the constructive laws; his mind shapes the course of events, prompts him, gives him the opportunity to commune with his fellows. Through his mind he creates continually, Body and Soul, and he is guided in all of his activities, through conformity to laws which the mind permits him to understand. Mind is the starting point, the guide through the entire creative process.

Through the use of his intelligence, the law of Cause and Effect says to man that as he sows, so shall he reap. He knows that he cannot build without a plan, and he takes into his heart the highest ideal which he can conceive, and sowing love, beauty, purity, thoughts of the highest of which he can dream, he builds ever onward and upward toward the attainment of that ideal in his heart. As he grows, gradually the mind becomes refined, and the soul is built into the image and likeness of God. The mind then gives place to the Soul, and as the Soul is manifest, the body becomes quickened and spiritualized, imperishable, and the ultimate of creation is reached, the final Evolvement, the Perfect Man. Intuition then has taken the seat of reason, and communion, conscious communion with God is established, and the Soul wings its way upward and still upward into etherial realms, until it can say, with the Master, "I and the Father are one."

This is the purpose of evolution. All nature proclaims that it is a possibility and must be accomplished, and the wise man and woman will take the hint which has been given by the evolution of the centuries, and set the feet unfaltering, steadfastly upon the path which leads to the "Mark of the high calling of God," even the Christos, the Son of the living God.

INITIATION

Initiation is not, as it is popularly conceived to be, a system of believing, or system of ritualism. Ceremonial initiation is really no initiation in the generic sense of the word. Ceremonialism has its proper place. The inculcation of moral lessons and ethical principles helps men to a broader outlook of life, and to formulate their ideals. But, in and of itself, it has no power to make the candidate different than what he was before the ceremony. Ceremonial initiation is merely the outer symbol or the picture of the inner growth every individual must experience. It holds up to the candidate an ideal of life to strive for, if he would become better, healthier, happier and attain mastership. It is a symbol to the candidate of an inner growth to be experienced by putting the true teachings into practice. Otherwise, ceremonial initiation is meaningless. Just as we employ in the kindergarten pictures with which to instruct the childish mind, so is ritualistic initiation necessary to picture in concrete form to the candidate abstract truth which he is otherwise incapable of grasping. No matter how beautiful the system of morals may be which is taught through ceremonial initiation, if the candidate does not put into practice the lessons he is taught, if he is not helped to understand them, if he is not shown how to apply them in his daily living by a system of living and training, and if thereby he does not experience an inner growth, he does not receive the inner meaning of the degrees. By no stretch of the imagination can you conceive of an individual becoming a master-man through a ceremonial initiation. Yet thousands of intelligent men pay a fee to some Fraternal organization with the idea of being raised to the plane of Mastership in a few minutes and through a ceremony. And the Fraternal organization that promises to give the candidate "Light" and make of him a master-man, and fails to do so, is obtaining money under false pretences. No one can bestow upon you any power, growth or increase your status in life by a mere ceremony. Can you conceive of an artist, a musician or a successful business man being made such through a ceremony?

Real initiation is inner growth and development. It is the process of eternal becoming. It is the acquisition of intelligence and wisdom. From the cradle to the grave man experiences growth and change, physically, mentally and spiritually. Physically, our bodies are continually undergoing change; mentally, we do not think today as we thought yesterday; and spiritually, we are ever receiving "more light."

When man is consciously guided by his intuition and wisely directed by a system of teachings and training which accelerates his growth and unfoldment of his spiritual faculties we have the true initiation which the True Rose Cross Fraternity offers its students. True initiation teaches the laws of health, development of mind and the building of an illuminated Christ soul. In true initiation the student earns growth and advancement only through effort and through living of a life in conformity with scientific principles tried and tested; and true mastership is earned through development of soul. The candidate becomes the master in fact and in not in name only. In true initiation, higher self-hood is gained through self-development; while in ceremonial initiation titles and degrees are conferred and bestowed upon candidates for so much pecuniary consideration and without any effort of self-mastery on the part of the candidate. How foolish and childish for men to think they can obtain advancement in the unfoldment of their being without development and overcoming. No artist ever reached his goal without having worked for it. No man in any line of endeavor ever attained the topmost rung of the ladder of success except through work and self-mastery.

Within every man are implanted latent faculties and potentialities for him to make use of and unfold. Just as the potential rose is in the plant, so is the master or Christ soul in embryo in every man. Just as the seed has the potential plant, so has man the potential master-man. But, whereas, the seed has no free-will to develop itself into the plant, but must wait to be put into the ground for germination, man, the highest in the kingdom of life, is endowed by his Creator with free-will and free-choice, which enables him to unfold his potential Christ and raise himself to a higher being, whenever man wills and chooses to do so.

At birth we are given our working tools—a body, a mind and a seed, a Divine Spark from the Father, a potential Christ or soul. And we are given a span of years on this plane of life within which to employ our working tools for a purpose, and that purpose is to develop the germ soul into the master or Christ soul and attain sonship with the Father. And when the candidate is helped by a systematic training to accomplish this purpose, we have true initiation.

This is the meaning of life. We are not born to suffer and stagnate and die, but to live and grow and develop from plane to plane, ever higher and higher. The working tools, body, mind and soul—are not given us so that we can make of them stinking temples and employ our minds to generate power for selfish purposes. True initiation has no other object in view than the soulual development of the individual.

Initiation is birth into new and higher understanding. It is the development of one's intuition, enabling the individual to grasp a larger measure of truth. Alas, how densely ignorant is mankind of intuition, that divine channel in man which is the connecting link between himself and his Creator! We gain knowledge through the mind, but wisdom and Divine direction is obtained through intuition. Initiation or the introduction into higher truth is by way of intuition.

Truth is as infinite as God. Therefore, truth cannot be circumscribed within a narrow circle for the convenience of man. There is no limit to the wisdom of God, and there is no limit to our growth in understanding and the acquisition of wisdom, unless we limit ourselves and refuse to grow. When a man denies that there are higher possibilities for him by that very thought does he exclude himself from a higher life. When a man says he cannot do a certain task even before he has tried, by that very thought has he sealed his failure. The great mass of mankind build around themselves a fence and refuse to venture out. How are they going to know what is beyond if they fear, to do, to think and to try? No one limits man but himself. Man is the individual point within the circle of his vision of truth. If his vision is narrow, his horizon of truth will be narrow. The more we unfold, the greater we increase the circumference of the circle of our vision, and the greater expanse of truth we come in contact with.

The storehouse of God's wisdom is vast, and it is there for our use and for us to draw on. But if we have not developed our faculties, what have we by which we can draw on that storehouse? The savage and the musician both listen to the same divine melody, but how differently are they impressed, due to difference in the development of the musical perception. As the connecting link between us and God's wisdom is intuition, it is our duty to develop our intuition, so that we can absorb more truth and wisdom. The unfoldment of our intuition is initiation.

True initiation is evolution on the soulual side of man. A man may have physical perfection, he may acquire mental acumen and his mind may become a storehouse of facts, and yet be far from truth and spiritual understanding and from mastership. Many men reach a high plane of mentality, and yet are evil at heart, where is their wisdom? Physical culture is good; it brings health and physical well being. But physical culture alone cannot bring us spiritual understanding nor does it teach us how to build an immortal soul. Mental culture enables us to become acquainted with the physical sciences and mental laws which are useful to man. But mental culture cannot develop intuition. The greatest progress the human race has made and is making is on their spiritual side which concerns itself with internal growth. Man evolves from darkness and ignorance into light and truth through the development of his soul, and this is true evolution and initiation.

The greatest progress of the human race is not done in the physical laboratory, but in the laboratory of the human heart; In the heart base passions are changed into pure gold of love. When transmuting evil tendencies, refines his nature and develops good-ness or God-ness, he is fulfilling his mission in life and is treading the path of evolution. When man can advance from hating his enemies into loving them, he has made the highest progress he is capable of. We can measure the reactions that take place in the test tube, but who can measure the wonderful reactions that take place in the laboratory of the human heart? What difference is there between the uncivilized and civilized man? Is it a physical difference, a matter of flesh and bones? Is it a mental difference? The ignorant man can be taught a great deal of the mental culture of today. Is it not rather a difference of the spiritual make-up? The savage cannot grasp abstract truth such as virtue and forgiveness. This understanding of the abstract dealing with morality is not a mental process. Were it so, then the criminal would not be a criminal. The criminal class are mentally capable, but spiritually they are dark. The difference between the race of today and that of the Roman Empire is not due so much to mental culture, but in a change of heart—which is the spiritual side of man. We can no longer sit in an arena and derive pleasure and entertainment from watching wild beasts mangle human beings. What is true of the race is also true of the individual. True initiation aims at a change of heart in the individual.

True initiation is through regeneration and purification. Regeneration is rebirth or birth into a new life. To become regenerated is to become born again, not only in mind, but in body as well. It is possible to create a new body, younger and healthier. Purification is freedom from grossness, from impurities and from base and vile habits. Purification is not only of the body, but of the mind and heart as well. The ideal man, the one who has developed the Christ soul, is he who is of pure and healthy body, of sound and powerful will and of loving heart that throbs for hunmanity. A master-man is as wise as a serpent and innocent or pure as a babe.

Initiation is life. Life is a school. Life is an opportunity, and every moment of our life is a change—a variation of opportunity. This we must become conscious of. If we let our opportunities go, we are the losers, and we go down the scale of life by some degrees. Every man who is born to this world, whether he knows it or not, treads the initiatory path of evolution. The difference between the average man, and the man who takes up the path of inner initiation or soul development as taught by the great and true Rose Cross Fraternity is that, whereas the average man goes through life blindly, not knowing what he is aiming for, nor whither he is drifting to and permits his divine possibilities and potentialities to remain dormant and undeveloped, the student or Soul Science is constantly conscious of an ideal before him towards which he concentrates every ounce of his strength and every minute of his life and is scientifically directing his energies towards the development of his latent potentialities. The student is hastening his freedom from karmic conditions and from slavery to bound destiny and is working towards soul illumination or Christhood. The first is like a piece of driftwood in the grip of the rushing current, helpless to direct its own course; while the latter is like the able swimmer, who breasts life's currents and is able to direct his course whither he wills against tide and wind. Which do you desire to be, drift wood, or a masterful swimmer?

Life is not only an opportunity, but a gift. It is not a curse and a misfortune as some believe. If you believe in a loving God, would he curse you by giving you life? If God is love, then out of love for man has he given him life. Then life is a blessing. This life of ours is one grand opportunity given us to unfold, to grow, to gain experience, and through experience, wisdom. It is a school on a great scale; and every experience we encounter furnishes us with a problem to solve—and solve we must. For, Nature, unlike a lenient and forgiving teacher, knows no excuses and expects from us an accounting and a correct solution to her problems. Then why run away from the problems of life, when you know you cannot escape them?

Initiation is by way of the crucifixion of the son of man. That is, the earthly man with his false appetites, his prejudices and vices, his sensuous loving desires, and the craving of the flesh to be indulged in appetites that degrade and pull down, must be hung upon the cross. Man has indulged his body so long not with what he desires, but with what it desires, that he has become a slave to its desires. And the average man's mind is like a runaway horse. He has no control over his thoughts. The thoughts control him and they are for the most part destructive in character. Just as long as a drug fiend feeds his body with drugs the apetites are satisfied; but let him deprive these appetities of their stimulants, when they will fight for their very lives. And in like manner, as long as the individual sees no necessity of depriving the appetites of his body and mind and keeps indulging them, he is unmindful of the slave that he is. But as soon as he begins to assert his mastery by depriving those appetites of their desires then he faces a battle which requires strong resolution and indomitable will to gain mastery. As long as the individual has no desire to reach perfection and gives in to his body and mind, there is no struggle; but when he begins to nail upon the cross the unnecessary and the useless things, then does he find out what a slave he is. This is not a struggle for a day. It is a matter of time, of patience, of perseverance and of continual trying. But each time he gains strength and the appetites lose their power.

Progress on the path of initiation is by way of sacrifice. But do not think it is necessary for you to sacrifice anything that is worthy and good. What is required is that you give up the things that are unnecessary—the things that are so much dead weight. Just as we expect the growing child to give up its toys as it reaches the adult state, so do we expect that the man who desires progress on the path of initiation to give up the childish and unimportant things. When man has lived a life of delusion when from infancy he has been taught to regard the impractical as practical, and the practical as impractical, the things that are not necessary seem essential.

Initiation is the great climb up the steep and rugged ascent to God. It is a rough and rugged journey. To make progress one must divest himself of all unnecessary impediments. The higher you climb this path, the more one must free oneself of unnecessary luggage, otherwise they weigh the candidate down and prevent his ascent. And on this steep ascent, to make headway, the candidate must overcome beasts that are stationed along the journey and that fight his progress. For instance, you will have to overcome the beast of pride.

Pride stands in your way of obtaining wisdom. It makes you cling to things that are not necessary to your growth. It blocks your path and would keep you down in ignorance. It is no easy matter to kill the beast; you will have a long struggle with it; but you will have to overcome and utterly destroy it, if you desire to ascend the path to wisdom and God. After all, pride is not necessary to your welfare. If then it becomes essential that you part company with pride, will you love it so much as to prefer its ignorant association to making progress on the path?

Then you must meet the beast of laziness. To the death with this beast. It would have you temporize and procrastinate. It whispers into your ears soothing words lulling you to sleep. It would make you believe that there is no hurry to climb life's path, that there is plenty of time, that somehow or other you will advance without putting forth effort. This is a hard beast to overcome. He is subtle in his arguments. You are offered a life of ease and indulgence. Laziness would convince you that no climbing is necessary to advance on the path of God, and that nature will take care of you. Mental laziness is the strongest beast that rules humanity. The people will not think, but let others do the thinking for them. Do not listen to the seductive pleading of this beast. Realize that growth and progress is to be had only at the expense of effort and work and systematic training. Nothing that is born or produced is born of laziness, but of struggle and of effort. A muscle is developed through exercise; a voice is developed through hard work. If no effort was required for our evolvement and spiritual unfoldment, and if all were equally created in the image of God, then at present every individual of the race should be on the same plane of development. We should be all alike, think alike, feel alike. If nature takes care of us and evolves us, whether we want to or not, then nature would have taken care of us all alike and we would be now on an equal footing. But the fact of the matter is that no two individuals are alike and every one is on a different plane of evolvement because every one puts forth different effort. Some are farther on the path of evolution than others, not because nature has been partial to them. Effort and practice and self-mastery is the keynote to growth and progress. To make headway in spiritual unfoldment is to make effort *now,* wisely and systematically.

We will not enumerate the many beasts the traveler on the path of initiation must overcome to reach the summit, which is mastership or Christhood. But the effort is worth while. Power and wisdom is gained only through experience in overcoming. Understanding of Divine law is gained through application and practice in our daily living. True initiation is conservation of our bodily and mental forces and concentrating them for building character, manhood, soul and attaining Mastership of Christhood. Ordinary living leads to diffusion of our forces, stagnation and death. While true initiation is concentration and leads to power and immortality of life.

Soul building recognizes that man is a triune being—body, mind and soul. In order to obtain the most efficient results, each department of man's being must be given equal attention through co-ordinating and harmonizing the training so that one-sided development may be avoided. The aim of initiation is perfection, and to attain perfection, man must begin with his foundation or body. For upon the strength of the body rests the strength of the nervous system and the power of the mind; and a powerful mind is required to build the Christ soul. Just as in plant life, we have at one end the earth and at the other end the product of creating, the beautiful rose, so in man, the foundation is a strong and healthy body, and the product of our living, creating and developing is a beautiful soul. As in the plant the essences of the earth go for the production of the rose, so in man, the strength of our body should go in building soul. But if the plant has parasites living off it, the essences of the earth go to feeding the parasites and never build the rose. And in man, if he is a slave to his parasites, the beasts that are in him, the essences of his body are wasted in feeding the appetites of the beasts, and there is no energy left with which to build the soul.

It is possible through a systematic training of the body, mind and soul to accomplish in one life what it would take thousands of lives to do. We can if we will by concentration of our efforts on one ideal hasten our development from a plain ordinary unregenerate mortal to a sinless Master-man or Christ soul. This is what all the great Masters, prophets, Messiahs and Christs have taught and it is taught today by the true Rose Cross Fraternity.

True initiation is an inner growth and unfoldment of one's spiritual faculties leading to Illumination and immortality of soul while external or ceremonial initiation is pure ritualism and merely symbolic of the inner initiation or growth. We declare that the "initiation" as practiced by most fraternities, societies or orders of today is external initiation only and is purely ceremonialism and ritualism. These bodies have long lost the true "word" or the true logos or science of teaching the candidate inner development leading to illumination and immortality of soul. In pantomine they conduct the candidate through a ceremony but they do not know how to teach that Divine science which enables the student through years of training to develop himself into a master soul. Most of these bodies, fraternities and societies, so-called mystic and occult, can offer their candidates only ritualism and external initiation. While the true Rose Cross Fraternity, insists now, as it has always in the past, that the seeker after truth, first of all, pass through the inner initiation or growth before the ceremonial part shall be conferred upon him.

The true Rose Cross Fraternity is first of all a school of spirituality, but it is also an order, in that it has a ritual and a ceremonial initiation. However, it is not a degree peddling institution. It does not take money for its instruction nor does it accept money for the conferring of the ceremonial work.

THE SECOND COMING OF CHRIST

The law of evolution is a reality. Nowhere is it more evidenced than in man. But Man must comply with this law, which is the law of growth, in order for him to experience the operation of the law of evolution in his life. In other words, in order for us to manifest the law of growth, we have to comply with Divine law and live in accordance with its rules. We have to assume an active, positive and co-operative attitude towards the law, and not remain passive or indifferent to it. Passivity is stagnation and not growth. Growth implies activity and change. A close study of mankind, its various peoples and races, the savage, the semi-civilized and civilized—discloses to us the operation of this law of evolution. And by it also we account for the differences between individuals. Some have more heart and more intelligence than others, and, in consequence, are further advanced on the evolutionary path than others. Of the white race today, there are those, who, in their unfoldment and growth, have far outstripped the rest of mankind. These are the thinkers and leaders, who mould human thought and give direction to civilization.

In the study of man we perceive that the law of evolution is operative principally on his spiritual side. The more highly evolved the man, the more spiritual he is, or the more soul or goodness he displays. As soul in man is his highest plane, and the connecting link between him and God, the more soul he has, the nearer God man is. And the more Godly a man is, the more of soul he is.

In the vanguard of the human race, there are those individuals (a few only) who have far outstripped the rest in development of their souls, beyond the imagination of the average man. As the difference between an Edison and a savage is immeasurably great, so the difference between an average man of today and an evolved Master Soul of Christ is still greater and beyond the common conception. If we admit that the race has evolved spiritually, from the savage to the civilized state; if we admit that the race today manifests more of heart, goodness, justice and mercy; we must admit the truth that if the race has evolved thus far, it is capable of evolving still further. And when we accept this proposition we must accept the statement that there are those individuals, who through living a life in conformity with Divine Law, and who, through training in soul development, have so much advanced in the evolvement of their souls, that, to the average man, they indeed have become supermen, angelic beings, master souls, Christs and Gods. As the race is evolving towards God, naturally these highly developed men stand nearest to God.

From time immemorial, there has been an organization of these highly developed souls, banded together for one common purpose—to teach mankind Divine law to show mankind how to live their lives in conformity with Divine law so as to hasten their evolution towards Godhood, to warn them against false teachings, to originate movements tending to improve conditions, and to train men to lead the race into the paths of righteousness. This organization or Fraternity has existed in all ages, under different names and exists today under the true Rosicrucian title. It trains men to become master men, master souls, Christs and Messiahs. It has always guarded the pure teachings of the masters from profanation. It has never taught openly; for it recognizes that the race is not as yet prepared for its sublime inner mysteries. Its esoteric teachings are only for the few of the race who have evolved to the point where orthodoxy, creeds and ritualism no longer satisfies, whose motives are pure, and whose desires are holy, and who hunger for a meatier spiritual diet. It has ever kept its sacred teachings of its master uncorrupted and beyond the profane, the vicious and the ignorant. Today as never before, in a spiritually more enlightened age, the true Rosicrucian Fraternity offers its sublime teachings to the worthy and the true student.

From this great Fraternity of great souls have been sent trained master souls, great Messiahs and Christs to lead the people back into paths of righteousness, when the people had wandered away from the truth. When a time arises when the people through false teachings have drifted away from Divine law and have sunk into misery and degradation, and when it becomes imperative to point out to them the true path, these great leaders come to teach Divine law and how to apply the law so as to evolve oneself to Christhood.

Every age and every people have had a great Messiah or Christ or Saviour, sent by the Great Fraternity. The Chinese had their Confucius; the Scandinavians Balder; the Egyptians, Osiris; the Greeks, Hercules, Bacchus, Apollo and Hermes; the Indians, Krishna; the Persians, Mithra and Zoroaster; the Hindus, Buddha, and the Jews, Moses, the prophets and Jesus.

These great teachers having been instructed by the same Fraternity, taught the people the same mysteries of the Kingdom of Heaven. A close study of all the great religions will disclose to the earnest student that the basic principles are the same in all, since their origin is the same.

During the life of these Masters, only a few of the people, disciples and students, understood their teachings. But the great mass of the people never wholly accepted the teachings. After the masters passed away, as the teachings spread, designing and ignorant priests substituted the word for the spirit, creed and dogma in place of Divine truth, and so corrupted the true teachings that the mysteries of soul building were lost to the people. As in the past so today, the churches have lost the grand science of soul building and can offer only blind belief, creed and dogma.

The teachings of the Masters or Christs concerns itself with the science of soul building. But ignorant and selfish priestcraft of every age, having lost this grand science, and desiring to control the people, have substituted a worship of form and ceremony and idols. Instead of teaching the people Divine law, they have set up these great teachers or Christs as Gods for the people to worship. So that the Chinese worship Confucius, the Jews Moses, the Egyptians worshipped Osiris, the Persians Zoroaster, the Grecks Apollo and Hermes and the Christians worship Jesus.

Today, after two thousand years of the last great Master Teacher or Christ, we meet with conditions if not more serious than at any time in the past are at least as bad as any history records. We have vast fertile acreage, yet the people are landless; we raise more food than we can consume, yet large numbers of the people are hungry; we have an over production of wearing apparel, yet many of the people go naked. Never in the world's history was education so easy of access, and our libraries so full of books, yet the mass of the people are ignorant. Courts dispense injustice instead of justice. We have self-seeking and corrupt politicians instead of wise and just statesmen and councilors. Religion is not a matter of science and philosophy with the people. It has become a blind faith in creed and dogma. The priestcraft having lost the spirit of the true teachings of the masters, having become ignorant of Divine law, and not knowing how to teach the people the science and philosophy of soul building, and observing that their grip on the people is loosening, are attempting to revive and gain back their authority through frenzied emotionalism called revivals. Poverty, misery, disease and early death stalk the streets. Society is miserable, sickly and unhappy. Surely, no apologist can be found who is so dull as not to admit the utter failure of our present civilization.

Instead of considering the Master Jesus as a leader come to teach the science of soul building, the people worship Him as a God. And by deifying the Master, they place His life and His teachings beyond them. For they reason with themselves, "who can do like Him he being a God or born of God?"

The great teachers or Christs never claimed anything for themselves but that their mission was to teach the people "the way, the truth and the life" of the initiatory path, leading to development and immortality of soul, through living of a life in conformity with Divine law and training in soul building. These Christs were trained leaders, who were born in the flesh like you and I, and who through development and training only in accordance with the teachings of the great Rosicrucian Fraternity, had developed their soul and attained supreme illumination or Christhood. Christhood was earned by them, and so can you earn it if you will live the life that they did.

What is Christ? Christ is the illuminated or developed soul. Every man has the potential Christ in embryonic form, which through training can be developed into an illuminated soul or Christ. And this training is offered today by the great Fraternity of Masters. So that when we speak of Christ, or Messiah or Saviour, we mean those great teachers of mankind who attained their position only through training in Soul Science. And their mission among mankind was to teach this glorious science and philosophy of soul building, and by their exemplary life be a model to the people. The difference between the average man and a Christ is in soul growth. The average man pays no attention to his divine possibilities, while the Christ, through a life of training under Master teachers, has unfolded his soul and made himself a Divine being.

The Fraternity of Masters or illuminated souls has always existed and exists today. They are ever ready to point out "The way, the truth and the life." But they cannot force their teachings on an unwilling public, nor do they desire to court death at the hands of ignorant mobs. "Seek and ye shall find; ask and it shall be given you; knock and the door will be opened unto you." The individual must of his own free will and accord seek soul development and wisdom, and a way is found whereby the earnest seeker will meet the true teacher.

Jesus said, "Think not that I come to destroy the law, or the prophets; I am not come to destroy, but to fulfill." The Divine laws were given to the people by Moses, as by all other Messiahs to all people in every age. But after Moses passed away, the people turned their backs on Divine law and drifted back into materialism. When Jesus came, no one among the people including the priesthood, understood Divine law and the science of soul development. The mission of Jesus, then, was to fulfill the law and the teachings of the prophets, for he was in harmony with them; and by his exemplary life to show them "The way, the truth and the life" or how to unfold their soul and reach supreme illumination or Christhood.

The question arises, can a Messiah or Christ change the mass of the people? History proves this has not been done. For, consider, the many great teachers who have appeared before the people to bring them out of darkness into light. What have they accomplished with the mass? The people in the present, as in the past, still worship form; they still cling to creeds and ceremonialism. If in the past they worshipped the golden bull, they worship today the golden calf. They still think that they can gain salvation and heaven through mere blind belief only in the divinity of one man, forgetting that "the way, the truth and the life" is not based on belief alone but on soulual development and training.

Common sense leads us to see that no Messiah, not even God himself, has the power to change the people from one state into another. God having endowed man with free will and free choice, and having constituted him a free moral agent, it would be a contravention of His own laws were He to compel mankind to mend its ways. Man must of his own free will and accord square his actions by the square of virtue and thereby gradually grow into divinity. If God has not been able these many thousands of years to turn the people from their erring ways, how can anyone, who is less than God, do that which God has failed to do? And to claim that a Christ can transplant the people bodily into heaven whether deserving or not, is to place a Christ on a higher plane than God and stamp God as a failure. But God is not a failure. He desires his offspring to come to him of their own accord in due time and season. And coming to God is a matter of growth and soulual evolvement and training in Soul Science, and not a matter of compulsion or overnight conversion. God is soul, and to know God, one must become soulually developed, which is a matter of years of training in soul science under a Master teacher. How foolish it is for the people to still think that they can be converted and become regenerated through blind belief alone.

The race today still thinks that when a Christ will come, he will lead them direct to heaven and save them from their sufferings, and forgive them their sins and give them plenty and bestow upon them growth without their working for it, if they will believe in his Divinity. It is a fantastic dream, this idea of waiting for Christ to relieve mankind of the responsibility of paying for its sins and of working for its growth. If we subscribe to the golden rule, "As ye sow so shall ye reap," and if mankind has sown plentifully of sin, who will do the reaping? Can God set aside his own laws? If God is all law, how can he set us an example of law breaking? Mankind must pay the penalty for transgression of Divine law and no one can stand between us and Divine law. All that these Christs can do for us is to teach us the initiatory path of soul development and how to gain immortality of soul now and here but they cannot live this life for us nor pay our debts, nor grow for us, just as much as no one can eat or drink or sleep for us.

The Masters never taught that the Messiahs through their sacrifice would bring salvation to mankind. This pernicious doctrine has been given to the world by a designing priesthood for selfish reasons and has been acquiesced to by the people who are only too glad to believe in doctrines which will promise them most at the expenditure of least effort. Man is lazy and he likes to believe in teachings which best suit his lazy notions and which do not require from him effort. Set up a system of thought whereby one can be absolved from reaping what one has sown by mere blind belief, and you have hordes that will follow you; but teach the people individual responsibility, and they will stone you.

No one, no matter how Godly he may be, can live the life for others, or relieve them of their burdens or bring them salvation. If the people had the right kind of manhood, and felt a Man's responsibility to their God, their neighbor or themselves, they would not expect any one else to pay their debts, or the Master's death to save them from just punishment. Yet millions of mankind today, as in the past, are waiting for some Messiah or Christ to come down from heaven, to lead his Godly life and to die for them, so that they, without doing anything worth while for themselves, can reap health, happiness, growth and immortality of soul and be transplanted into some far off place called heaven.

The law of God is individual responsibility. Every man must first rise to that plane of intelligence where he feels his individual responsibility for his thoughts and acts. And when he arrives at this stage of his evolution he no longer sits idly by waiting for some Christ to drop down from heaven to relieve him from his burdens, forgive him his sins and make an angel of him.

All these Messianic expectations arise from the erroneous teachings given to the people by ignorant priesthood who having lost the science of soul development teach the people that these Messiahs are Gods and that if they, the people, believe thus, they will be saved and absolved from past errors. What a frightful thought to hold and how blasphemous it is of God!

Let us understand clearly the meaning of Messiah or Christ. Christ is not a man. Christ or Messiah is the developed or illuminated soul in a man. All the great Masters and teachers of the human race Moses, Buddha and Jesus, were born in the flesh, like you and I, and who through training in Soul Science as taught by the great Rosicrucian Fraternity today, as it has done in the past, had become the Christs or Illuminated Souls. But every man has the same opportunities and the same possibilities of becoming Christs. If only one offspring of God could become the Christ, and it were denied the rest of the race, and if the race were denied soulual development and were doomed to death and extinction, then it were better for the race not to have been born at all. But the great teachers never taught that they were the only begotten sons of God. On the contrary, they pointed out the path of attainment and Christhood for all who were willing to overcome and work for immortality. Jesus said, "Verily, verily, I say unto you, he that believeth onto me, the works that I do, shall he do also; and greater works than these shall he do; because I go unto my Father." Jesus did not mean blind belief, active faith supported by works. His disciples were were earnest students of soul science, builders of their spiritual temples, who lived their lives in conformity with Divine law and who were in training under him. They were not mere blind followers. And he promised them that they would do greater works than he was doing. If it were possible for his disciples to do the works that he was doing, why is it not possible for others to do likewise? Do you think that the science of soul building as taught by Jesus and the other Masters of old has been lost? It has been lost to the people who have never accepted these teachings, but they have not been lost to the few earnest students in every age, who have always kept the pure Christic teachings alive.

Jesus said plainly, "The kingdom of God cometh not with observation. Neither shall they say, lo here, or lo there. For behold the kingdom of heaven is within you." Each individual is a Christ in the making. Christ is soul. Each man has the germ or christ child within him. It is his Messiah or Saviour which through training under a Master teacher will make of him a master man with Christic powers. It is for each man to bring forth and unfold his saviour, and no man can do it for him, just as no one can eat for him. And the kingdom of heaven is within each individual. It is for him to find it. "The kingdom of God cometh not with observation." No one ever attained his Christhood by waiting for some other Christ to do his work, just as no one ever became a ball player by watching some other ball player play.

Two thousand years ago Jesus came to teach the people soul development. He attained his illumination of soul or became the Christ. It is now up to the people to accept his teachings in spirit, to become students of soul science. And when the people travel the path of initiation of soul development, they will have become the Christs, and then does the Christ come to them a second time.

Do not wait for some external Christ to come. The saviour or Christ is within you. And it is ever ready to become manifest in your lives when you are ready to take up the training of soul development. But remember that belief in immortality of soul is not sufficient to make of you immortal. The great Fraternity of Masters want students who are willing to work. They do not care for mere followers who are satisfied with faith alone. The great Masters are ever ready to help the earnest student who is desirous of unfolding his soul and become a Christ. And today through Soul Science we are offering these teachings in all their purity and simplicity.

"Behold, I stand at the door, and knock; if any man hear my voice, and open the door, I will come in to him, and will sup with him, and he with me. To him that overcometh will I grant to sit with me in my throne even as I also overcame, and set down with my Father in his throne."

How many of you realize that your soul is urging you for its unfoldment? How many of you hear its voice and are willing to open the door to the Christ within yourselves?

AUTHORITY VERSUS INDIVIDUALITY

From time immemorial there have existed two schools of thought, the one standing for the suppression of the freedom of thought by the masses, and the other for the freedom of the individual, individual development and initiative.

For convenience sake, we will call the first, the Devolutionery school, and the second, the evolutionary school. The First School denies the principle of evolution as applied to the individual, while the second considers that the law of life, which is the law of growth, is for differentiation and individualization.

The Devolutionary school has no faith in the people, considers them incapable of governing themselves or thinking for themselves, and has no higher hope for the masses than a life of labor and slaving for the privileged few at the top. Those who belong to this school are men who have attained superior intelligence, but are selfish, self-seeking, ambitious for power, and are obsessed with the desire to rule and govern. They are the backbone, brains and power of the dominant church and political parties, the two main instruments of power that have controled and are controling and governing the public mind. And whenever possible and convenient, the church and the state, which is usually a political machine, have united to share the power of control over the people. For both recognize that they are dependent upon each other to maintain their authority over the people. The church by teaching fear and respect for authority can influence the people to become submissive to the governing powers, and the state by passing laws can protect the church from untoward influences. The established church has always stood for every movement which would curtail the freedom of the individual and make him subservient to its authority. In every age and among every nation we find this to be a fact.

The Devolutionery School has the greatest contempt for the intelligence of the masses and believes that the greatest good for the common people can best be obtained by centralizing the power of government in the hands of a few individuals, whom God created with superior attainments for the express purpose of acting as his viceregerts on earth. They would deny the people freedom of thought and of choice, and consider themselves best fitted to think and choose for the needs of the masses. They consider individual development and initiative as inconsistent to centralized power and dangerous to its authority. They are self-appointed God's agents on earth with powers to forgive sins, remit transgressions against Divine law, and give a ticket of admission to heaven or condemn souls to hell depending on the attitude of the individual to their authority.

On the other hand the Evolutionery school stands squarely for individaul effort and initiative, and individual freedom of thought and of choice. They consider that the law of evolution as applied to man is for differentiation and individualization, and that any interference with this law brings about dire results. For a time only can authority hold back the progress of the masses in individual unfoldment. But as this is contrary to the law of nature, nature has its way of ridding itself of intollerable conditions, resulting in cataclysms, revolutions and wars.

The evolutionary school would work in harmony with nature and allow the individual full liberty of unfoldment, freedom of thought, belief and choice, in so far as it would help him grow, without interfering with the freedom of others and with no injury to society. This school thinks that the world can be made better and mankind be best benefitted *only through* the development of the individual and that as he grows, unfolds and is made to understand and recognize individual responsibility, is he in position to help himself and his fellow-men. When man is taught that as he sows, so will he reap, that every act and thought produces definite results, good or bad, according to the deed and thought, that no one can stand between him and his Creator and delegate to himself authority to forgive sins committed, and that every sin committed brings about just punishment commensurate with the performance of the act, then the individual will begin to feel moral responsibility and will be careful as to his mode of living. The danger in allowing a few persons to control the public mind and conscience lies in the fact that it breeds an opportunity for developing selfish, self-seeking and power-mad men. Such men are unfit to be entrusted with the interests of the people, for they can use their power for evil and for self as against the best interests of the people. Such men would keep the people in darkness and in ignorance and would stifle individual effort, lest the masses wake up and remove them from power.

Authority is the result of a few individuals at the top delegating to themselves powers and prerogatives, and constituting themselves the control to judge, to rule and to dominate. In time you may be sure they will see to it that they will instill and foster respect from the people for their authority.

And in time the people come to worship this authority as a fetich or idol to such an extent that they fear to think for themselves. So that if any new teacher arises or new ideas are pushed forth which might be contrary to the teachings of the established church and political machine in power, no matter how beneficial it might prove to the interests of the people, the authorities perceiving the danger to their power, immediately endeavor to suppress the new teacher and his teachings, on the grounds that the new teachings are heretical and inimical to the welfare of society and the teacher is an enemy to the people. And the people having become like sheep, having lost the power to think for themselves owing to mental paralysis from fear, cannot think or judge for themselves as to the truth or falsity of the new teachings; but, comparing it with the established or authoritative teachings, and finding no harmony, condemn both the new teacher and the new teachings. Remember the experience of the Master Jesus with the established church of his day and its authorities. And this has been the experience of every great teacher in every age.

So effectually have the self constituted authorities taught the people for thousands of years respect for their authority that the masses have lost the power to think for themselves. They have become slaves to authority, which robs them of free-will and free-choice, and which denies them freedom of action, and stifles initiative—the greatest factor in man, which if rightly exercised, leads to the greatest amount of good. As long as the people are rooted down to authority, they are helpless and at the mercy of unscrupulous and selfish men in power.

The greatest weapon in the hands of authority, which enables them to control the masses, is fear. The people are imbued with fear for this or that, are born into fear, live a life of fear and die with and on account of fear. And those in authority have encouraged the people to fear, for herein rests their control and power. If the authorities would encourage the people to think, instead of fear, they would soon lose their hold on the public mind.

The people actually sleep away their lives through fear of being awake. They fear to breathe, they fear to think for themselves, they fear to cross authority, they fear to live their lives in accordance with the dictates of their conscience and live rather in accordance with opinions outside of themselves. They fear disease, they fear death, they fear to express themselves and they fear to assert themselves. Fear has become so rooted in their nature as to paralyze their thoughts and make of them mere automatons subject to the control of authority. Many grand ideas have been stifled and many noble desires have been suppressed because of public opinion which is really authority. For, strictly speaking there is no such thing as public opinion; for few people have a mind of their own, but think and do what their authorities desire them to think and do.

The subjection of the people to authority is manifested in every department of life. Through fear the people are in bondage to the authoritative school of medicine. The people submit to inocculations, to unnecessary pain and torture on account of their submission to authority. In science, in religious thought and in every phase of life it is remarkable how tremendously powerful is the control of authority over the masses. This condition has always prevailed. Individual effort and freedom of thought has always been in conflict with authority.

Every great thinker, every great master and teacher, has been subjected to the greatest trials, and in many cases have met death, for daring to teach the truth and to assert their individuality. Remember the experience of the Master Jesus with the authoritative school of his day. "And when he was come into the temple, the chief priests and elders of the people came unto him as he was teaching and said, by what authority doest thou these things?' And who gave thee this authority." Moses had the same experience, "And Pharoah said, who is the Lord that

I should obey his voice to let Israel go? I know not the Lord neither will I let Israel go."

The Devolutionery school in all ages, represented by the authoritative church and state, has never been friendly to progress! and if any advancement has been made, it has been accomplished in conflict and in spite of authoritative teachings and not because of its support.

Ah, if the people would only have the courage to do, to think for themselves, to live a natural life and to act in accordance with the dictates of their higher promptings, what a beautiful world this would be.

If the people would only be taught to exercise their God given faculties instead of depending on authorities for their welfare what a change in the social economic and religious thought of the world we would witness. But the Devolutionery School desires the masses to be dependent upon them so as to strengthen their power over them. And this pernicious teaching has been inculcated so long that it has become imbred with the people to the extent that they are satisfied with things as they are and assist the authorities in fighting any change no matter how beneficial it might be to their interests. Jesus said to the people, "And think not to say within yourselves, we have Abraham to our Father." What matters it what the people believe in? One system of authoritative belief is as good as another, as long as the people are compelled to blindly worship a system, instead of truth itself. No belief, no matter under what name, or in what age, unless accompanied by works, and unless it encourages independent thought and individual unfoldment, has ever accomplished any good in this world. It is not what the people believe in that counts but it is what they *do* and how they *live*, and how happy and contented society is. And judged by this standard, all authoritative systems of the Devolutionery school, depending on the blind worship of the masses, are negative and destructive in tendency.

The only authority one needs to guide one's footsteps and the safest one to go by is the conscience within each person. God has placed in each human breast a greater judge than any mortal judge, and that is the conscience, which is the voice of God speaking to us through our soul. Man is endowed by his Creator with free-will, free-choice, a conscience and a mind. Evidently

God intended us to exercise these faculties—to think for ourselves, to choose for ourselves, to will and to judge for ourselves—otherwise, had he not intended us to use these faculties, but expected us to depend on authorities, then why has He endowed us with those faculties at all? If a man is made in the image of God—to will, to do, to think and to create—he will attain his higher self-hood only through the exercise of his God given faculties. And this pre-supposes individual unfoldment.

Under most authoritative teachings, these faculties are asleep in man with the result that the people are compelled to depend on their authorities to do their thinking and choosing and deciding; whereas the scheme of creation is for individual unfoldment of faculties and the exercise of same for individual advancement and growth. Conscience if rightly exercised and frequently consulted will never fail us in determining the true from the false the right from the wrong, the essential from the non-essential. There is no higher Authority than God. God having created us, He has not forsaken us, nor has he left us without a guide. And this guide is our intuition. But man chooses to turn his back on his intuition and God and listen to authoritative advise outside of himself which in most cases is not to his best interests.

"A noteworthy thing about the teachings of Jesus and the power he manifested is the fact that he never theorized. *He spoke as one "having authority."* And the authority he obeyed was the God within him, represented by his Illuminated Soul. His mission was to teach men to use their God given faculties. And because he champions the cause of the individual as against against the interests of the authoritative church and state of his day, he was put to death. It has ever been thus.

The hope of mankind is in the welfare and intelligence of its individual members. Those nations who have given their citizens greater opportunities for initiative and intelligent unfoldment are more efficient and further advanced in civilization. History is replete with examples to illustrate this point. And nowhere is it more evident than in the present great conflagration in Europe. And this conflagration if it will teach the world any lessons will advance the cause of individualism and bring home the truth that a people's greatness and efficiency lies in giving the individual freedom of action and freedom of unfoldment restricting this freedom only to the extent of preventing intereference with personal rights.

Any attempt to dam a stream results in a flood. And to attempt to prevent the individual growth of a people is as futile as daming a stream. Evolution is for differentiation and individualism. We perceive that the more civilized a people the more unlike are its members. In proportion that a people have encouraged individualism in just that proportion have they prospered; and in proportion that a people have been suppressed, in that proportion have they shown barbarism, stagnation and decay. History is replete with examples of the downfall of nations because of the suppression of individualism.

Individual unfoldment is the only solution for the welfare of the race. It is the law of growth. It is nature in its constructive operation. If the world is to become better we must start with the individual; and as he unfolds becomes more responsible, a moral being, he raises his envionment and influences for good of his fellow-men with whom he comes in contact. He becomes a "lighted city on a hilltop." A man who evolves towards Godhood, and who becomes a morally responsible being, realizing his accountability to God for his thoughts and acts, will be a more law abiding citizen, a better Father and husband, and will display more respect for the rights of his fellow-men. Individual unfoldment teaches a man self-respect and respect for the welfare of others. The greatest nations in the world have been those who have zealously guarded the principle of life. liberty and the pursuit of happiness for all its citizens. This nation was founded on this principle and this nation has thus far prospered because it has protected its individuals in their pursuit of life, liberty and happiness, and has offered its citizens the greatest opportunities of individual expansion and assertion. And this nation will go down, if it ever will, because it will have trampled this principle in the dust and attempt to suppress individualism.

We recognize that governments cannot by compulsion and legislation bring about a condition of goodness, virtue and intelligence among its people. We recognize that this is an individual problem, and that it is a matter of growth. We recognize that the function of governments is to give its people the greatest individual freedom of thought and of action.

We have heard so much that men are born free and equal. This is not so. There is no equality of men. We are born free to live to use our will for the accomplishment of laudable undertakings to choose a worthy life, to attain noble ideals, and to exercise our Gcd given faculties; but we are not born equal. No two individuals are alike because no two individuals have lived alike or developed alike. The law of nature is for differentiation. The only equality that men possess in common is the equal opportunity to do, to develop and to accomplish. We all have the same opportunity to enrich our hearts with goodness and love and to evolve towards Godhood. Men and despotic governments may deprive us of material wealth and enslave our bodies, but they cannot rob us of spiritual wealth nor enslave our souls. We alone are the masters of our soulual destinies. We alone can free our souls from material despotism. We alone can make our lives a blessing to mankind or an abomination to our fellow-men. We alone are Gods or devils in the making depending on the path we chose to travel. God has given us *all* Divine faculties, which through our own efforts and the training in soul building offered by Soul Science can help us overcome all adverse circumstances.

In our lectures here we speak a great deal of self-development and unfoldment. To the one who is not entirely acquainted with our teachings it might appear as if our teachings are selfish in that the individual is concerned with his own welfare only and might become so rapt up with his own particular growth as to forget the welfare of his fellow-men. There cannot be true individual development if based on selfishness. True individual unfoldment is based on true unselfishness. There can be no progress except through self-sacrifice for mankind Only through service for our brethren can we gain wisdom and power and our growth on the path of attainment will be in proportion to the amount of service we give to mankind. There was no selfishness in the life of Jesus. He attained his greatness and power through a life of self-sacrifice for mankind. And the student who desires to grow to do and to accomplish must pattern his life after the life of Jesus. The person who truly seeks self-development does so with the thought only that by his growth and attainment he can do more for his fellow-men. If he desires to help his fellow-men will he not be of greater help, if he becomes stronger, healthier, happier and wiser? We can give only as much as we possess; if we possess little we can offer but little; but if we possess much, how much more we can be of help.

The Master has said, "whosoever will come after me, let him deny himself and take up his cross and follow me." The individual who desires to be of real and true service to mankind, must first deny or give up one's baser or lower self, and take up the cross of self-sacrifice and be prepared to be crucified on the cross of authority. Just in proportion that the individual gives of his time, labor and life, in helping his less fortunate brethren to a realization of a better day, in that proportion will he receive from God wisdom and power.

Soul Science recognizes that the hope of the world for a better day lies in individual betterment. In proportion that individuals become self-helpful, morally responsible, thinkers, independent of external authority, exercising their free-will and free-choice, will the world become a better place to live in. Our environment is what we make of it, individually and collectively. Our environment is the reflection of internal states or conditions within ourselves. And when we improve ourselves, we improve our environment. Therefore the starting point is the individual. And Soul Science teaches the individual to help himself, to become real men and real women, for women have an equal share in the world's work. Soul Science teaches men moral responsibility and individual accountability; it teaches men to become free, free from the domination of external authoritative teachings, free from slavery to debasing environments. Soul Science teaches intuitional developments, that inner voice of the soul, that Godly authority within us. For man's unfailing and infallible authority is within himself, and not outside of himself. If man is in full possession of all of his Divine faculties and if he develops intuition, he has within all the authority he needs to guide him to righteousness, to wisdom and power and to freedom.

"Blessed are they who hear the voice,
"Thrice blessed are they who obey it."

REINCARNATION

Tho' little thought or attention has been given the Law or Reincarnation among the peoples of the western hemisphere, it is neverétheless a fully accepted and established law among many of our brothers of the eastern climes. Nor is it strange that our eastern brethren should have perceived and accepted this practical solution to all of life's questions long in advance of the peoples of the western world. For it is from the East but interperted by the West, that every true philosophy and religion has come. It is from the East that we must look for all the spiritual knowledge and enlightenment that is to enlighten and illumine the western mind. So from the East, from whence came all true prophets and teachers, all true religion and philosophy, shall gradually come to all mankind the only true and practical teaching that shall redeem the world—that embodying reincarnation.

And what is reincarnation? Reincarnation is that process of change and rebirth by which the soul, or ego, takes on a new life, a new body. It is the rebirth of the soul into a fleshy body, thru' which body the soul may take on such experiences, may accumulate such knowledge, may attain such growth, as will further its advancement towards its destined goal—back to the Father from whence it came.

For in the beginning the soul was with God, and in its desire to know and experience both good and evil, was sent forth into the world of flesh; there to be tried and tempted of the flesh; there to know, and experience—and to overcome. And with the soul, both as its protector and its judge, God sent forth his great Law of Justice, or Karma, "As ye sow, so shall ye reap."

Governed and guided by this great law, each soul has gone forth from the Father of all, to come down into the very depths of materiality and sin, there to experience, to know and to overcome, and finally thru' overcoming to come again unto the Father. For by this experience this knowledge of good and evil and by the overcoming of good over evil, the soul proves its divine right and comes as the true Son, back to the house of the Father from whence it came.

In this light, this earthly life of ours may be likened to a wonderfully equipped and systemized school, thru' the many grades of which we must creditably pass before we can hope to pass on into the higher heavenly schools. And what are the lessons to be learned, but the experiences thru' which we pass? If we learn our lessons well; if we profit by our experiences; then we pass into a higher grade where other lessons, other experiences, teach us greater truths and fuller knowledge.

But if we refuse to learn and study; if we refuse to apply our experiences, can we expect to pass on into the higher grades of truth and knowledge? No, Life's school is as our material schools. When the short term of one life is over, if we have failed to learn our lessons; if we have neglected to study and apply our experiences, then we must again return to the same lessons, or experiences, until we have mastered them, and become eligible for a higher grade. And how, may I ask, are we permitted to come again into life's school to study again its lessons of experiences, but thru' the process of reincarnation.

As souls, we have been placed in God's great school of life, but the soul can only experience and learn life's lessons while in the body of flesh. Governing this great school is the one all sufficient law, the Law of Justice, or "as ye sow, so shall ye reap." Since all flesh, or material, is subject to change, should that change called death for one reason or another come to us before we had met every requirement of this great law, think you we would be permitted to leave this great school, with our lessons but partially learned; with our desire for true and higher knowledge but partially satisfied?

No, in his love and mercy, as well as in his requirement for the fulfilment of the law God permits us to again take on the earthly body—to again pass thru' the state of physical birth, thus re-enetering life's school, reaping the experiences of past sowing, and sowing the seeds of greater experiences in time to come, thus giving us the opportunity of learning life's lessons and coming up into a higher grade or class of understanding and truth.

In this light, is the law of Reincarnation then such an

absurdity? Is it not rather the only plausible solution to life's numerous and mystifying problems? We are taught that God is just, that he is love and mercy; but without reincarnation as the explanation can we look upon conditions as they exist among us today, and truly believe in His justice and mercy? No, a thousand times, No. Is it justice that one should be born into the squalor of poverty, misery, and disease, while another, thru' no apparent worthiness on his part, is given all that life has to offer in health, success and happiness? Is it justice that one should be born a genius, gifted with unlimited talent, while God should see fit to send another into life with not a single means of attaining the desired things of life? Can you see the innocent and pure in heart polluted and wronged by veritable demons in the flesh and with no explanation, no reason why, with no hopes of compensation to the wronged or just deserts to the wrong-doer can you close your eyes to such conditions, and believe in the love and justice of a merciful Father?

Such is indeed a blind belief. For no man whose eyes are open to the unhappy, sinful, evil conditions existing among us today can refrain from calling unto the great God of us all and exclaiming with all the anguish of his heart "Where, Oh Lord, is justice?" And to this man of deep and sorrowing heart this man of love and compassion to his fellow man comes the solution—Reincarnation. To him comes the realization that in this great world of ours are many souls of varied states of growth and experience. Souls buried deep in the depths of materiality, sowing seeds of hate, malice, licentiousness and destruction. Other souls, reaping the result of evil sowing in past lives, suffering seeming injustice and undeserved punishment. Some sowing seeds of labor and effort to be enjoyed in lives to come, while others are reaping a life of success, as a result of past efforts.

With this solution he can look upon the world of peace and happiness to some, and misery and degradation to others, and say that God is indeed a loving and merciful Father permitting each soul to reap only that which is just, whether good or evil, according to that which he has sown.

In this light, he sees and understands why one individual may come upon earth and with seemingly little effort on his part, attain the very heights of success and fame. Take, for instance, one such as Mischa Elman, who at the age of twenty-one was considered and recognized among the world's master violinists. Can we believe that all that expression, heart, melody, and musical perfection was brought out in just one life, and at such an early age? No, in the light of Justice, one sees that such an one has no doubt suffered, labored, and deprived himself of the necessities of life in lives gone by, for the mastery of his profession. That thru' his hard work and earnest desires in this life he is reaping the reward of the sowing in the past. For in the light of Justice he knows that the present is but the reaping of the past, and the future will be but the result of the present.

But, you ask, if there does exist this law of Reincarnation, and if we have lived before, why have we no memory of our past lives? If we are strong enough to look back and read our past history God would have endowed us with that faculty. But we are weaklings and if we were to see our failures our misdeeds of our past we probably would not have the courage to work and strive for better and nobler things now.

Man spends time enough as it is reviewing and repenting of the events of his past, often holding himself back from further advancement. What then, were the incidents, the blunders, the events of our past lives suddenly revealed to us? Not only would we be restrained from pushing forward but without doubt we would give way under this great mental strain, and end our lives in the madhouse. Again we see the justice of God. The Wise Creator wants us to see the present and the future—to look ahead not backwards. In time thru' a gradual strengthening and cleansing of the soul, we may some day be sufficiently strong to look upon our own soul and know what that soul has been in the past. But that should not concern us now. It is a mark of wisdom to forget the past and not harp on what has been, but to take up a new life, and through good works we will be able to amend for the blunders of the past and build peace and happiness for the future.

Reincarnation is by no means a newly advanced idea or theory. Rebirth, or reincarnation was taught by Jesus. In speaking of John, the Baptist, he said, "And if ye will receive it, this is Elias, which was for to come." Jesus told the people that John was the reincarnated Elias. Elias was one of the prophets that lived five hundred years before the birth of John.

As today, there were few among them who realized the full meaning of Jesus' words. But there were, and are, those who sought the inner meanings of these words and recognized the truth.

No master, or teacher, has ever taught the law of Justice more clearly than Jesus. His golden rule, "Do unto others as you wish that they should do unto you," is but another way of expressing the law, "As ye sow, so shall ye reap."

Again we find him admonishing his followers to agree quickly with their adversaries, lest they be cast into prison, from which there is no release until the utmost farthing be paid. Here again is the law of absolute Justice, showing that if we sow seeds of wrong-doing against our brother, we shall not be released from the effects of this wrong doing until full compensation is made.

Jesus taught absolute individual responsibility. He taught that each individual thru' his own sowing of deeds, reaped the result of such sowing, whether good or bad. Never did he teach that he came to release them from the effects of their own reaping thru' mere belief in him. Jesus came to "show the way." In other words, his mission was to teach mankind how to sow, in order to avoid undesirable reaping. He never taught that belief in him would cancel their past debts. In fact, he plainly stated that "should they be cast into prison, they should not be released until the last farthing was paid." He told others to follow Him and they too should do even greater things than he, and should also come into sonship with the Father. He also told them there was no way but by the cross, implying that each one must bear his own cross.

In none of Jesus' teachings do we find a basis for the orthodox belief of vicarious atonement. Viewed in the light of justice, it is clearly perceived that such a belief is a false one; one contrary to Divine Laws. If Jesus taught that as we sowed, so should we reap, could he deliberately contradict this law by teaching them the doctrine of vicarious atonement? Could he teach them the individual responsibility of their every thought and deed, and then take this responsibility away from them by offering to atone for their sins if they would but believe on him?

The true mission of Jesus was to show man his relation to himself, to God and to his fellow man. Jesus came to show man how to think and live that he might come to a better understanding of himself——that he might know his purpose on earth and might be brought to a realization of his own individual responsibility in shaping his own life and destiny.

Some there were who accepted these teachings in their true meaning, who applied them to their own lives, thereby becoming true masters and leaders of man. But many there were who were not willing to apply the Master's teachings as they really were, who were not ready to recognize such laws as would bring them to a realization of their own responsibility. These it was, who set up the false standards of religion, who preferred to set Jesus, the man, before them as one to be worshipped and adored, rather than take his teachings into their hearts and become like him.

Like cowards they sought to hide behind his merits and good deeds. In blind faith they held up his life before them and claimed it as their own. They would steal Eternal Life by permitting Him to bear their sins, while they went unpunished. Thru' their cunning and deceit they would defy the absolute law of Justice and defraud God himself, by receiving the man instead of his teachings, which they knew would bring them to a responsibility of their own sins.

It is the same in the present day. There are those masters and teachers on earth who would teach man that he is absolutely responsible for every word and act. Those who would show him that as a soul sent forth from God, he must come again unto the Father, not thru' the efforts of another, but thru' his own efforts and experiences. There are those who know and understand the Divine Laws governing the growth and development of man, who can bring man to a knowledge of his own soul thru' that system of living which the Master Jesus taught.

Today, as Jesus, there are those masters and teachers of the Divine Law, who are earnestly striving to bring mankind to the real Truth, that he may know and understand the workings of the immutable law of Justice and bring his life into harmony with this law. Who know that only thru' the recognition and understanding of the law of Reincarnation is it possible to perceive the workings of the law of Justice. For then and then only can man realize that everything about him, his conditions, his environment, his success, his failures are his exact due, brought about thru' his own efforts in time gone by.

Such a teaching naturally necessitates that man put aside all cowardly thought of evading the consequences of his own deeds thru' various forms of belief and repentance, and places him in the position of a true man, strong in the love and justice of God, ready to grapple with his own life's problems, and thru' his own suffering and untiring efforts, to come forth the victor over every weakness, every sin. It is such a teaching that discloses the fallacy and uselessness of any ceremonious doctrine, creed, or belief, which would lead man to believe that he could gain anything, even Eternal Life, thru' the efforts, or at the expense of another. It teaches clearly that every individual is a separate being, apart from his fellow man, in that he is absolutely accountable to God for his own soul, its growth and development into sonship with the Father.

Such a teaching is *Soul Science,* for as its name implies it teaches the science of training, developing, and knowing the soul; showing man how the soul was sent forth from the Father into the world of flesh that it might take on experiences, comprising both good and evil, that it might overcome, and thru' overcoming become the Christ, the True Son of God.

Soul Science has as its basic, fundamental principles the law of absolute justice, or "as ye sow, so shall ye reap," and the law of reincarnation. It recognizes that the one is not complete without the other, for without Reincarnation, there is no Justice. Reincarnation is the only solution of the law of justice. Reincarnation explains why a certain condition, a certain event, or happening, is just. And without such a solution man may indeed look upon the conditions and scenes of misery about him and see only the workings of an awful and unmerciful God playing with man as his fancy sees fit.

Like the true Christic teachings, it shows a man how to sow that he may reap desired results, both in the present as well as the future. It guides and trains him in this school of life, teaching him to stand upon his own merits, to honestly pass his own examinations if he would creditably finish the course. It shows him the utter folly of wasting his study hours in idleness and mischief and then stealing and copying from another when examinations come.

Soul Science holds before its followers the one standard, that of Love; helping him to love his neighbor as himself. This is made possible thru' the understanding of the law of Reincarnation. For when others persecute him or seek to wrong him, like Jesus, he can say "Father, forgive them for they know not what they do." He realizes that they are brother souls, who thru' past as well as present mistakes, have not as yet reincarnated or come up into the higher classes of this great school of life, where they have the knowledge of the higher laws of love. He is then more able to overlook their misdeeds and show compassion and tolerance towards them, for full well he knows the law, that they shall reap as they are sowing and that in time they shall be their own judges, and that in wronging him they are but sowing Karma, which means accumulated indebtedness to the law of Justice, for which they must compensate at some future time.

In this light it is easily understood how an individual can come to hold no ill will or malice against his fellow man, and can come to love and forgive, to serve and guide his erring brother just as Jesus loved and served his fellow man.

And this is the life that Jesus came to teach the people to live. Is it any wonder that the forces of evil tried to frustrate his plans by inducing the people to accept the man Jesus instead of his teachings. For had the people accepted the true teachings of Jesus two thousand years ago, the evil powers should long ago have lost their hold upon their hearts and the Kingdom of Heaven, the Universal Brotherhood of man would be established among us.

How successful the forces for evil have been in blinding the people is easily seen in our materialistic sciences, our religions of blind faith, doctrine, and ceremony of today. How cunningly they have fixed the attention of man on the exterior, meaningless issues of life, preventing him from seeking his center, his soul, his God within.

They have shown him a God outside and apart from himself—to be feared and dreaded, instead of allowing him to know that God dwells within his own bosom as his guide and strength. And when any great teacher, such as Jesus, dares come among the people to show them the real truth, how quickly they snatch the kernel of truth from the mouths of hungry men, and give them but the shell of doctrines, creeds and ceremonies, upon which to feed the starving soul. How deftly they center the people's mind upon that which is apart from themselves by holding up the man, the teacher, as a God to be worshipped, rather than his teachings which they know would lead man to know himself and his God, and which would end their hold on the hearts of men forever. For full well do they who are evil know that once man is brought to see real truth; once he is brought to a realization of his soul or God power within, the charms of evil will no longer tempt him, for thru' the strength of the developed soul within he is master, not slave—he is conqueror, not victim.

Does it surprise you then, that the power of evil permeates our materialistic sciences, even our religions and philosophies of today?

Do you wonder that our sciences embody and support such ideas as those of chance, of fate, and of destiny; that they consider and measure man's success by his ability to outwit his fellow man? That they permit such outrages as vivi-section, causing the harmless and innocent ones of God's lower kingdoms inconceivable pain, in the blind pretense of helping mankind? That they support such practices as vaccination, thus innoculating the human race with the vilest of poisons?

Are you surprised that our religions of today teach everything but Divine Truth; that they would hold this false belief and that before the eyes of the people to keep them from seeing their true selves and their divine possibilities? Do you wonder that such doctrines as those of vicarious atonement and remission of sins have become the fundamentals of our religion today?

When true religion has been lost to the people, and when conditions become almost unbearable, there is a desire among them for a Messiah or Saviour to lead them back to the simple teachings of the Masters. The people have been led to believe by false teachings that when such a Messiah would appear, he would be sent by God to rescue them from their sufferings, restore order and bring peace, prosperity and happiness to all who believed.

At the time of Jesus the Jews were looking for a Messiah to come. Throughout the centuries they have been looking for a Messiah and today some of them are still looking for one to appear. And in like manner many Christians today are looking for the return of Jesus. Every people in every age have had Messiahnic expectations. They have been led to believe that their troubles would be over when these Messiahs would appear; and that by some magic process these Divine teachers would forgive the people their sins, and would make them wise, beautiful, healthy, happy, and transplant them direct to heaven without, the people, being required to do more than professing a belief in the divinity of the Messiah or Christ.

Such is the race belief fostered and encouraged by false teachings. Yet what is the witness of history? If we are to believe that civilized Man has been on earth for the past hundred thousand years, and we have authority for our statement, there have come at various times great teachers to instruct the people in Divine law and how to live a life in conformity with Divine law. They have failed to interest the majority of the people. Only a few understood the teachings and lived them. While the mass blindly believed and set up the Christ as a God, and never practiced what he taught. These Christs failed to bring lasting peace. Most of the great teachers have been stoned, persecuted and crucified. Neither Lao-tze Confucius, Zoroaster, Buddha, Moses or Jesus brought peace on earth or succeeded in getting the majority of the people interested in the science of soul building. The people have always found it easier to believe in dogma and creed and have shown a marked disinclination to practice Divine law. And you may be sure a designing priestcraft in every age has seen to it that the people were encouraged in this for selfish reasons.

And our modern philosophies! Who can estimate the evil results of the teachings of the thousand and one "so called" religious, destructive philosophies and cults of today? Philosophies that teach negative and destructive systems of living setting forth such theories as will lead man into the great sea of nothingness, of no use to himself or his fellow man.

How deceptive is Evil! Truly it comes as a wolf in sheep's clothing.

Let us seek then for the real Truth, the Truth that shall redeem the world. The truth that embodies such sciences as recognize the workings of the Divine Law, both in man's treatment of his fellow man and God's creatures of the lower kingdoms: such religions as teach man's individual responsibility and the Universal Brotherhood of man: such philosophies as propound only positive constructive modes of living and thinking, bringing him into the higher development of body, mind and soul.

And where shall we look for such a truth—where shall we seek the light that shall illumine the world? We are told that "as the lightning cometh out of the East and shineth even unto the West, so shall the Coming of the Son of Man be." Let us turn our minds and hearts then towards the East, towards its morning light of truth, and let us bow down in reverence and obedience to the great and divine laws it would teach us, coming forth from the very source of Truth itself. For from the East shall come our redemption.

PRAYER

There is not an individual, no matter how materialistic or atheistic, during a crisis or when in great trouble, but consciously or unconsciously will turn to God or the Invisible Cause of all, with a prayer or appeal for help. As long as conditions are favorable, the materialists and skeptics, who scoff at God and religion, will never think of prayer, but let them face a crisis or find themselves in dire distress, when they consciously utter, as the first words, "Oh God! Help me!"

The nations in Europe who are at war and who are denying God by breaking every commandment of God in this most unholy war, are yet appealing to God with prayers for help and success. No matter how low and degraded an individual may be, yet by his desire for life and for better things, is unconsciously praying to an invisible power, God or Nature, for help, for strength, for life.

What is prayer? Prayer is desire. True prayer originates in the heart and is always referred to the heart? True prayer is true desire. The desire or hunger which begins in the heart, for life, for happiness, for help, is the prayer of the Soul. Prayer is the voice of the heart and soul calling to God for the things man needs and by his helplessness is unable to obtain.

If our prayer, our desire, is strong enough, it leads us to put forth effort to obtain that for which we pray. But if our prayers or desires are feeble, they are too faint to be of force or power. A feeble electric current will not produce sufficient motive power to move a street car, but a powerful current is productive of results. And so it is with prayer and desire. If prayer is too feeble, it does not move us or anybody to activity, to bring about a fulfillment of what we desire. But if our prayers are powerful they are productive of results.

While prayer or desire begins in the heart, we use our minds as instruments to bring about the realization of our prayers or desires.

Intense desire of the heart is real prayer, and the greater

the intensity with which we desire or pray, the greater power is there in our prayer.

There are two kinds of prayer, selfish and unselfish. Selfish prayer may also be divided into two classes. There is selfish prayer or desire for the self irrespective of the desires and wishes of our fellow beings. Thus, if a raincoat merchant prays for rain, which rain would benefit him but would prove injurious to others who need clear weather, it constitutes selfish prayer or desire. Needless to say that such prayer, which would bring harm to others, is contrary to Divine Law, and is never answered or fulfilled. It is regrettable, that most people pray selfishly without a thought as to the welfare of their fellow man. And it is just and good that such prayers are not answered, and works for the protection of the selfish individual. Were selfish prayer to be answered, working harm and depriving others of what they desire, the man who prayed selfishly would be responsible for the harm to others, and he would be sowing evil, the reaping of which would prove burdensome to him. We have no right to pray selfishly for those things, which in their fulfillment, would prove injurious to others. Common sense and a sense of justice would indicate to the individual that selfish prayer is most undesirable and contrary to God's plan.

Then there is prayer for the self, the higher self. This class is proper and laudable, for it is true desire or prayer for the welfare of the real self within us. Thus if we pray for spiritual light and understanding, for health, for happiness, we are not desiring the things which would be against the interests of our fellow man, which would harm our neighbor.

Unselfish prayer is the highest form and most worthy of all prayer. Where we pray or desire things for the welfare of others, without a thought for ourselves, it constitutes the noblest kind of prayer and works to our greatest benefit. Contrary to popular opinion, the prayers which result in greatest good and benefits for man are not the selfish prayers but those unselfish desires for his fellow man. *In giving is when we receive.* In praying for the welfare of our neighbor, we assume that attitude of our being most conducive for the reception of an inflow of goodness to ourselves. When we are praying unselfishly in the interests of our neighbor, we are really praying for our own best interests; and when we pray selfishly for our own interests without a thought or care of our neighbor, we are really praying against the best interests of ourselves.

True prayer is true, earnest, intense unselfish desire—a desire to live a better life, which will bring us nearer to the heavenly Father and enable us to become our brother's keeper and help our brother carry his burdens. The desire or prayer to be of service to God and our neighbor, to help God reclaim his wandering children, is the desire of our soul, when once it is awakened.

There comes a time when every man feels the necessity of prayer; and that time is when he, like the Prodigal Son, tired of living a materialistic and sinful life, begins to return to the Father. It is then when he needs prayer most—prayer for light and truth and guidance to light the wearied footsteps of the wanderer back to his Father's house.

Prayer does not necessarily have to be formal, for there is no particular efficacy in some set or formal prayer; but the power of prayer is in the earnest desire and concentrated force of that desire. When praying earnestly and sincerely, it is not necessary to repeat the psalms of David or any other prayer from the Scriptures. Nor shall we be as the hypocrites that Jesus speaks of; for he says, "And when thou prayest, thou shalt not be as the hypocrites are: for they love to pray standing in the synagogues and in the corners of the streets, that they may be seen of men. Verily I say unto you, they have their reward. But thou when thou prayest, enter into thy closet, and when thou hast shut thy door, pray to thy Father which is in secret; and they Father which seest in secret shall reward thee openly." "But when ye pray, use not vain repetitions, as the heathens do: for they think they shall be heard for their much speaking." "Be not ye therefore like unto them: for your Father knowest what things ye have need of, before ye ask him."

True prayer is true desire, and an instinct of refinement prevents us from voicing our deepest desires openly. Whether the desire is for something we need for ourselves or it is for the good of another, it becomes true prayer only when it comes from the heart and soul. Such prayer cannot be voiced in public.

If you feel strong and intense on some particular thing, can you go about telling it to others or will you reserve your feelings and enter into the silence?

Seek the Father within you. Commune with your soul, which is of the Father. It is not necessary to look for God in a church or synagogue. God is everywhere. Wherever there is life there is God. God does not dwell in some particular building only, such as a church, to the exclusion of the rest of the universe. God hears our prayers wherever we may be, on the mountain top or in the valley, within a church or without it. Whether we express our desires publicly, with eloquent language, or we assume an attitude of kneeling or standing in apparent devotion, we are merely soothing our intellect and are issuing forth lip service and not true prayer. If the prayer does not come from the heart, it avails us nothing. Our Father in heaven will only hear such prayers that come from the heart or soul.

If we pray just to be heard of men, we are hypocrites, for we are then posing and not truly serving God, but the baser self. The mumbling of a few passages and the singing of a sacred hymn does not help us or bring us any nearer to the "Kingdom of God." A hymn is sacred only when you make it so by the intense and unselfish feeling you put into that hymn. When there is no earnest desire in the heart for either the development of your own higher self or for the good of your neighbor, behind your prayers, those prayers are not effective.

What material food is to the body, so prayer is food for the soul. The oftener we pray, and the greater sincerity and earnest and intense feeling we put into our prayers, the more food we give our souls, and the greater peace we feel within ourselves. If the body needs sustenance for its upkeep and upbuilding, then the soul, the real and lasting part of ourselves, also needs sustenance for its peace and upbuilding. Those that have gone through the experience of having lived an atheistic life without prayer and have turned to soul development and prayer, know the difference between the two paths and the value of prayer as a factor for peace, happiness, health and success.

Many pray selfishly and when they do not realize what they pray for, become disappointed and lose their faith in prayer. Do these realize that possibly the things they selfishly desire may be injurious to them, and it is really a blessing in disguise if they do not obtain their desires. A child may desire a knife, and may be disappointed in not getting its heart's wish; but after all, is it not for the protection of that child that its desire is not granted? In most cases individuals pray for things that either may injure them, or for things they do not deserve, or have not earned.

One person may desire riches without his putting forth effort to obtain it. This prayer is not deserving of answer, for the reason that it is a selfish desire. In such a case the person has not earned riches, has not deserved it and has not worked for it. Wealth in this instance would prove baneful to this individual since it might lead him into a life of luxury, idleness and evil, which would not only injure him but might also bring harm to others. We are apt to appreciate and value more that which we have worked and struggled for than that which we have obtained without any effort on our part. God helps those that help themselves. And in proportion that we help ourselves does God give us help. God denies us nothing. It is we who deny ourselves health, strength, youth, wealth and soul development, by our not desiring or praying strong enough for these things, by our not striving hard enough. True, earnest prayer will lead us to work for that which will earn for us the things we desire. From this we learn that the fulfillment of our prayers, our desires, can be obtained only through work. Work and effort does us good.

If we pray or desire health, we must earn it by living that kind of a pure life most conducive to health. Some who are sick pray for health. If all sickness is due to wrong living, unless the individual changed his mode of living and thinking and prayed for wisdom and understanding whereby he might be led into living a purer and better life leading towards health, any cure would be merely a temporary relief, and would not do that individual any lasting good. So that prayer for health without being accompanied by a change of living and thinking and the putting forth of effort to gain health is in most cases not answered or fulfilled. And justly so; for the reason that only that will do us lasting good and will advance us in deveolpment and raise our status, for which we have to work and to strive for. Because it is in the putting forth of effort is where we advance ourselves and not in mere wishing.

When Jesus healed he always tested a man's faith, and after healing always remarked, "Go thy way and sin no more." Jesus knew that it was impractical to heal a person and at the same time permit him to continue in habits that foster disease. He did not cure their mental, moral or physical ailments by some magical power, thereby robbing them of the exercise of their faculties and capacities. But he instructed them and showed them that in order for their prayers to be answered they had to change their mode of living and thinking and had to work for what they wanted.

The person that prays for health and does not stop "sinning," or does not stop breaking the laws of health is foolish to expect the realization of the fulfillment of his desires.

Faith without works is dead. Prayers unless accompanied by constructive thinking and doing are not answered. It is well to have faith in the Father and feel that we will realize our heart's desires; but are we always worthy of the things asked for?

Are you working to elevate yourself and free yourself from materiality, or are you satisfied merely to ask and not to give? if we desire to receive, are we always willing to give? Remember, the giving must precede the receiving. Works and deeds that we do for others constitutes the most effective prayer.

The heart knows its deepest needs. It knows what others need. The heart's sincere desire is always simple; it requires no repetition; it requires to be held silently and soulfully. Through such prayer does the heart realize that the Father knows and understands.

Silent prayer is true prayer. When in the silence we can meditate and concentrate more deeply. When trying to figure out some problems, where have you found the best place to solve them? Is it in a crowded room full of discord, or alone in your private room or study? The best time to communicate with the Father is when alone and in the silence. Shut the door and be alone. Close the door to the outside world, the world of materiality and discord, and commune with your soul.

Is there any particular place where our prayers will be heard more than in any other place? The answer to this question is covered in the conversation of the Samaritan woman with Jesus:

"Our fathers worshipped in this mountain; and ye say, that in Jerusalem is the place where men ought to worship." "Jesus saith unto her, Woman, believe me the hour cometh, when we shall neither worship in this mountain nor yet at Jerusalem, worship the Father." "But the hour cometh, and now is, when the true worshippers shall worship the Father in spirit and in truth: for the Father seeketh such to worship him." "God is a spirit: and they that worship him must worship him in spirit and in truth."

The same conditions that existed in the time of Jesus exist today. Today as in those days, the people still cling to the belief that one place is holier than another; that God dwells on the mountain and not in the valley; that God dwells in a church and not without; and that therefore their prayers have some magic power when uttered in a church. We build beautiful temples to worship in, and think we have shut up God in a place of our own making, and believe that this place is more sacred than any other building.

God is everywhere. Just as the sun shines on every leaf, on every plant, on every living creature, so does the love of God shine everywhere.

The prayers that the people offer in a temple do not become more sacred than if they were uttered in the home or some other place. Is the prayer of the hypocrite more acceptable to God just because it is spoken in a temple? Can the thief, the liar, the adulterer, find grace with God by merely praying in a certain temple?

God does not care where we pray, or how we pray, or in what tongue, so long as our prayers come from the heart, are sincere, are unselfish, are for some worthy aim and ideal, and are accompanied by faith and works.

Man in his ignorance ond superstition thinks that some particular place is more sacred than others just because he wishes it so. But some day he will wake up, "the hour will come," when he will realize that no particular place is more sacred than another. The Father seeks those that worship him in spirit and in truth, and he cares not for our lip service. Man may ever be so humble, may live in a hut, may wear rags; but if his life is pure, if he loves his enemies, is kind to God's creatures, is forgiving, is ever ready, to help his neighbor and is truly living a life of service to God and his fellow-man—such a man is truly worshipping the Father.

If God is like unto ourselves, he will discriminate between the worship of the pauper and the rich man, between the worship offered up in a temple or in a humble cottage. But if God is All-Love, All-Goodness, All-Truth, All-Mercy, Omnipresent or present everywhere, he judges us by what we think and what we do, rather than by what we say and where we say it.

"The hour cometh, and now is." There is no particular time or day in which to worship the Father. Why wait for Sunday or Saturday or some other day? Is God asleep the rest of the week? "The hour cometh and now is" when man will realize that he must not wait for a certain day to worship the Father, and that the rest of the time he can remain content just because he has repeated a set prayer on Sunday. Every day should be a day of consecration for us to worship God and serve our fellow-man.

The time comes to every individual when he awakens to the truth that not what comes from the mouth, no matter how beautiful the words, gives him salvation, but what he thinks and does and how he lives.

Just as the flower, the leaf and every blade of grass turns to the sun, the visible manifestation of God, for light and life, so every soul turns to God for consolation, for comfort, for light and for love.

"The hour cometh and now is" when man realizes that only through the fulfilling of the law of love can we understand and know Divine law. But in order to understand this higher love, the love that overcomes and forgives all, we must live the life which gradually will initiate us into the understanding of this law. We must rise up to that plane of Divine understanding before we can become conscious of the law of love. The more of love we have and practice it, the more of God we will possess and the more Godly we will become. This constitutes true worship of the Father.

To do the works of the Father—to help the afflicted, to forgive the sinner, to love our enemies—is manifesting in our daily living true love. This is true prayer and true worship of the Father.

We gain nothing by entertaining thoughts of hate and ill-will towards our fellow-men. If we send out thoughts of love, we naturally attract love. We must expect the same equivalent if we send forth thoughts of hate and malice towards others. *If our minds are full of constructive thoughts of love and purity towards all, we insulate ourselves and thoughts of hate will be powerless to affect us.*

No matter how trying circumstances may be, we must not forget to control our thoughts, emotions and acts. We must always be ready to forgive those who wrong us. If the Father continually forgives us our trespasses and gives us many chances to rectify our mistakes, why then should we not be more than happy to forgive those that wrong us? It is our duty to return good for every evil act.

Many individuals seek retaliation for evil acts committed against them. They still cling to the old belief, "An eye for an eye and a tooth for a tooth." This they interpret literally. Moses never taught man to return evil for evil. This law of Moses is the same as the law of justice taught by Jesus, or "as ye sow, so shall ye reap." If you think evil of others, and return evil for every unkind act towards you, it stands to reason that each time you will reap what you have sown. If you curse another, you are cursing yourself; if you judge another, you are judging yourself; if you condemn another, you are condemning yourself.

Ignorance is the root of all evil. Those that persecute us or despitefully use us are ignorant of the laws of action and reaction. They do not realize what the effects will be and what they are bringing into their own lives. If we have knowledge of the power of love, and live in accordance with the Divine Laws, we then will often be able to turn our enemies into friends and we will receive health, life, wholeness to the body; purity, goodness and power, to the mind; wisdom and illumination to the soul. That is how we will pray for those that despitefully use and persecute us. Not merely think about it and in our minds temporarily forgive them but in our hearts send out thoughts of love to them—that is *real prayer*. You are progressing and at the same time helping your brother for he cannot help but feel your vibrations of love.

In the Lord's prayer of Jesus, in his sermon on the mount, we have the summing up of what true prayer is and should consist of. Our Father which art in heaven, hallowed by Thy name.

First of all where is heaven? Most people think it is a sphere or another world we go to after death. Heaven is a state of existence or a plane of being. You make your own heaven or happiness. It is for you to seek the Father in heaven or the conscious soul within you. As the Father is in heaven, so is the soul enthroned within the temple of man. If we violate the Divine laws and sin against the Father we are cursing our own soul by the same act. The soul in the temple of man, like the Father in heaven is supreme. Whatever we do to our own soul will leave a mark thereon, and we will suffer the consequences. When we do wrong to the soul, we do wrong to the Father which is in heaven.

"Thy kingdom come, thy will be done in earth, as it is in heaven."

The world has been led to believe in a kingdom of heaven after death. The world is also waiting for a Messiah to come to establish a kingdom of God on earth. But this kingdom cannot be universally established on earth until all men obey Divine law. The kingdom herein referred to is the establishing of the rule or kingdom of God within our own selves. It is up to us individually to do the will of the father on earth, and thus find the kingdom of heaven here and now. We know that heaven is not a place, but a state of being, and all men have the privilege of reaching this state. As the Father in heaven is perfect, so can all men become perfect, if they seek to establish the kingdom of rule of heaven within themselves—this is finding the soul within our own temples.

"Give us this day our daily bread."

Jesus here tried to show the people that bread does not come for the mere asking; but, if we have faith in the Father and if we are willing to do the work He gives us to do, we will receive the bread that is our due. God is not a parasite; He is a worker. If man will cease trying to live the life of a parasite, and will do his duty he will receive his bread, that is, his just reward. "Give us this day our daily bread," is equivalent to saying: Give us this day some worthy task to perform. Daily bread is not only of the body, but also of the soul; and as man obeys the law, or the Will of the Father, he will be given the bread, or the food, that satisfies the hunger of the soul. Just praying for something won't get us anywhere nor bring us our wants. Asking is not enough. Set out and do the thing and you will get it. Ask for the strength to perform the task and not for the food or work to fall from heaven.

"And forgive our debts, as we forgive our debtors."

If we desire our Father's forgiveness, we must forgive those that wrong us. Forgiveness does not mean freedom from suffering for misdeeds. If we do wrong, if we do that which harms another, which defames him mentally or physically, or if we deprive his children of bread, for such things we must suffer the natural consequences. We may receive forgiveness for the wrong, and yet, under the Divine law, we must suffer for the act. We have sown, therefore we must reap what we have sown. Unless we forgive others the Father cannot forgive us; and, even if the debt is paid and the wrong righted to all outward appearances if there is not full forgiveness of the heart, the soul will not blot out the memory of the act. In this prayer the Father is identical with the verdict of one's own soul.

"And lead us not into temptation, but deliver us from evil: For Thine is the kingdom, and the power, and the glory, for ever. Amen."

God does not lead a man into temptation, nor does he deliver him from evil. God gives man the law and it is up to man to follow and obey the law. If God were to lead us into temptation, he would be no more perfect than our worst enemy. "Lead us not into temptation" is a request to the Father, or to the soul, to guide us, and to lead us in the way of righteousness; it does not imply that the Father would purposely lead us in any other than the right way. This prayer is an appeal to the Voice of the Soul, to our Intuition, to show us the right of way, and to lead us in the path of Truth, Justice, Love and immortality.

If we pray in the above manner, then surely will our prayers be realized. Have Faith in the Father and his works first then live the life that wil lhelp you to realize your oneness with the Father. True earnest prayer is but a step toward the goal, the finding of the kingdom of heaven within us, or the soul of man.

BODY, MIND, SPIRIT AND SOUL

Man is a threefold, a triplicate, and yet a fourfold, being.

This statement may seem contradictory and inconsistent. How can a man be both triplicate, a perfect representative of the triangle, and also, at the same time, a fourfold being, a perfect representative of the square? Seemingly, this is impossible. Actually, it is true, and admits of the closest and most scientific investigation and analysis. Then, let us consider man as body, mind, spirit, and soul.

The body is the foundation of the whole being. The seeker after spiritual things, or the things of the Soul, has a tendency to discount the body. Nevertheless, to him who seeks the things of the Soul, to him who seeks Immortality, and especially, to him who seeks Mastership, the body is of first, even of supreme, importance. Mastership cannot be reached unless the body is in normal condition.

Let us reason for a moment from the analogy of building a house. Suppose you, my reader, desire to build a house. Let us suppose that you have sufficient means to build a magnificent palace. Moreover, it is your desire to build such a palace. Therefore we work on the supposition that you have both the means and the inclination to build a palace.

If you are wise, your first step is to go to a first-class architect. To be sure, to do this, you must first make up your mind to be willing to pay his price. For, bear in mind, all men who have mastered their trade, art, or profession are expensive men. Mastery and expense always go together, they cannot be separated. For this reason, we say in the Sacred Schools, "You always pay for what you get." Having placed your plans before the Master Architect, it remains for him to work out these plans and personify them on paper in drawings. But bear this in mind, you must follow his plans; otherwise, so far as you are concerned, all his work will be in vain.

I am thus plain with you and thus precise, because I will

emphasize these particular points again when we come to apply them to the Great Work of Building the Soul.

Now, after receiving your perfect plans and drawings from the architect, you will, if you are wise, go to a first-class contractor, or builder, one who is known not for his cheapness, but for his ability and his skill. When you confer with the expert contractor you will note one thing above all others: he will insist on having a firm foundation. In fact, he will give his first and most careful attention to the foundation. And why? Because the entire palace must rest on the foundation. And no matter how perfect, no matter how strong, the super-structure, it is actually no more nearly perfect and no stronger than is the foundation.

The question of building a house, and this argument, will appeal to you as a fact, for the simple reason that it is a material subject, something you know from experience, something you can see. Or, if you have no practical experience, you can easily get the facts by going to a master-builder for his opinion.

Now, my Brother, just exactly as it is with the building of a palace that is to stand, so it is with the body and the Soul. The body is the foundation on which Soul Building rests. It is the house itself, in fact. And just as is the house so may be the Soul. Note that I do not say, As is the body, so will be the Soul. Neither do I say, As is the body, so is the Soul. For it is possible for the body to be put in perfect condition, and then stop there. To put the body in perfect condition is necessary as a preparation for Soul Illumination; but, in and of itself, it is by no means sufficient. It is correct to say, As is the body, so may be the Soul. When the body is brought to a state of normal functioning in all its parts, it should be accepted "as a sign unto you" that the Soul likewise may be brought into a state of normal functioning in all of its departments. Physical development, and a normal physical condition, is the foundation of a perfect Soul Structure. And this foundation must be built before you begin to erect the super-structure. To be sure, the body as it now is, in its abnormal condition, may be used as a basis of Soul Building. But, in this case, you are doing exactly like the foolish man who rears a grand palace on the sand as a foundation. To be sure, the sand is some sort of foundation. But you remember what the Master Jesus said about the man who built his house on the sand. The fate he predicted is the probable fate of him who is foolish enough to attempt building on the sand. The house may stand for years. Yet again, it may become a wreck or be swept away by the first storm.

Thus it may be with the one who is foolish enough to think that the body has nothing to do with the building of a Soul. To begin the work of developing the mind, and to begin the process of Soul Illumination, without having first prepared a firm foundation whereon to build, is like building a house on the sand. And, sad to say, there are very many who are thus foolish. They only find that the first storm, the first great test, leaves the body a wreck, and the Soul without a fit habitation.

The preparation of the body for Illumination of Soul needs just as careful an architect and builder as does the building of a palace. The wise student will take care in choosing a system of development. He will not follow just any system of development that comes to his attention. He will be careful in his selection of an instructor. He must make sure that the one who gives him instruction in regard to physical perfection is one who has had a large experience and marked success in restoring men and women to a normal physical state.

And, as the building of a palace, bear in mind that it will not benefit you to receive instructions, no matter how skillfully prepared, unless you follow them to the letter. They are given for the purpose of being obeyed. They are given for the express purpose of being applied to the needs of the individual life. Unless this is done, the building will be imperfect, and become useless in time; and your work may be worse than if it had not been done at all.

Let me repeat, then, the body is the foundation in the Great Work. And the attention you give it, is every bit as important as the attention you give to the Illumination of the Soul itself. From some points of view, it may be even more important that the building of the Soul, being basic and fundamental to it.

There is but one difference between the building of a palace and the building of a body as a fit habitation for an Illuminated Soul. In the building of a palace, you go to an architect for the drawing of your plans. In like manner, you go to a Teacher to prepare plans, or a system, for restoring the body to normal functioning. But, unlike the case of building a house, you can not go to a builder to erect your Soul structure, or to restore physical perfection. These you must do for yourself. You yourself must do the work of physical development. A teacher can give you the instructions, the plans, the program, of daily routine to be followed; but he cannot build for you. Even the knowledge of *how* can do nothing for you unless you obey instructions and apply the knowledge to your own case. You must build according to the plans. This means the living of the life itself. When you live the life you grow into the power that such living confers on him who so lives.

So much for the body, the foundation of the building. We now come to a consideration of the mind. The mind has much to do with the building of an Illuminated Soul. It has much to do even with the building of bodily strength; for it is the mind, as a reasoning and thinking power, that decides upon the truth or the falsity of a statement or a system of teaching. If the mind fails to accept or to approve of a system, naturally the individual has no incentive for following or obeying that system. Consequently, in that case, nothing can be accomplished.

The mind is that in man which accepts or rejects a statement, that which decides in regard to the truth or the falsity or the plausibility of methods and ideas and principles. The mind in man is that part of his nature which exercises free-will and free choice. The mind also gives the impetus or the desire and inclination to act according to the decision made regarding any matter. The mind also furnishes the will-power to execute thought in accordance with desire. In the last analysis, these three great departments include all the functionings of mind: thought, feeling and will. For ordinary purposes, mind may be defined as that in man which thinks, feels and wills. Every mental state or mood may be reduced to a thought or a feeling or a condition of will, or rather to a combination or a blending of thought, feeling, and will. A given thought stimulates or provokes a corresponding feeling and a corresponding state of will. The acts of a man's life correspond to the triple blending of thought, feeling and will, which dominate him at the time of acting.

It is taken for granted not only that you, my reader, are interested in Soul Culture, but that, to a greater or less degree, you believe in it. In order to believe in a thing, you must know enough about it to have a basis for belief or a reason for belief. Knowledge, which gives basis for belief, is of the mind. The thought and the attention and the interest you have given to Soul Science are evidence of the working of your mind. The mind, that in you which thinks and feels and wills, has accepted the principles of Soul Science so far as you comprehend. Your attitude of mind toward Soul Science is a blending of thought, feeling, and will. Interest and a desire to know more and to understand better, and the desire to follow and to obey the principles of Soul Science come under the category of feeling. The purpose and the determination to live in harmony with these principles, the force and the energy that enables you to execute your determination—this comes under the category of will-power. Your understanding of the principles involves thought and reasoning and judgment. As you become more and more interested in the subject, you give up old ideas, habits, and beliefs, and accept new ideas, habits and beliefs. To be sure, your desires and purposes are not strong enough to enable you to give up the old life entirely. But, in time, as you study more and more deeply, you will believe more and more sincerely in the principles of Soul Science, until at last your faith and desires are strong enough to force you to give up the old life for the new.

The processes of mind action, being metaphysical, are difficult of explanation. But the process of leaving off one belief or desire or habit and the taking up of another is virtually the same as change of habits through the influence of associates. It is largely a matter of association. In the case of reading and study, it is association with ideas instead of with persons. Ideas, thought, and feelings are environments as truly as are persons and conditions environments. The seeker after truth changes his thought-environments to constructive, elevating associations; and the process taking place in the mind is virtually the same as the process of change in one's character through a change of personal association.

Mind is the directing power, the builder of Soul. Mind is not the architect. The mind is not qualified, in its unawakened state, to map out or plan its own building. To be able to do this, it would have to be a perfect mind in a perfect body and would, thus, being perfect, need no super-structure. But those who hunger for something better are the ones who have been living the abnormal life. The abnormal life is not capable of devising or mapping out plans for a restoration to normal conditions. The patient is not capable of prescribing for himself. The mortal must have the Immortal to perfect plans and methods and principles for mortality to follow, in order to attain Immortality. The body is the foundation on which the Illuminated Soul is to be built, yet the mind is the directing power in rebuilding and in regenerating the body as well as in building the super-structure of Perfected Soul. Mind gives the understanding, the purpose, and the will-power necessary for following a system of teaching.

In the school of life there must be teachers. The owner of a ship would not think of taking a man from the streets and entrust to him an ocean vessel, even though the inexperienced man has a compass in his personal possession. Before allowing the man to sail the seas and the oceans, the owner of the ship would instruct him and train him and give him practical experience in the use of a compass. In like manner, though the truth-seeker is sure of his desire to know the true life and to live the Immortal life, he must not get the idea that he is sufficient unto himself. Because he desires aright is not a sure sign that he is capable of going aright. He must realize that he needs instruction and guidance, that his being is abnormal and therefore incapable of devising for himself a perfectly normal career or chart of instructions. Therefore he needs a Master Teacher, one who will be a safe guide for him until he is capable of sailing the seas of life, a free and independent being.

In the vast multitudes, the mind centers in the head. In the head, that part of the brain where the nervous system centers, the mind has its throne. During the process of regenerating and rebuilding the body, and during the first stages of Soul Building, the mind has its seat, its home, in the brain. Be it known to all men, a truth first given out by the Rosicrucian School, that the brain, the nervous energy, and the reproductive power are all of one and the same material; and that which affects and weakens one of these will affect and weaken the other two. They are one and indivisible. They cannot be separated one from the other. And, furthermore, they are the physical base of the Immortal Soul.

The mind is constructive or destructive in its operations, according to the philosophy of life accepted by the individual. Ordinarily, man unquestionably accepts the philosophy as taught from time past, which admits that we are born, we live, and we die, and that after death we inherit bliss or damnation according to whatever we accepted or rejected the sacrifice of one who voluntarily gave his life a ransom for us. This system of belief is destructive because it leads us to lean, not on our own God-given power, but on that which was done by another centuries ago.

At just this time when there has been exposed a scandal in connection with the military schools of the country, we find in it basis for an argument. In a certain military school where many young men are being trained for military service, the students availed themselves of plagiaristic methods of passing the examinations. Instead of relying on hard study and honorable means for mastering problems in the military branch of government, they employed illegitimate means of procuring the answers to questions. Not being willing to work for themselves, they accepted the work of others, giving the impression that it was due to their own efforts. As a result the whole country is horrified at this sample of thievery, and regards that manhood, the choicest manhood in the country, is degraded thereby.

Yet something similar to this has been the basis of a religious or philosophical teaching which is accepted as honorable or even godly. You demand how. You accuse me of degrading the race. You ask for proof. Here it is. The Master Jesus came to earth and lived a life that effected certain results. He lived it as an example and an undeniable illustration of the fact that such a life will bring such results and that such a life can be lived by man. What has mankind done? It has held this life up before us as a perfect redeemer of others, teaching that Jesus lived such a life for the sake of saving those who believed the fact that he did live a perfect life. They teach that merely to believe in the perfect life and death of Jesus will save a man whether he himself lives the perfect life or not. In other words, it is not necessary to live the perfect life oneself, if only one believes that Jesus was the Son of God and that he lived the perfect life and gave it by his death to the world. This doctrine advocates that we simply take the life of Jesus and claim it as our own, and that we thereby "pass our examination" creditably. In exact parallel, humanity is doing and has done, in so far as the true life, the Immortal life, is concerned, exactly what the military students have done in their preparation for military service.

This principle is destructive. The thoughts and the conclusions and the acts growing out of such a doctrine are destructive in their tendencies. It is for enlightened man to teach his fellow men that this doctrine is perverse. The doctrine of accepting from another salvation that has not been honestly earned for oneself is a destructive doctrine, and leads to a destructive life. If enlightened man does not endeavor to counteract the destructive tendencies of a teaching by instilling true principles of life and conduct in the hearts and the understanding of mankind, then destruction is at hand for the nations, just as destructive doctrines were the cause of the fall of the greatest empires that ever existed, Egypt, Greece and Rome.

The vast multitudes have accepted this doctrine, this destructive doctrine, of the divinity of stealing the life of another and calling it their own. The result of this perilous teaching is seen in the European war now waging, the most destructive of any war that has ever been known. It is full of hatred, full of cunning, full of the foulest deeds that man can think of. At the basis of it is this erroneous principle, that men may do, during life, all the foul, deadly, damnable things in the category of wickedness, and that, when examination time comes, they may hide their "flunking" by claiming the perfect life of another as their own. This thought held in mind, this destructive principle, causes men to live and to act in accordance with the thought and the principle. As a man thinks, so will he act. This is shown in the fighting of the millions of soldiers, who have been brought up in the thought that to steal the life of another is just and right and will be honored by God when we cross the Border.

We stand, each one, as an individual creature. As an individual, each one must work out his own salvation. We cannot lean on the merits of another, not even of God Himself. We must become masters of our own thoughts and acts, and must work out our own Regeneration, our own Immortality. Like boys in military schools, we must solve our own problems. To refuse to do so, and to accept the work of another and use it as our own, will bring its own appropriate punishment. The penalty is death to us as individuals; we must return to the melting pot of nature and become part of the whole, which God will have to rework in order to bring out something worthy of Him.

This more than anything else will convince the truth-seeker of the one, of many ways, in which thought destroys the soul. As we think, so do we act. And, according to the life, so will be the Soul. It is not thought directly which destroys the Soul. It is the acts caused by the thoughts which cause destruction. The mind thinks and feels. These thoughts and feelings, if strong enough, cause us to act; and the acts destroy. The Master Jesus taught that the Soul that sinneth, it shall surely die. Thoughts cause us to act. Acts drain the body and the Soul of those forces which give life and strength to both body and Soul. If they drain body and Soul of life and energy, in time they cause the Soul to die.

How can we drain the Soul, you will ask. Not so difficult to answer as you may imagine.

The brain, which is the base of the mind, and the nerves and the generative forces are of one and the same material. There are many acts, or rather one act performed in many ways, which drain the system of this force. Now, bear in mind that the Soul can not exist unless it can draw its life from these centers. When you realize that these are acts which can drain dry the brain and the nerves and the generative centers, you will understand that when these three centers are drained dry, the Soul can no longer draw from them; and therefore it becomes starved in like manner as the body starves when it has no nourishment. Remember the Law of Hermes: "As above, so below." The law of the body is in harmony with the Law of the Soul. As there is food for the body, the supply of which can be exhausted, so is there food for the Soul, the supply of which can be exhausted.

How terribly destructive the throwing away of nerve, brain, and generative forces may become, is indicated in the Bible in the history of Moses in connection with the Children of Israel in the wilderness. The ravages of this destroying power had become so great that Moses had to find a remedy, and a method of teaching his people how to conserve the forces that build Soul and Immortal Life.

In the ordinary individual, the mind centers in the head. As the individual overcomes self, and nears true Mastership and Illumination and Immortality of Soul, or, as our Church Friends say, as he becomes "saved," the seat of the mind is changed. As the Soul awakens gradually, so does the power of the mind give way and become centered in the Soul. Thus it will be that, when Illumination actually takes place, the thoughts no longer center in the mind of the brain, but in the mind of the Soul. Thus the seat of government for the individual is moved from the head to the Great Center where centers the Soul, and reason will have given place to Intuition. Be it known that Intuition is the Voice of God. It is the Voice of God that speaks through the Illuminated Soul. While the voice of man and imperfect reason speaks through the mind of man.

The Spirit of man, being non-individual and impersonal force, is the connecting link, which holds together the different departments of man's fourfold nature. It is the link that holds the Soul to the body. When this connection takes place at the first drawn breath of the infant, the functioning of the brain takes place, and there is mind.

In this is found the reason for holding, as does the Great School of Soul Science, that man is triplicate, the Equilateral Triangle, when perfect, and that he is also fourfold, the perfect Square. He is actually body, mind, spirit, and Soul. But he is, in actuality, also body, mind and Soul, since the Spirit is not an individual entity, but is merely a connecting link, a pervading energy or life force which animates and functions through the vital organic processes of body, mind and Soul. The Spirit is really God or a part of God. Without the Spirit nothing can exist. Spirit is Life. Spirit is the Life Principle. It is impersonal, universal, non-individual. It is the personal property of no one, for it is God. The lowest and the most unsightly creature on earth as well as the most Godlike man has part of this Spirit. It is the life of both just as the life of the fruit gives life to man and to beast, and as the deadly poison is enabled to send the most enlightened man to the Beyond.

The Spirit, or Life Principle, is confusedly rendered in the Bible. This leads to misunderstanding, and inclines one to consider Soul and Spirit as the same thing. It must be remembered that Spirit is not peculiar to man. It cannot really be called a part of man. Therefore, in true knowledge, man is a triplicate being, a perfect representative of the Triangle. Spirit is impartial and imparticaled, belonging to all living things, good and bad, destructive as well as constructive.

It remains to give special attention to the Soul. Roughly considered, man is simply an animal with the possibilities of a god. He is, roughly speaking, a personality, with the possibility of becoming an individuality. When he develops individuality he is developing Godward. All men are born as personalities. They are given the privilege of becoming individualities. The seed is within them. The food for the seed is within them. And they are given the privilege of using both the seed and the food of the seed.

It may be crudely stated that all men are born with Souls. But, in taking on flesh, the Soul is covered by the flesh in the same manner as an acorn may be covered by and buried in the ground. The acorn is the oak in embryo. Planted in the earth under proper conditions, it will germinate and develop into the oak. In like manner, the body is the ground or the soil in which the soul is buried. The ground or the soil of the body is as necessary to the germination and development of the Soul as is the soil of the earth necessary to the germination of the acorn. The body, being material substance, is heavier than the Soul; and the Soul sinks into it and is covered. There is one part of the Soul which is not completely covered—that is, the longing for something better and higher. This longing, this cry, makes itself felt and heard from time to time.

In many lives, there are several forces at work. The Soul cries for better things. But environments, associations, religion and philosophy tend to cover the Soul still further with hindrances; and, in the vast number of cases, they succeed in covering it so fully that even the conscience, the cry of the Soul, cannot be heard. Then nothing remains but the mind, which is purely intellectual, and heeds nothing except the religion, the philosophy, and the standards of life usually accepted by mankind.

On the other hand, in some lives, the cry of the Soul to find light and its proper sphere is heeded; and the person comes in contact with books and teachings which have to do with the Immortal life. The cry of the Soul acts as a stimulus and an incentive to the brain and causes the mind to accept the truths presented. In the acceptance of these truths, there is the possibility of a gradual awakening of the Soul; and then man becomes the possessor of an individuality. He becomes, in fact, an individuality plus a personality. He is reaching toward Godhood.

The mind is the judge in the lower court of existence. It is cold intelligence. Mind is ever cold. It is not in touch with things immortal, because it is itself only mortal. It therefore accepts and comprehends only the things of the mortal plane, things accepted by the majority. As mind, it may become all-powerful; but it cannot become Immortal. In fact, it may be said that environments always control it, because it has no power to step beyond the limits of physical comprehension.

But the Soul has an urge; and if the mind reads and studies concerning the Soul and Immortality, or if the mind is slightly awakened to the truth; then, this, together with the urge of the Soul within, will cause it to question. In the questioning, in this possibility of dissatisfaction with material and merely intellectual things, is found the salvation of the Soul. Gradually it may come to seek deeper and deeper until finally the Soul becomes the ruling power.

In regard to fineness and density of substance, mind is next to physical matter. It is to be classed as a force rather than substance, and is far finer than is the material body of man. Like the nerves and the generative forces, it is not spirit, neither is it matter. It is the link between the two. But the Soul is finer than the mind. It is a Fire. The purity or the grossness of the Fire depends entirely on the purity of the Soul. As man understands immortal principles and begins to live the true life, this Fire, which is at first completely hidden in the material and is very gross, gradually becomes more intense. As its intensity increases, it burns away, not only its own dross, but the dross surrounding it. In time, it becomes a Living Fire. Then it is part of the Godhead, and lives or exists on the Throne of the Temple. Where this Throne is, none but the Initiate can know. This information cannot be imparted by word of mouth. It must be found by the individual for himself. Like Moses, man must find it in the Burning Bush.

Yet let it be remembered that mind is of supreme importance in that it is the directing power. When the mind accepts a constructive philosophy, it will gradually cause the entire being to work in harmony with that philosophy. The more the being works in harmony with such a philosophy, the more purified will become the Soul. As the Soul becomes purified and vital and dynamic, it gradually usurps the place of the mind. At last, the Soul itself rules on the Throne; and the mind acts only as the *acceptor* of the things that are to become part of the Soul. The reign of the mind is at an end. John, the Baptist, has been imprisoned and beheaded to make way for the Christ.

To sum up: man is composed of body, mind, spirit and Soul. The body is of the earth, earthly. Its tendency is downward. This tendency man must overcome. To overcome this tendency is the price man must pay for becoming discontented with his original oneness with God, and desiring to experience conscious Immortality. The body has the appetites of the flesh, which are contrary to those of the higher realm. These man must overcome, these and his earthly desires and appetites. In the overcoming will he receive strength to *be*.

Next comes the Spirit of man. The Spirit is of God. It is impartial, impersonal, universal. It is in all things, but returns to God as things die. Thus, the rose is given the spirit of life, which it retains so long as it lives. At death it returns to God, not as the spirit of the rose, but as the spirit of God just as it came from Him. Being impersonal and impartial, the Spirit is neither good nor bad. It simply *is*. It is God because it is life. It is given to all so that all may work out their own destiny.

The mind is the ruling power. Mind is given to man, not because it is of God, but because man has the right of choice. The mind has the power to choose. Like life, it is neither mortal nor immortal, but is the result of combination. The Soul alone belongs to man, as his very own. Properly speaking, the Soul is *man*. Before the earth life, it existed as an Immortal Being, not knowing love or pleasure, being unconscious as to sensation. It was not satisfied to *be,* but wanted to become a conscious individual. This dissatisfaction forced it from the Kingdom; and, as it can know only by taking on flesh, it entered flesh and accepted the earth life. But this condition was imposed upon it: it could not return to the Kingdom until it had worked out its own salvation, by making the mortal part of its nature immortal. The Immortal must raise the mortal unto Immortality.

The Spirit, being life, is of God. But the Soul is free from God in that it has free choice, and man must raise it to God through his own efforts. It is the fundamental Laws of the four-fold culture of body, mind, spirit and Soul that the Illuminati in its Soul Science teaches. Moreover, it is this four-fold Philosophy that is the base of all teachings in the Sacred Colleges as now being instituted throughout the world.

INVOCATION OF THE HIERARCHIES

In the early Christian church and in the religious life of the early Christians, the Invocation of the Saints, as it was termed, was accepted as an important part of life. It is one of the fundamental doctrines of the Apostles' Creed, and there stands as a monument to this feature of religious service.

Gradually, as men wandered away from the true religious life—the life of service and helpfulness—the secret of the Invocation of the Saints was lost. By the vast multitudes who are devoted to the church today nothing is known of the Invocation of the Saints except the mention of it in the Apostles' Creed; and to this little thought is given as to its real meaning.

By no means did belief in the Invocation of the Saints originate with the early Christians. It was handed down to them from a still earlier religious practice. In its original form it was known as Invocation of the Hierarchies, or Invocation of the Guardian Angels. This feature of religion was powerful in primitive custom, especially among the Egyptians. Adherents of this practice believed that all interests of human life and all elements of nature are under the care of superior Hierarchies, or Guardian and Ministering Angels.

With the ancient Initiates, religion was more than a formulated creed. To them it was a reality. To them it was life. A certain part of their time was given up to religious practices, just as certain portions of time were devoted to manual labor, to eating, to sleep, and to procuring the necessities of life. They understood the soul and its mysteries. They understood that man is a composite creature, and that the body is only a part of his being, that body and soul are co-equal each with the other, and that body and soul have each a duty to perform—the body to nature and the soul to God. This understanding of the composition of man gave them a clear comprehension of prayer as a means of putting soul and body in correct relation with God and nature.

The Initiates, however, did not follow a formal system of

prayer. Prayer to them was more than lip service. They understood Hierarchic celestial rulership, and recognized intermediary powers and potentates in the management of the universe. As in the government of the people there is one supreme ruler with many officers of subordinate rank to execute the laws of the supreme ruler, so, according to the conception of the Initiates, the universe is the product of one Supreme Creator and Ruler, one Supreme Divine Being, but with Him is associated a corps of subordinate being and powers through whom the work of the one Supreme Ruler is performed. These subordinate beings were termed Hierarchies, or celestial Potentates, or Guardian Angels. They guarded the destinies of men and performed the Will of the Infinite in all things.

This unquestioning recognition of Hierarchies or angelic hosts made prayer to them an actual Invocation through which they came into conscious touch with the Hierarchies or angelic forces. Thus, when they proved worthy and were sincere in their demand, they received help in accordance with their Invocation. By the Priesthood of Egypt, Initiates were instructed in the laws and the principles of Invocation. By the priests of Melchizadek also were Invocations fully taught. Indeed, the laws and the teachings of Melchizadek were the foundation of Egyptian Initiation. It was these teachings with which every neophyte must become familiar before he was permitted to minister to the public. So long as the great Priesthood of Egypt continued to exist, up to the time of the usurpers, all kings were trained in these principles. And no one could become a king until he had first become an Initiate. For this reason they were called Initiate or Priest-Kings.

It must not be thought that the people generally understood the Invocation-religion. The people then as now repeated formulas, witnessed beautiful and impressive ceremonies, and believed in them, with meagre comprehension of the truth on which formulas and ceremonies were based. Today, however, it is a question whether even the minister at the head of the flock knows what is meant fundamentally by "Invocation of Saints."

At the beginning of the Christian era, there were not many of the Initiates left. It was an age of change, an age in which the old had to give place to the new because the old had been abused. Yet, so strong was the belief still held in the Invocation of the Hierarchies that it was incorporated into the Creed of the Apostles, founders of the early Christian church. Instead of being retained in its purity as an article of faith in the Invocation of Hierarchies—beings and forces pure and powerful in the service of the One Supreme God—it degenerated into a mere verbal expression of faith in the Invocation of Saints—men and women who had gone on before.

Some may claim that it is more reasonable to believe in the Invocation of Saints than in the Invocation of the Hierarchies. Let this argument beanswered by questions. How did God effect the progress of the world and of mankind before saints existed? How is it that the world continued to exist and the work of the world was performed before the Chrsitian church was founded, when so-called heathenism is supposed to have reigned? Or, if the world could exist and progress enough to make the coming of a Messiah possible, why could it not continue in the same manner without the help of saints?

Moreover, it must be remembered that God does not canonize men. Men are canonized as saints by men, mere human beings. And history shows that the lives of many who have been registered as saints were by no means exemplary according to accepted standards of uprightness. Is it reasonable, then, to suppose that any good could come from invocation to those who may not be superior even to the invocant himself? How can we expect good from the practice of Invocation unless the ones whom we invoke are on a plane far superior to human knowledge and power? A marked contrast indeed between Invocation of Saints and Invocation of Hierarchies is seen when it is remembered that the Hierarchies are none other than the Eloim, creative forces and potencies associated with the Infinite.

There is every evidence for the belief that Invocation of Saints, as referred to in the Apostles' Creed, has descended from the Egyptians. Its form has been modified, and it has degenerated into an article of faith merely, whereas formerly among the Initiates of Egypt it was a sacred daily practice, a feature of worship, or, better, a feature of life, essential to each day.

Through all Sacred Scriptures, whether it be the Bible of Christianity, or Buddhism, of Brahmanism, or of any other religious system, is to be found the doctrine that there are guardian or ministering angels watching over the destinies of men. It is a fact generally admitted that men of the early church when under persecution were guarded, guided, sustained, protected, by angels, or angelic presences and influences. Not only these, but, according to general acceptation, prophets and seers of all times have been administered unto by angels sent by the Lord to save them. By priests of the Church of Melchizadek and by Egyptian Initiates these ministering spirits were called Hierarchies, or Eloim; and Invocations to them were in harmony with the specific work performed by the particular Hierarchy addressed. Now it must be remembered that prophets and seers and holy men of old invoked the help, guidance and protection, of Higher Potentates long centuries before the Apostles' Creed was a possibility.| Therefore, it was not saints—canonized men of the church—who saved and helped those who appealed to the Higher Powers.

These things indicate that Invocation to Higher Forces was not original with the early church. From every point of view it seems plausible to claim that it was a modified form of the old Initiate-Priest service of the ancient Egyptian Priesthood.

Nevertheless, Invocation of Saints, as a relic of the Invocation of Hierarchies rests upon a true and a firm foundation. In its essential features, Invocation of Hierarchies should be revived and become a part of the religious life of every human being. It *must be revived* before religion can be what it once was, a *living, powerful, life-giving reality.*

In the ancient worship, a part of the service was devoted to the Invocation of the Hierarchies that have guard each over some particular territory of the Kingdom of God or the Kingdom of Nature. Thus, in sorrow, in sickness, in failure, in misfortune of any kind—in fact, in all things which affect the destiny of man—there is a particular Guardian and Ministering Angel, or Hierarchy, which has charge of that domain of human life. Moreover, there is also an Invocation adapted to the needs of each department of man's nature. This Invocation, issuing in humility, faith, and sincerity from the heart of the suppliant, and being directed to the Hierarchy exercising guardianship over that department of human interests, unfailingly secures the help of the Hierarchy invoked.

Superstition this! Possibly. But in that case let the church at once proceed to cut out of the Apostles' Creed its expression of belief in the Invocation of Saints; for it is one and the same thing stated in different words.

The new church, the coming church of man, recognizes the truth that underlies Invocation of Hierarchies, as practiced in its original simplicity by Initiate-Priests of all ages. It regards that Invocation of the Hierarchies is a possibility, *a verity,* which should be understood and practiced by all men. It is in fact, the very foundation of true religion. It is the essence of true religious life. It is the secret of true prayer.

Mankind generally is coming to recognize this great truth. Aye, even the established church is coming to see it. But the established church cannot now step backward and make Invocation a part of its service. It has waited too long and such an innovation is clearly impossible.

The Right Reverend Arthur Ingram, Bishop of London, recently, in one of the annual services in the Church of England Congress held at Southampton, made a plea for the restoration of the saints. He made a plea for the restoration of that aspect of the doctrine of the communion of saints to which every Christian reciting the Apostles' Creed is pledged.

It is well said that history repeats itself, and that there are cyclic returns of customs and practices. Let us remember, however, that history repeats not *verbatim,* or word for word, but that, through the experience of a lapse from a worthy practice, history revives the practice in purified form.

For many centuries, aye, for ages before the Christian era, Invocation of the Hierarchies existed as the foundation of religious worship and religious life. In measure, the early church recognized the facts underlying Invocation of Hierarchies, and attempted to incorporate the principle of Invocation in their religious system. They failed, however, to make it an actual living fact, apart of daily life. They failed to instill into their adherents the necessity of daily use of Invocation according to individual need. As a result, the practice degenerated into a formality, and, being deprived of life, became lost to view, until at the present time little is known of it except the incidental mention of belief in communion of the saints as recorded in the Apostles' Creed.

And now, after many centuries, leading men of the church are beginning to see what humanity has lost through being deprived of this essential feature of religious worship. Man has gone from one extreme to another, from irreligion to irreligion, until he has no firm foundation on which to stand. He keeps waiting for something to come to him which he can accept, something which, to his reasoning mind, has a firm basis. All this, some few of the established church are forced to admit. And the plea of the Right Reverend Ingram for the re-establishment of the Invocation of the Saints voices the conviction of these few.

But the established church, having long ago parted with the service of invocation, cannot restore it. They have lost the Key, the mystery, to it, the real significance of it, and it is to them a dead letter. Moreover, even if they possessed the Ritual of Hierarchic Invocation, they could not reinstate the service, for the reason that their adherents would not "stand for" such a radical, though natural, innovation. Consequently, the church will be forced to do the best it can until the new church—the church with the ritualistic, invocative service—will have become strong, so useful, so natural, that the old church will be absorbed in it.

By no means is the established church to be condemned for having lost its hold on Hierarchic Innovation. It has done all that it could, all it knew how to do. When the change was made from the so-called heathen era to the Christian era, everything had to be given up that was of the old; and, though much of the outer form of the old was given up so as not to savor of the discarded worship. Consequently, that which had been a living, vital reality became no more than a part of the creed of the new church, a doctrine to be accepted as correct teaching, but not a truth to be lived.

The age in which Hierarchic Invocation is demanded by the people is not far distant. In fact, it has already begun. The old Ritual of Hierarchic Invocation, of which history gives little information, has been faithfully preserved and is in the care of the new church, the church now in process of formation.* This means the ushering in of a new era, an era made possible by the cyclic ebb and flow of human progress, an era in which history revives in purified form a religious practice formerly honored and cherished by Initiates of old. It is to be an era in

*The Order of the Magi, Degree "Priests of Melchizadel" uses the complete, ancient Ritual in all its beauty.

which men will demand that the priests or the clergy of the church to which they belong shall be conversant with the entire ritual of invocative intercession. More than this, they will demand priests who are qualified to use invocative prayers in their behalf. They will be satisfied with nothing less than priests, teachers, ministers, or leaders, in whom they have unwavering confidence both as regards purity and sincerity of motive and as regards superior ability in the effective and the intelligent use of invocative power.

The time is come in which men and women generally, seekers after truth, demand as leaders and teachers those who are qualified to give authoritative instruction and to impart vital knowledge. The people demand basic knowledge concerning religious practices. They require the reason, the why, and the wherefore, for religious customs. When they are convinced that a certain religious practice is based on undeniable principles and that it is powerful and effective for the needs of daily life and that it is regenerative in its influence, they will be satisfied with nothing less than definite and authoritative instruction in regard to it. They will demand the knowledge that can be tested in personal experience. They will demand the knowledge that enables them to make intelligent use of the practice according to thir own needs. Such knowledge, such instruction, will soon be in demand regarding Hierarchic Invocation and Invocative Prayer.

The new church of the present age will not fasten creeds and articles of faith on its adherents; but it will teach vital truths, truths which are not only to be believed but also to be lived. The new church will consider daily life and daily needs. Its Invocations will be such as have to do with the conditions in which its members live. Invocation will be something which calls for the help that is required by frail, groping humanity. It will bring its people into touch with those powers which they seek.

In accordance with the cyclic rhythm of historic changes, the time is ripe for a replacement of emphasis on Hierarchic Invocation. Mankind is reawakening to the beliefs held by the ancient Initiates. It is well to know that God is all, and that without Him is nothing. But it is also well to know that He works in a multitude of ways, that he works through these which are less than He, and that He ministers to mankind through powers and potentates, which, though inferior to the Infinite and intermediary, are specifically qualified to satisfy human need. As God works through human agencies, so does He also work through Hierarchic instrumentality. And no part of the multiplicity of human interests is left without its appropriate guardianship and protectorate from the invisible forces.

Here again, by way of analogy, may be brought into use the Law of Hermes, "As above so below, and as below so above." As in human government, so in celestial. To gain a hearing in any given department of governmental administration, a man does not appeal to the supreme power direct, but to the subordinate power to whom has been entrusted authoritative supervision in that particular domain. For a matter of importance that concerns the army or navy or the treasury, we do not think of directing our communication to the President, or supreme ruler of the nation. Rather we address the department in which our concern is classified. If we do not know the name and title and how properly to address the one to whom our communication should come, we seek the desired information, and make our communication in conformity with accepted usage.

Similarly, it is reasonable to think of God as the Supreme Ruler of the universe with subordinate powers as co-workers and co-rulers. In celestial powers there is this difference. They are true to their divine nature, true to God, and true to their work; their motives are clean, pure and unselfish; they must grant or refuse a demand according to the justice or the injustice of the request. Whereas, in national and in state management, officers and executive are biased and hampered by human frailties and weaknesses.

It is likewise reasonable to think of Hierarchic powers, or Eloim, as having appropriate titles and designations by which man must appeal to them and by means of which he must invoke them. The title or name or designation of a Hierarchic power is important, however, not as a mere arbitrary requirement. It is to be thought of as the Key to the vibration to which that particular Hierarchy responds. Thus, to use the correct appellation of a deific potentate and to make use of a suitable formula serves as a means of bringing the invocant into contact with the power sought. Titles and degrees, as designations of honor or station or authority, have no place among the Eloim. To inform oneself of the correct title and the appropriate formula by which to address a given Hierarchy or deific power, and to become skillful in the use of it, is *to awaken in the invocant that subtle vibratory force which puts him in harmony with the par-particular power invoked.* On the human plane, address to a superior power must conform to correct usage for conventional reasons; on the celestial plane, for reasons vital and fundamental. without which it is impossible to reach the vibratory realm in which that deific power dwells, but with which it is possible to strike the chord of his vibration.

All these things the Initiates who have been faithful to the true laws have long recognized. All these things they have privately taught, though usually under a code, or secret system.

But at last the time is at hand in which it is made possible, and in which it has even become necessary, to speak plainly and openly. Even the modern church Father is beginning to recognize the truth and the reality that underlies customs followed in the days of primitive religion, customs which the established church of the present day never had; for, though reference is made in the Apostolic Creed to the Invocation of Saints, the fact remains that Invocation of the Saints has never been observed by the church. And, on account of the failure of the church to teach and to practice a vital religon and a religious life, it has failed in its aims, which, admittedly were of the best. And men are leaving the church with no thought of returning to it.

But, in the horizon, in the East, as the sun rises on a June morning, comes into view the new church, the new order of things. The Illuminati and their Inner Priesthood are again beginning to teach the people a living, pulsating vital, livable system, a system throbbing with force and power. They are again establishing among the children of men a religious system as glorious, as divine, as life-giving, as was ever practiced by the ancient priesthoods when religion was pure and undefiled, when the priests of the Temple, admittedly, had great power, and were the teacher-healer-rulers of the people.

Let it not be thought that when such a church is established the service will consist of an Invocational program merely. Nothing of the kind, the service will admit of variety and will appeal to the varied interests of man's composite nature. There will be place for music which will lift the souls of men from the commonplace to the divine. Sermons should be lectures or addresses of real instruction, food for thought, of practical value to the soul, something more than flowery oratory which has neither aim nor end.

Let it be clearly understood that the establishment of Invocative Prayer to the Hierarchies would in no sense do away with prayers of devotion and adoration and gratitude to the One God, the Father over all. Invocative Prayers to the Hierarchic Powers, or Eloim, would be only for specific purposes, while the devotional prayer would continue to be addressed to the One true and only God. Invocative Prayer to the Hierarchic Powers and Potentates would be in case of sickness, in case of sorrow, or in the many other specific cases; but the spirit pervading the entire service would be devotion, and worshipful adoration and gratitude, directed to "Him in whom we live and move and have our being." One form of prayer would supplement the other. The two forms of worship would be in full harmony with each other, and not, as some might think, a false worship or worship of false gods.

In short, prayer of worship or adoration or gratitude would not be directed to Hierarchic Potentates, for all worship is direct to God. Invocative Prayer differs from the prayer of worship or adoration in this point: it is distinctively and exclusively, as the name indicates, a prayer in which a particular Hierarchy *is invoke* for a specific purpose and with a specific request. In passing, it is worthy of mention that the most beautiful and impressive magical rites and Invocative Prayers in the system of the ancient Initiates are those which invoke the Hierarchies for "wisdom and an understanding heart." This is definite and specific, and who can question the desirability of a specific Invocation for wisdom and an understanding heart?

Furthermore, another great change is to be advocated—that is, the inauguration of true family worship. The time was when there was a family service once, twice or three times a day. The head of the family acted as priest for the home. He led the members of the family in daily worship, following a formula, or a system of worship.

THE SONS OF OSIRIS

Listening, we hear; looking, we see; in the silent spaces long vanished scenes and events are before us. Passing from the busy sounds of outer events to the inner stillness we hear the murmur of the rising tide of human souls breathing upon these western shores, and afar the music of wave beats as this human sea of souls is driven in this present age, seeking evolvement higher on the spiral scale here and now; souls from the long past; the many bearing stains and darkened records of former misspent incarnations; some blackened and seared by awful deeds; some dwarfed and misshapen through former warped and selfish lives; some just beginning; some utterly lost, their individuality appearing in their present bodies for the last time; and the *few* bright and shining ones who have afar back "washed their sins away in the 'Blood of the Lamb,' (the meaning of which is: blood symbolizes regeneration; the 'Lamb' is the Universal Christ—Principle; hence "washed in the blood" means—regeneration through attaining to Christhood, which can be done by no man except with the help of the Great Brotherhood, after he himself chooses and wills the mastery over his own lower self; and even the Master Christ, Jesus, required such help). Each human is to a large extent what his soul makes him together with his traits inherited from his physical ancestry; on the other hand his soul is just what he has made it himself in his past lives, and will be for the future just what he is now making it and will make it in his present and future lives; this implies most certainly that whatever is his lot he has made just that for himself. This brings us to the fact that the Great Master Jesus was not such because He was originally any greater in soul than any other beginning soul, but that He was in that incarnation just what He made *Himself* in *past* lives, no matter how few or many they had been. Moreover, the physical ancestry which each soul seeks in reincarnating, in so far as such can be supplied by the world at the time being,is determined by the character which its past lives have given to that soul. Hence both the soul and personality of which any humans find themselves possessed and whatever Karma may be attached thereto are just what they themselves have made them. We see through soul vision an ever increasing host of souls reincarnating in a powerful and growing civilization; growing in knowledge, prosperity, material power, and to a certain extent in spirituality. Born again into the flesh; to the darkened vision of their unillumined fellows and to themselves these present bodies and this life, changing, fleeting, and soon passed, appears to them as the whole sum of their existence, and as the beginning and end of their experience in *this* world. But the Illumined Brother, through the soul's eye which has opened for him because of his own self-evolvement either in this or in his past lives, beholds in each personality a hidden being which in its beginning was endowed with potentialities capable of attainment to either Godhood or to Devilhood just as its subsequent lives in the flesh might choose to follow the right hand or the left hand way, and accept the opportunities for good, or for evil, constantly being offered in every life, and on every hand. Thus the Illumined Brothers of the bright and shining souls among this host perceive in every human this Being, in varying states, according as it has fared at the hands of its previous personalities, in some it is bright and shining like unto their own; in others it is revealed in every grade of evolvement or destruction, for as it has been builded so is it; for this Being, lost to many who are now living for the last time, and grievously disfigured in others, and in those who have climbed the heights—shining as the stars of the firmament—is the human Soul. And conscious, higher visuality, reveals in each human soul its past; and some there are in whom this inner hidden Soul-Being has reached its end and this life is the finish, for deeds of darkness and sin, or too long procrastination in seeking the right hand way destroys the Soul. In the many immortality is still within their reach if they so will; while the White Souls need return no more to this vale of tears unless it be to further help humanity. And so we view the great host in their reappearance in physical incarnation; the skies bend above us, the broad land receives us to her bosom, our beautiful Isis of old is here with us, her beauty is apparent for those who know her, our long lost power and glory and riches is again returning to us here in the flesh, we eat and drink and are merry as we have done so many times before; but let us remember that each time we return and fail to follow the right hand path, or procrastinate our seeking the way, our souls suffer and atrophy accordingly, and the "balances will find us wanting" even though we do no great wrong; for the balance becomes increasingly wanting in greater degree each life we fail, and this must be equalized sooner or later when the final adjustment is required though it removes both soul and body out of existence to meet the deficiency; for there are two great forces at work in the universe; they are good and evil. They are guided and directed by intelligent beings for above the human. Neither of these may interpose *directly* in our lives, for the law of being of the human determines that he shall be entirely free to choose either of these forces as he may himself elect; but the law also determines that he shall be fully responsible for his choosing and must *himself* meet the consequences of his choice, be it immortality or eternal death. Plenty of opportunities are given by the directors of both forces to each and every human; they come to him in the seemingly ordinary affairs of his every day life, though to the undeveloped personality they are never understood as such directly, or as representing the Universal Christ forces as one aspect, and the Universal Devil forces as the other. Only the Illuminated human interprets in each person, and event, and circumstance, their real meaning and the source from which they come; for the profane world knows nothing of the universal laws nor of the intelligent beings who operate them. But though unconscious of these higher laws every human endowed with a soul which has not been destroyed and therefore a conscience, and a mind and reasoning faculties is capable of knowing through intuition, and of choosing between right and wrong. For the law as well as the "Progenitors of the Race" from which man has derived his free choice, have also given him the faculties to do his own conscious and intelligent choosing. A single real injustice occuring anywhere in the universal whole would destroy all there is, for a universal unbalance would result. Man does indeed cause great injustice to his fellows and to the lower living things but the Law of Karma is equalizing these re-establishes equilibrium, and thus whatsoever a man suffers for his misdeeds either in the life in which they were committed, or in lives following is just. Man is the only portion of infinite creation that creates injustice, and sins; for even the evil spirits depend upon Man to accept and carry out the wrong which it is their office and aspect to revise in potential, but which it is his free choice to refuse *if he will,* and this therefore makes him wholly responsible for the effects. When the sum of injustice he creates sufficiently accumulates, its equalization may involve the destruction of the whole planet upon which it occurs as with Lucifer, or the very land beneath his feet as with the lost continents of Lemuria and Atlantis of this earth. It is for these reasons that Man's injustice, which is the only injustice anywhere, does not wreck everything there is, for if he is constantly causing injustice, through retribution he is as constantly required to equalize and re-establish the balance he has perverted. While it is the individual Karma caused by the individual which brings sorrow and destruction to the individual, it is the general Karma accumulated by the whole race which reacts as general suffering upon the just and the unjust, and destroys planets and continents. And so we view the incoming host from the past; a host of souls of every grade, and state, and degree of perfection or destruction; some bright and beautiful, some hideous and distorted and warped according as they have fared during their sojourn in their past bodies and earthly lives, some lost beyond redemption. Between these high and low soul states we perceive every possible variation of evolvement and development among these souls; as they have been builded so are they now according as the lives have chosen good or evil, kindness and love, or injustice and wrong as to whether these have made them bright and shining, or dark and sorrowful, or black with despair. O hidden memories of the great past! like a long river flowing on through ever changing scenery, now through broad meadows sunlit and calm, again through rocky defile rushing with spray and roar, shadowed between high and dark mountain walls, on and on toward the great sea of the absolute through rise and fall of empires and dynasties and always the same souls; some not far from the end, some the headwaters just left behind and others becoming lost in the desert sands.. These memories, for the majority, lie buried in their sleeping souls which have never yet been awakened by them, for the soul cannot be awakened by lives lived for physical bodies however passively good these may be, or how much worship is devoted to an unseen and unknown Deity in the abstract; it can only be properly awakened by seeking the masters to be found associated together in the Great Mystic Fraternities, such as that now known as The Fraternity Sons of Osiris, is among the best and oldest. It is safe for no man to attempt soul awakening alone. He will be assailed by the Black Brothers on all sides and without the protection of the true masters is almost certain to fail and perhaps be lost. Without the true training before the awakening, the experiences of that awakening together with the pressure of the terrific flood of memories of his past lives will sweep him either into the "madhouse or the grave," in his unprepared condition. How much less will lives of wickedness and selfishness and sin awaken the soul; indeed such lives serve to sink it deeper in unconsciousness and finally the fatal coma from which it can never be awakened and the soul through sin, and procrastination as well, go out into the eternal night of oblivion. For others, these memories and the soul awakening is yet a long way off and largely through failure of the carnal to seek the way of life which requires constant determined search and denials and efforts to find, and the sacrifice of worldly pleasures and ease and selfish aggrandisement, and the giving up of visible things for such as are invisible for long, until the awakening reveals them in glory and beauty, which cannot be shown, however, to the man "dead in sin and frittered away lives." There are others we perceive who have sought the "way of life and light" and have entered the path and are faithful disciples; to these each day brings them nearer to soul awakening and illumination and the eternal memories locked within them. For the few who *have* awakened, memory stretches back across the span of ages through life after life, and race beyond race upon this earth and afar back to sunken continents and lost civilizations. To these the world's story is an open book and the history of mankind has been repeated over and over again and always ending the same in failure and retribution, and always for the same reasons, and always through his own fault and voluntary failure and because he has chosen to follow the left hand path and has accepted the things of the "Black Brothers" which pleased his carnal nature and afforded him wordly advantages but which in the end have invariably destroyed his soul. This host now appearing upon the arena of this growing civilization and coming hither for a new trial; through soul-memory we view the experiences which they bring of far off Lemuria, of beautiful Atlantis, of sublime Egypt, of ascetic India, of Magian Chaldea, of philosophic Greece, of cruel Rome, of Mosaic Judea, and of other countries and epochs. The memories of those forgotten ages brings before us the awful mistakes which first destroyed the great continents of ancient Lemuria when the world was in her youth; where Mother Earth writhing in torture and burning with unquenchable fire, because her children had turned her green bosom into a human slaughter house and a den of iniquity, finally gave up the struggle to save them and dropped into her ocean grave. And later on rises before us beautiful Atlantis, Queen of the Sea, man's paradise on earth where the human attained to physical perfection and beauty never before attained and never again to be equalled in this Manvantara, and where his knowledge and attainments have never to this time reached so high a plane; here again the same host of souls coming over from lost Lemuria and incarnating in the beautiful bodies of the Atlantean Fourth Race created so tremendous an unbalance of injustice and sin that the safety of the whole planet demanded adjustment. Then it was, that, unable to harmoniously equalize the balance and meet the sweep of eternal justice for the prodigious Karma created by those she had cradled and sheltered and given freely of her plenty, as the stroke fell, staggering under the terrible load of wickedness and accumulated evil, unable to longer withstand the shock of the cosmic forces lashed into fury and struggling for equilibrium; our mother land, lovely Atlantis with all her wonderful achievements, sank beneath the blue waves in death and oblivion, that the injustice of her children might be atoned through her destruction as well as theirs. For when great unbalance has been accumulated through the wrong actions of men the whole earth is affected by the general Karma; when this becomes sufficiently great that it cannot be balanced through destruction of the inhabitants themselves then the very earth itself beneath them will also be torn and convulsed and disappear as to its former conditions. But though all went down and destruction overtook the dwellers of Lemuria and Atlantis, and equilibrium in nature was re-established, yet the Karma against them has not been fully requitted even yet, nor the balance of past misdeeds equalized. There is still in the "cup of sorrow" for these now appearing here portions to be finished, both from those long ago races and from later ages. We see again in the panorama of memory these same souls in later civilizations building, in other bodies, empires and kingdoms, and greatest among these, Egypt the fallen. Down through the long dynasties of Pharaoic glory memory recalls the scenes of magnificent beauty, of sublime wisdom and knowledge, the mighty civilization of the flower of the Atlantean souls reincarnated; the "mantle" of the occult power of Atlantis laid upon the shoulders of the Ancient Osirian (Priesthood) Brotherhood. However, compared with the majority, these were few in numbers; advanced souls who had evolved along the pathway upward to mastery and illumination, and wholly worthy and true. And what is recalled of the great multitude of souls down through these ages? During the earlier dynasties the rulers themselves were also initiates; and the people were guided and taught in the higher things and righteousness reigned and all things were well, and Egypt in those days bloomed as the rose and was green and fertile. But the blackness of the past gradually awakened; more of the souls of wicked ones of the past reincarnated, it was easier, as before, to follow after the evil things of the flesh and aggrandisement of self of the left hand way. The wickedness of former lives on the lost continents was still in them; the throne became corrupt and no longer lofty souls came down to incarnate and rule the Empire; many of the Priesthood walked the left hand path and became a band of sorcerers and black magicians, and only a few illumined souls any longer reincarnated and these were persecuted and their bodies often destroyed because they opposed the prevalent evils. Wrong and injustice accumulated and again, as in the forgotten past, piled high against these souls, and here it was Egypt who had received them this time and nurtured them who must share the consequences with them for what she was innocent; for O what death and ruin has come upon every land upon which this galaxy of souls has appeared, which is now appearing upon this North American Continent; it is only the true Mystic Brotherhoods who hold the keys to the knowledge of the vast desolation in the wake of these souls; it is we, knowing these things, who now strive and pray that we may prevent a repetition of these awful calamities again here. It is we alone, who knowing, work day and night to bring some measure of enlightenment of these things before these souls that they may be saved, which no amount of worship of intellect, or *belief* in any man or personal God or any other means short of *true soul awakening* which brings into conscience the memories of these past experiences will ever do. The mighty unrest and spiritual awakening now seen on every hand is truly a cause for thanksgiving; but the land is filled with false teachings prompted by writers and publishers, who, noting the general trend, are taking advantage of the call for light by writing and publishing purely spurious and imaginary doctrines simply for the money returns they bring. Moreover, self-appointed teachers abound plentifully who seek through imparting "original" teaching of what they conceive will be most acceptable to the largest number of students for the largest amount of tuition to incidentally gain notoriety and an easy living. In this western civilization nothing can be accomplished without money; for few there are indeed who will perform the slightest service without material compensation. The personalities of these souls of the past who so much need real enlightenment around us here have money for everything else except the promotion of the truth which our fraternities alone possess and which it is impossible to publish or teach without adequate means. While the mercenary who are traveling the left hand path still, as in the past, do employ every scheme and shrewdness of plan without stint to make a goodly showing before men as well as a financial success for themselves; the great law rules that no Brother of the right hand path, who must give up these very things of the world to attain the full illumination, may use his influence to acquire personal gain or honor before men, unless these be voluntarily offered by others in the interests of the great cause of enlightening the race, for such enlightenment must not be bought nor sold for gain. And so we see great sums freely given for public buildings and show, for education of the intellect, for relief of the sick body, for war to murder, for personal pleasures and appetites and worldly honors, for greater comforts and conveniences, for speculation; but nothing to bring before this great army of souls, enlightenment of their past, the meaning of the present and the fatal dangers of the future. O where is the great soul with abundant wealth who will arise to the occasion of a greater emancipation than our beloved Lincoln ever dreamed? The emancipation of a world! Mankind has hitherto refused to investigate or believe anything of the invisible; his consciousness and conceptions and perceptions and *thinking* have all required images, visible either to his outer eye or inner mind; anything beyond these he has never known anything of; to attempt to teach the generality of men truth requiring perception higher than these images visible to his eye or mind is to make him an unbeliever, a skeptic, and too often an enemy to the one attempting to teach him. And yet, the only *real* perception is higher than any image or picture possible to be formed before the eye or mind, and hence no physical eye or mind ever yet conceived a reality but merely an image of it corresponding to the individual's ideal, which he, unable to perceive above his own ideal therefore never perceives the truth, and he moreover, unwilling to be led "across the unknown" to the higher plane of perception, remains forever in the darkness; and this is the main reason why the world has always repudiated the mystic, and followed the "flesh and the Devil," and has required visible churches and means of worship and religions, and has constantly fallen by the wayside, and piled up accumulated Karma and brought destruction upon the very earth they inhabited, and why these souls must further suffer, now here on earth, in these present and in future bodies, for the long lurid trail of destruction and desolation and still unrequited Karma which has followed them all along the way in the past; and this is why this race, as a whole, will continue to dwell in spiritual darkness unless they can be reached and enlightened and raised to the higher plane of perception; and why they will continue to accumulate more Karma and sorrow, and eventually destroy these lands whereon they dwell just as they have destroyed everything pertaining to them in the past; for these are surely the same souls in new bodies coming up out of that long past. Illumination then, is the attainment through evolvement of the inner faculties of perception, of conscious and *real* knowledge which does not require visible images or forms for the operation of thought or memory; though indeed, where images are formed, at will, from such higher perceptions, they will necessarily be truth, and not illusions formed from individual ideals as is the case with the unenlightened. Who then will open their eyes? The churches have set up a man as an Idol to worship and teach simply that belief on Him, like "looking at the brazen serpent" in the wilderness, will save them, and leaving them in darkness as to where they really are, or who they are; though all praise should be given the churches for whatever good they have accomplished which has been much, *perhaps as much as man would heretofore receive.* Science has failed to reveal to man practically anything of his past; or of his real nature; she is now blundering at the border-line of the unknown and must either accept mysticism as authority, or go away back again and try it all over, though discoveries are soon to be made of occult forces with which we were perfectly familiar in Atlantis, that may compel her to acknowledge the immaterial. Of what avail was science or formal religion to Lemuria or Atlantis in their dying throes? Had some of her influential and rich citizens devoted themselves more to promoting true mystic teachings among the people toward their enlightenment, rather than to their own sinful pleasures and position in the eyes of men, they might have been saved to this day; and all men recognize that if the Jew had listened to Jesus and honored Him that Palastine would still be fruitful and fertile as it was then; but the rich follow after the science which busies itself with external things and repudiates the *real,* and reveals nothing to man of his soul which suffers on and on hoping for a day when it may enter a personality which will seek and find it and save it, for an ignorant personality long ago, when it began, may have filled this soul with such unfavorable things that it could reincarnate next only in another unfavorable personality who still further filled it with unfavorable things and so it has been from bad to worse. And millions are freely bestowed upon the churches, and the rich man sits in his pew each Sabbath, and listens to eloquent discussions of vicarious atonement whereby the Master Christ died that his "Blood might wash away all men's sins" if they will simply believe that He was and is the "Son of God." But he never hears anything about *all* men becoming Masters and Christs (which they must finally do or be lost) nor does he hear anything giving him the slightest guidance or enlightenment toward the knowledge or finding of his own soul that he may become such a Master and thus find *real* salvation which *saves* and in which there is certain immortality; nor does he hear that there is a way by which he may gain full knowledge and come into possession of complete use of his own soul *while he is still in the body*. And finally these millions have not as yet been taught that *all* men are "Sons of God" equally with Jesus if they, like Him, choose as He did, and like Him enter the door to the Mystic Brotherhood, which is the only way of truth and ever has been such, and through the teaching of the Brothers become, as He did, Christs and Masters and Sons of God. What is the meaning when we say that Jesus or any other human is a Christ? It means that He has become, through evolvement on the "Mystic Path," a *Master of Love!* For the Universal Christ, and the Universal principle of *love* are the same thing, and any man who has attained to be a Master of this has become a "Christ." And no man ever attained to be a Christ except through the door of one of the Mystic Fraternities, and the Master Christ, Jesus, was a member of the Essene Mystic Brotherhood from whom He received His initiation. Who then is there among us that will, from his abundance, furnish the means that will carry the torch among this host of souls sitting in darkness upon these shores whose personalities in the future will pile up a Karma more deadly to this fair hemisphere, even as they have before in other lands, than pestilence or famine; for they will surely destroy their own bodies and the soil beneath their feet as before, unless we can succeed in teaching them and leading them to the truth and light, and the real facts of their past. Already the old traits are appearing among them and with the present awakening spiritually, the time is at hand "and the Bridegroom cometh" but there is little money to buy oil for our lamps, and the law demands that such money must be supplied voluntarily from those who are to be taught and saved, for they must first seek us as evidence of their sincere desire to know the Way of Immortality. In the long ago in ancient Egypt these same souls in other bodies committed great iniquities and wrongs and injustice, and the balance was broken as before, and the Karmic retribution overtook them and all things besides, and the tribute exacted by the law threw our Egypt, the mother, which we, her sons, loved well, into the crucible, that the universal whole might be saved from the consequences of evil deeds through her destruction and sacrifice in the purifying fire of equalization. And the fire has burned and seared our beloved mother whom we of the multitude so greatly wronged, and her glory and magnificence is no more, her proud Empire is in ruins and desolate and alone, and only dead, gray sands, the ashes of her former beauey, are carried by the winds over her still burning desert wastes, and fair Isis has departed for aye, and all that remains, as in the long ago, is the lonely Nile which still flows past the scenes of other days. O what lessons these memories teach to those who have awakened soul vision to see. And now in these later days the ancient scepter of power has passed to thy hand, O America; the same power is transferred to thee that was given first to Lemuria, then to Atlantis, and to later civilizations. Those same souls from past ages are here reincarnating again but higher on the spiral according to their accumulated experiences. Many great souls are coming down to us from higher spheres to redeem the race. In the better days of Atlantis there were many of these great souls incarnated who represent both the rulers and the priesthood; and so long as the people listened to their higher teaching all was well, and harmony and peace and plenty abounded on every hand. But in later days they harkened no longer to the voice of wisdom and justice, but turned away and wickedness flourished and but few of the great ones any longer came to them. But after the destruction of Atlantis the same great souls carried much of the wisdom and knowledge, reincarnating in later civilizations, principally in Egypt, though by no means in her alone, where they were in representation, with as many disciples from the people as elected to like evolvement which were in early ages a great number; all these were organized for mutual co-operation into a general Order known as the Brotherhood of Osiris, the inner circle of which was known to the elect as The Grand Lodge of Initiated Masters, which has never ceased to exist to this day. In later dynasties the Brotherhood became known as the Ancient Order of Osiris. It was really through this great Order that Egypt became what she was. All of the ancient symbolism originated in the Order; all of the wisdom of this classic land was taught through the Osirian Brotherhood brought down from ancient Atlantis through enlightened and evolved and reincarnated ones of the Atlantean White Souled Priesthood, some of whom had acquired these things through untold aeons and evolvement reaching back into past Manvantaras. In later ages undoubtedly the greatest of these was the Great Master Soul reincarnating in the man Jesus to fulfill the Messiahship of the age just passed, which soul began its evolvement several Manvantaras afar back. And in these latter days we bow our heads in memory of the great dead past; for Egypt has fallen; no longer do the great soul-host of the past seek reincarnation upon her sacred soil; the Ancient Order of Osiris is no more as of old, though not entirely extinct, for the few still return to that land of ruin and loneliness. That host, once animating the great Egyptian people is coming here now and reincarnating on this free soil to act another great drama; they represent every state and aspect of character of soul according to the experiences each soul has acquired in the long past. (There are also many others here from other lands, and many great ones of other past Orders of Initiates not of Egypt, and who we duly revere.) Among this host now coming here are many good and noble souls who have never received the true enlightenment or entered the path but who have preserved in past lives goodness and purity without evolvement toward real soul awakening. There is little of individual Karma overhanging these, and if they could be brought to the full knowledge of themselves and of the real meaning of their lives the mystic pathway would surely open before them toward the glories beyond, and the question arises, how shall we reach them? If all had been like unto these in the past even, destruction of the whole would not have taken place. But the wickedness of the majority created vast general Karma and these who were good and pure suffered at the last for the transgressions of the wicked. And moreover all of those wicked ones of these times whose souls have not been lost are returning again here, how then shall we avert the disaster ahead which these will surely cause unless we find the way to bring enlightenment to sufficient of their number that too great Karma be not accumulated? Looking out over this broad country we see many of the great souls of the Ancient Order of Osiris reincarnating in America, and many of these are uniting in the order whose name has been here changed to The Fraternity Sons of Osiris, with centers in the United States and Mexico. To recognize these great ones from other men is impossible to the profane of the world; they come and go and fill all manner of professions and positions and labor like other men and women; their power and greatness is in the silent places and unseen by ordinary men; the law forbids these to produce phenomena or to use their powers for their own personal purposes, or to influence other men against their own choosing for this would be depriving them of their rights of free moral agency. (The Black Ones, however, are also all around us and do not hesitate to use their powers over any who will yield to them, as may be witnessed on every hand.) Were the White Ones not in authority the Black influences would speedily create such wickedness and Karma through humanity that everything would in a short time be utterly destroyed. (Reader, think not these are fanciful things; everything here written is perfectly visible and plain to any human being who will follow the teachings of the Fraternity and who has an undestroyed soul, and who thus attains to awakened higher vision and perception, and there never was an Initiate who was unable to see and know all this, and the only trouble is that we cannot get the majority to do the things necessary to acquire all of this knowledge and all of these powers also.) The Order, as in the past, seeks the enlightenment and illumination of the race. So long as Atlantis listened to their teaching was she great and good, and likewise later Egypt; when these turned from the Councils of the Brothers of the Order and yielded to the influences of selfish men (Black Forces working *through* these) both fell after a time and are to this day desolate. No matter how highly illumined a soul may become, when reincarnating in a new body, that body with all its physical and carnal aspects must be overcome before its mind can be awakened and true Initiation again occur in that life for that combined body and soul; and no matter how high the soul may have attained it is always possible for its carnal body to cause it to fall. We see here and now many of the high and white souls, and some of the Order who are not as yet awakened in this present incarnation and who are still unconscious of the great past and who will so remain throughout this life unless they come into touch with some of the true Mystic Orders and thus become enlightened. But there is danger of falling in with those of the Dark Path, and already the country is filled with religious cults and spurious organizations calling themselves Occult and Metaphysical; these are for the most part Black. The materialistic teachings and trend of the present time has developed a people wholly opaque and dark to the great transcendental realities pertaining to themselves and to their relationship to the past and to all knowledge of the souls within them, and indeed do they seriously question whether there is anything more than this material world and their carnal minds and bodies. This has created men and women inimical as ancestry for bodies suitable for reincarnation of great souls and to such an extent that it is a matter of almost impossibility for such to return to earth safely, for this class of humans furnish bodies for their children of such carnality, density and opacity to all soul influences and therefore of such difficulty of overcoming by the incoming illumined soul that it is in great danger of being overwhelmed and of falling again into bad Karma and spiritual darkness and being put very far back in its cycle, and of failing in this and subsequent lives of fulfilling its mission for long ages. Thus there are a goodly number of the Ancient Order and also of advanced souls who were with us in our mother land—Egypt—here now, who are unconscious of their higher beings but who rightfully belong to our great Order, The Fraternity Sons of Osiris. The question arises, How shall we reach them and save them from disaster? Knowing naught of the past or of their real selves, they constantly accept the carnal things of the flesh as an ordinary matter of course, and blindly follow after and grasp the tinsel and empty honors of a day, and the mercenary illusions of the passing days, and the deception of appearances, as realities, and in the darkness of dulled faculties acquired from materialistic ancestry, yield to the temptations devised and proffered in the guise of ordinary every-day events of life, by the Black Brothers of the invisible, left hand Brotherhoods; who constantly seek their overthrow. There are many who, if they could be made conscious of themselves and of who they really are and of the past, would surely seek the Order and its teachers and thus come into their own in this life. The trouble is that the clouded and perverted minds of these refuse to accept the truth when we strive to present it to them. So long as we keep within the realm of this material world and of mere reason and intellectual concepts they are interested; but the moment we cross the line and endeavor to lead them into the real view of the realm of the soul and their higher being, and to reveal the real meaning of their lives, and the story of the past, and the true doctrine, and the purposes of all things, then interest stops and unbelief closes the door to their souls. Indeed, we see many here with souls which in the past attained high evolvement, wholly engrossed in worldly and selfish things and each day falling to lower levels; so material are the minds and bodies in which they have incarnated that they care nothing for the future so long as they enjoy the sensual and illusory passing things of this life, and they care not if the whole earth is destroyed at some future epoch for the wrong doing of men if their present enjoyment or worldly interests are not interfered with. O mighty Monad throng; once more another great drama is before thee; though among thee hath ever been found the worthy and the good, yet beforetime hast thou utterly failed and thy long pathway is filled with ruin and blood and tears. "O Sons and Daughters of our dearly loved and once regal Egypt," here in number so many, would that we might gather thee within the guidance and protection of our great Order that hath o'ershadowed thee like a palm in a weary waste lo these aeons of ages of the past. "The present Order Sons of Osiris" is the same Order and directly continuous of the Ancient Order of Osiris which is as old as Egypt herself. The Order fully recognizes the supreme Mastership of Jesus the Christ. It accepts the disciple down on the world plane who is truly sincere, and develops him to the highest initiation and illumination and helps him to find the Christ *within* himself. As his consciousness awakens his past unfolds and in the eternal memory of his own soul he reads the story of his lives from the long ages gone before, and thus finds himself. His awakened consciousness becomes illumined and he comes into the attainment of universal knowledge, in which all things are made plain to him. He then realizes that the fleeting pleasures of the carnal fade into nothing when compared to such joys as these. The man of the world knows nothing of the friends and loved ones around him except as he has known them in this short life, and when he loses them at physical death, on his return to earth again in a new reincarnation, he knows nothing of them though they may be again with him in new bodies, while the awakened and illumined man knows them every one, body and soul. Reader, the door of the Mystic Temples is never closed to the true seeker; the great teachers are ever ready to lead and help you on the way to all of these things which your soul must realize some time or be utterly lost, for if you do not overcome the lower man he will surely overcome your soul and draw it down into the darkness of death. The choice is entirely with you; the teachers will never come openly before the world unless the world becomes wholly Mystic; and you must seek them of your own free will. May God be with you.

OSIRIS OF THE EGYPTIANS

Empire of the Nile; Land of the Eternal Pyramids; Domain of the Ancient Paraohs. What memories lie buried within thy bosom, O land of the tombs and mummy. To interpret the mysteries of thy vast past is to know the secrets of the universe. Thy magnificent glory and wisdom of the past is no more. The stir and bustle of thy great civilization is still, and sleeps with thee and thy dead. Vanished are the courts of the Pharaohs, with all their pomp and pride. The desert wind touches the cheek of the traveler, lifting his mantle and shifts the listless sand of wide wastes over which ever and anon phantom mirage, oases of green, with springs of crystal water, flit in panoramic review. Wide stretches of waste under the sky, its solitude unbroken, save as beneath the blazing sun, symbol of Osiris, across its desolate sands, fall shadow of pyramid, of lonely ruin, of caravan or Arab horseman. Wherefore art thou desolate and alone, green and fertile valley of the past? Whither has departed the bloom and verdure, thy glory, thy wisdom and thy supreme understanding? Aeons of ages ago, on the banks of thy silent Nile appeared a mighty and imperial people; and besides thee, ever flowing river, within stupendous temples was taught the Eternal Doctrine of the only Truth, of the Absolute, of all that *is*. Upon thy temple altars perpetual sacred fires told their story of man's immortality, the story of the soul's *fire*. But, alas, thou art gone and only heaps of ruins remain to mark where once arose the wonderful structures of thy building. Whence tarriest thou, O beautiful Egypt, Queen of the East, Daughter of Isis and Osiris? Hast thou taken a long journey to a far country and return'st after many days again to thine own Neilos? From far away upon the Shores of Time her voice answereth across the ages: Sons and Daughters of mine, because my children harkened to the voices of the tempter and of the flesh, and forsake not their evil ways, and heeded not the counsels of my prophets, therefore, must I forever remain a wanderer and return no more to my native land, which hath become desolate and forsaken. However, in these later days will I return again to earth among the children of men of other lands to such as shall heed my voice and serve our Great Father—God; and they may find me even the same Egypt; the same Isis and Osiris; manifest among the chosen, even among these of the Ancient Order of Osiris. And I will bless them abundantly, and watch over them, and teach them the way of Holy Wisdom and of Immortal Life, even as they were taught while we were together in our beloved country of days no more, Egypt the fallen. For behold my power and beauty and magnificence hath perished and departed in oblivious night in the long ago. Had my children listened to the voice of wisdom and turned toward the true light of Osiris, surely would my glory have endured forever; and throughout my cities and land would resound the music of the harps of a thousand strings; and over my arid wastes would yet be spread the mantle of exuberant fertility; and all the world would know me and honor me as in days departed. Yet though in power and glory I have departed from thence, there dwelleth apart, in the flesh, the remnant of that once mighty throng; few though the number may be, I say unto thee that its slender thread shall never be broken; neither shall the presence of Osiris depart from that land. For surely shall the Supreme Council of my Ancient Brotherhood continue to meet as in the past, to watch and guide the destiny of mankind; though thrones rock and dynasties rise and fall.

Had Egypt accepted the light and guidance offered her in days of her glory, her waste places and lonely desolation would this day blossom as the rose; but she would not, and, alas, how she hath fallen!

How often in the long ago, in that far off land, hath its watchers gathered to study the star-lit dome above, and read the destiny of the future upon the scroll of the firmament. Locked in the ages that are gone, this knowledge slumbers before the outer world, but it never shall be lost, for the remnant of that great people dwelling upon that desolate soil and land of solitude will receive the great light.

There is one all-pervading radiance, one presence, since

earth began; watchful, brooding, omnipotent. Upon that lonely land falls still the light as in the other days; the light of Osiris the glorious. Even upon all the world falls his radiance, visible to all who understand and *know.* Not in burning sun, whose rays sere and consume upon a desert plain; or yet a vivifying orb falling upon more favored (favored to man of the present, that he may turn toward the giver of all good things) lands, calling into manifestation living forms of vegetation, is seen the real Osiris. The Ancient Brotherhood of Egypt worshipped not the visible sun, which they regarded as but a symbol; the modern profane would class the Ancient Priesthood of Egypt and their sublime Wisdom Doctrine of Isis and Osiris as "heathen worship." Nothing can be farther from the truth. The Ancient Priesthood worshipped not the visible sun. Those ancient races were not benighted heathen any more than they were a part of the lower classes who knew not of the higher truths, through their own perverseness, even as there are plenty of heathen all about us even in these days. It is true that the vulgar and profane among those populations not comprehending the higher meanings of the doctrine; even as the same classes fail to comprehend in these later days; demanded that some religious formology should be taught them (some formal religion has to be given to the masses to correspond to their crude views). All that could be safely revealed commensurate with their limited under standing (limited through no one's fault but their own), was given by the priests, and the ignorant masses largely interpreted the teachings as worship of the visible sun and other visible objects. Those who were sufficiently enlightened to enter the inner circle ever bore high aloft the torch of wisdom and deepest knowledge of God and His universe and its mysteries. To those who sought the great truth the temple doors were ever open. The earnest seeker for the higher truth has never been denied the teaching; and every assistance has been his for the asking since man appeared upon this earth. But in every age and race the *real* knowledge and higher way of life has ever been rejected by the majority (precisely as they are rejecting it in these days), who have only themselves to blame for the awful consequences of their mistake. Witness the destruction, *for this very reason, of every civilization of the past.* Behold how great is the heathenism of the present day! The difficulty lies in the willful lack of understanding, in a self-blinded and materialistic race, which refuses the well of pure and living water, *within*, which is ever ready to spring up into eternal life and joy. Look out upon humanity of to-day and its desolate lives, a desolation more complete than Egypt's sands, and for the same reason. Search among our men and women, living in voluntary darkness, and only for self, where soul grows weaker every day, buried in material clay, perhaps already lost. Of what avail are a few empty honors, houses and lands, bank accounts, fine raiment? These are well when rightly used. Often do they become a curse to those who have devoted a lifetime to their acquisition; while perhaps in the very hour of triumph of possession, when the laurel-wreath of victory over worldly conquest is placed upon the brow of the seeming conqueror, will his hopes turn to ashes over some secret remorse, or God say to him, "Thou fool, this night shall thy soul be required of thee." For the bigot, the willfully ignorant, there has ever been only the outer husks of materialism, just what they can see and demonstrate through mechanical means and materialistic chemistry. Intellect alone can never grasp the higher light. For them only the empty symbol, the dead-letter reading of the book of nature as well as of the Holy Scriptures, and only the outer and external appearances of things must be their interpretation and understanding. To the Great Osiris, the Christ himself gave eloquent acknowledgement, and the influences of those days and their teaching and achievements will never be lost, for lo! impressed upon celestial spheres, stamped upon every ruin and stone and grain of desert sand is the indelible record of the past; truly the soil of Egypt is sacred, and from the long silence of her tombs the voice of infinite wisdom and omnipotent knowledgement is speaking for those who can hear. Materialistic science herself has reached the border line of the material, and is striving through the analysis of crude matter to pierce the veil beyond to find out what is beyond and back of matter. But the infinite can never be discovered by finite methods. She must either accept the facts pertaining to the universe, known and taught by the Mystics ages ago, or fail and continue to remain within the night of materialism.

Of our own race and time, what shall the record be? If humanity continues to refuse the freely offered light and Divine call, then will the race surely plunge again into an awful night of destruction and darkness, and from the few survivors the future race must slowly and painfully emerge and rise again. Every civilization of the past has repeated the same history. Each grew into power and greatness, and as it reached the zenith the opportunity was offered to turn from worldly sins and pleasure to the truth and light. All have failed. Will our present civilization fail? At present there is every sign that man is turning his eyes toward the true light. The world is filled in these days with "cults" who are striving to climb upward; and the long lost brothers—to the world—of ancient orders are preparing to draw nearer to the children of men. Let us pray that all may be well.

Brother, would you learn the path to immortality? Or will you cling to the world of change and illusions, of empty forms and dead-letter appearances of yourself and your surroundings—taking things and people for what they seem to be, including yourself,—or will you drink of the pure spring of water so graphically described by the Great Master—Christ? Who is there among you to enter the Great Stairway—F. O. S. O.—each step leading (progressive lessons from the Brotherhood) to lofty and sublime realms of spiritual wisdom, understanding and knowledge, to the understanding of the universe and of your *real* selves, to your realization of the Great Osiris?

SONS OF OSIRIS

The name Fraternity Sons of Osiris is synonymous with the Ancient Order of Osiris and a direct lineal descendant of the Ancient Priesthood of Egypt, which was known as the Fraternity of Pun-t. With all this, we have ever been the same no matter what the name may have been under which we labored or worshipped.

It is not an order of idle construction, but has ever been a leading hand in progress. Not born of superstition, but of wisdom. True, we *do* understand and master forces that to the uneducated appear as superstitious, yet, all is in accordance with natural laws.

We acknowledge that our archives hold the history of ages and nations, supposed to be lost to the world, and that the ancient wisdom is equally understood and practiced for the same initiation. That is, the *same* secrets that were given the initiate then into the greater mysteries are given the initiate of those degrees at this day.

In the past the object of the Sons of Osiris was to educate those who qualified to be received into the mysteries of nature, man's relation thereto, his mission upon this earth, his past incarnations and whither he goes at this departure. Thus knowing himself, his past, his future, he was no longer "a wanderer" upon the deserts of life, knowing not where he goeth or from whence he came, but became a useful factor in the great plan.

In the first part, at present as in the past, by practicing benevolence and charity and doing good deeds amongst one another, we prepare ourselves for grander and nobler work in the great arena of life. In the past the Fraternity was the one great source from which flowed streams of sweetest waters to quench the thirst of nations. And however great the amount of pollution, unthinking and evil persons have thrown into its crystal waters along its winding course, yet, the fountain has remained as pure as when the Egypt shepherd kings drank its waters and were blest. As it was in its past so is its future, for the Masters of the Fraternity have lived in harmony with the immutable law of heaven, and by so doing the wisdom has advanced apace with the world. Thus it was that its members have been the silent ones who have led the world when all seemed lost, for although silent and unnoticed, we have met to watch the heavens and prepare for coming events, centuries before the world knew of these occurences and to-day we meet as of old to prepare for another great change that will take place upon our earth.

In the battles of the past, both visible and invisible, it has met the destroyer on the field and wielded the sword of right with a power triumphant. As a tender parent she teaches us our daily duties to one another, she admonishes us when we stray from the beaten paths of *truth* and *right,* and like a fond parent in sadness or misery, folds us to her breast and breathing upon us her powerful magnetism, heals us. When stern adversity, like an arrow sprung from the bow of an evil one injures us, she soothes and comforts us. Throughout life, from the day we first kissed her fair lips she has been a faithful guradian and friend. When at last we lay down this material covering to enter into a more beautiful and clearer abode, we have her silent hand to lead us through those to us unknown worlds. We sigh not for the end, for she has taught us the mysteries of life and death. Neither do we fear at our departure for she has driven fear from our breast and implanted *hope* and *love.*

Born of the Gods eternal in the heavens when Egypt was in its glory, free from the cares of matter, she ever points to higher realms.

The present Order, now working under the name of Fraternity Sons of Osiris, while conveying the mysteries to the candidate in the manner and language of the day has not departed from the ancient aim of the Fraternity.

All sons of Osiris are practical persons who believe in progression and who uphold law and order in whatever land they live. They constitute what was once the most profound secret society known, and what is destined to become, in a few years, the same power for good that their number and strength was heretofore. Every inducement is held out to those who desire to unite with us that is consistent with our laws and usages. Every Son of Osiris is the sworn brother of every other brother throughout the world. Those who once partake of the rites of love in full sincerity are ever held as brothers. They may, in opposition to right and justice, cause us to debar them from our meetings, but they are still brothers.

In acts of benevolence and charity our hospitality is always extended to the deserving so far as within our power. Thus we have mitigated sorrow, helped the deserving to better and nobler lives, building the fires of emulation in each human breast, encouraging manly efforts, strengthening the weak and cultivating self-respect. The doors of our Temple are ever open to the honest, upright citizen, nor can any man or woman otherwise unqualified enter our temple because of wealth, fame, religion or politics, nor is any person debarred because of poverty. All who come with purity of mind, willing to obey the ancient customs and usages are bidden welcome into our ranks.

The training is such that it meets the demands of each and every student. Each one is started in a given way at the very foundation. The training then commences, and as the student solves the problem and reports, so will he receive such additional instruction as he requires. This is kept up until he has reached the final initiation.

FRATERNITY "SONS OF OSIRIS"

The Supreme Temple in convocation assembled, has re-adopted the name "Fraternity Sons of Osiris" as being more in harmony with the objects and teachings of the Order.

The Fraternity will again resume much of the complete secrecy as before, especially is this so with regard to the secret school of the Order which shall furnish the candidate the inner work of personal training.

The greatness of our Fraternity in the past wholly depended upon the greatness of its individual members, upon their powers as more than ordinary men and women, not as members of the Order, but as individuals. So must it again be in the future, as publicity exposes many of our grandest and noblest members to unnecessary risks, because of the malice and evil doings of evil destined organizations. Thus has decreed the first American convocation of the Fraternity. So must it be henceforth .

As to our origin, no exact history exists as to when the Order was founded. Some say by the priests of Heliopolis, others by the Aryan tribes. Again there are in the Fraternity (in the Outer Courts)those who claim that the order has come from the greatest of Esoteric priests—Thoth (Hermes Trismesgistus). Again others in the western world claim that it was re-founded by none other than Jesus, the Initiate (see the book "The Son of Man"). This, however, does not alter the truths, as truth, as such, is unalterable. Each prophet or messiah has uttered the same truths that we hold dear. Thus none of them can claim originality, even though different words were employed to express the same truths. We of the Supreme Temple say that the Fraternity, like truth, has always been and will always be, though its members may add to its ritual or subtract from it, yet the truth of its inner work *must* ever remain the same.

This Fraternity appeals to those who have outgrown mere organizations and realize that their advancement depends upon their own efforts now as much as it did when they first learnt their alphabets in school, though the Fraternity teaches those who make effort to learn, yet each must himself bring out of himself the greater truths.

This fraternity has no connections whatever with any other body, yet frequently joins hands and assists others to accomplish, the good they have set out to accomplish, and therefore we are not at enmity with any other body that may be interested in the welfare of the human family. Those who desire the higher thought and vibration, will be attracted to us and will remain true to the higher self. Such as belong to the mere curiosity seekers will never care for more than the teachings of the lower degrees, others again will cling to us as particles of iron cling to the magnet. These are the souls that have made the Fraternity a name to sound with an echo down the corridors of time.

THE END

OUR RECORD

On June 31st the last delegates who had been attending the Sixty-eighth (68th) Convocation of the Rose Cross Order left for their homes.

On the 1st of July we began to arrange the material for the book "Fundamental Laws," containing practically all of the Lectures that had been delivered during the Convocation and also giving a great deal of additional matter and information concerning both the work during the Convocation and the work of the Rose Cross Order.

As soon as all the material had been arranged, the book went to press and was ready for delivery within eight weeks from that date.

This book is exceptionally valuable in that every article in it is really fundamental and therefore of great importance to every sincere student. It is a book of over 200 pages. On very fine book paper (we could not get regular book paper), bound in silk cloth, stamped in gold. Price $1.25. Price of this book would actually be about $2.50 but for the fact that donations were made by the delegates towards the expense of Publication.

THE SON OF GOD

While the book "Fundamental Laws" or "Rose Cross Order" was in press, we arranged the third edition of the "Son of God." This book is too well known to need any description as it has been called the most important book of its kind ever issued. Moreover, the fact that this is the third large edition proves this.

The book is almost the size of the regular $1.25 books, but as it is used for propaganda work, the price was made at 50 cents in cloth or 25 cents in paper binding.

Paper is the same as that of "Fundamental Laws" binding also the same in every respect.

We shall endeavor to keep this book in print even though

an edition a month will be necessary in order to do so.

THE WAY TO LIFE AND IMMORTALITY

Less than three weeks after the book "Son of God" had gone to press, we found that not a copy of "Way to Life and Immortality" was left in stock, but that orders for it were coming in. We therefore at once put to press the second edition of this important book and are now able to supply all with copies who desire this book.

Bound uniform with the other two books. Is in silk cloth and stamped in gold. Price $1.25 delivered.

HISTORY OF THE ROSE CROSS ORDER

This we consider a book of extreme importance at the present time for the reason that within the past few years not less than five different Orders, calling themselves Rosicrucian, with slight variations in title, have sprung up, and all of these claim to be regular Rose Cross bodies.

The true Rose Cross was founded in America 68 years ago and has continued to exist ever since the foundation.

In the present book the Life of Randolph is given and many extracts from newspapers all over the world. It is shown that a United States Attorney had made the statement, to be used against Randolph, that he, Randolph, was Grand Master of the Rose Cross Order of the world in 1861.

The student who does not desire to be defrauded, who does not desire to join a clandestine body, thinking he had joined the true Order, should get this book at once.

It is printed on extra book paper, for reasons before stated, bound in beautiful silk cloth, stamped in gold. Price $1.00 while the edition lasts.

OUR RECORD

Our record, therefore, is four books within the short period of ten weeks. This will prove to all that there is a demand for literature such as issued by this house. *Order now.*

"ANCIENT MYSTIC ORIENTAL MASONRY"

The Mystic holds that Masonry is the basis of religion; rather, that the mysteries of Masonry are also the Mysteries of religion; that in Masonry is found the Key to the Mysteries and the Key to religion.

The book is composed of quotations from the highest Masonic authorities, and the mystical interpretation has been given.

The compiler and author has one of the finest Masonic libraries in the country, besides having unlimited privileges of consulting books and manuscripts on this subject.

This book is not an exposure of Masonry, but is, from every point of view, friendly to Masonry. It is a frank discussion, a frank interpretation, of Masonry in its highest and most sublime form.

It is a book for all those who are interested in the philosophies, but is especially valuable to the sincere Mason.

Printed on fine paper, in two colors, bound in beautiful cloth and gold. Price, $1.50.

A CATALOG OF

ROSICRUCIAN and SOUL SCIENCE AND SUCCESS BOOKS

TRY

All books herein listed are part of the teachings formulated and given by The Temples of the Illuminati and Illumination

Published by
THE PHILOSOPHICAL PUBLISHING CO.
ALLENTOWN, PA

THE SON OF GOD

THE MYSTICAL TEACHINGS OF THE MASTER OR

THE CHRISTIC INTERPRETATION

The old edition of the book called, "The Son of Man," is sold out; and so great is the demand for it that it has been completely re-written and much enlarged, and harmonized with the teachings as given by the Temple of Illumination.

Preface.

In the Preface is summarized the fundamental principles of the Christic Interpretation and the characteristics of the Christic Law, as advocated by the Temples of Illumination and of the Illuminati.

Jesus an Essene.

In this chapter is given an historic sketch of the training that Jesus received among the Essenes. The harmony is clearly shown that exists between the teachings of the Essenes and those of the true Rosicrucian Order; and the connection between the old Essenean Order and the Rosicrucian Fraternity as founded in America by Dr. P. B. Randolph is clearly shown.

The Son of God.

Here the expressions of Jesus, "The Son of Man," and "then Son of God," are used as the basis of interpretation. The esoteric significance of these terms furnishes the foundation of the Essenean Law and its interpretation.

The Sages.

In this book are given quotations from the great sages representing different nationalities, to show that the Illuminated Masters of all ages agree in regard to the essentials of a *living* Religion and Philosophy, and that all those who *lived* in harmony with the Divine Law reached the same state of Soul Consciousness.

The Cream of Christic Interpretation.

In this book is found the cream of the Christic and the Rosicrucian teachings. It is a book that should be given to your friends, whoever they may be; and it is issued with this especial purpose in view.

The Book Itself.

The book is printed on laid paper, beautifully bound in silk cloth so as to harmonize with "St. Matthew" and with "St. John." It is a $1.25 book; but, as we desire that it shall be used as a propaganda book, we offer it for 50 cents.

A limited number of these books are bound in paper, and can be had for 25 cents.

Some of the friends and the Brothers of the Illuminati have ordered as many as 20 copies in cloth, in order to use them as gift books. Do not miss obtaining at least one copy; and, if possible, order more to present to friends whom you wish well.

* * *

CHRISTHOOD

SECOND OF THE TEXT-BOOKS ISSUED BY THE TEMPLE OF ILLUMINATION

Christic Power can be awakened only through obedience to the Divine Law. When we obey this Divine Law, then is the Christ Child born within us; and, if we continue in the way, this child grows to manhood and enters into power.

The millions are today looking forward to a world teacher, to a new interpretation of the Law; for they instinctively know that to understand the law, to live the Law, is to give man power.

"Christhood" gives positive instructions concerning the power to be obtained through soul development. It not only hints at the powers, but it gives many clear instructions as to how to live in order that these powers may be obtained.

CONTENTS

The Christ.

Showing who and what the Christ is. The Son of God; His Work; the Inner Man; how *you* may become the Son of God.

The Divine in Man.

Showing that all men are Divine if they but awaken the Divinity within them. It elucidates the meaning of "Man being the Temple of the Living God."

Development.

Giving the laws for the inner development which lead to Real Initiation. It also gives many of the laws and rules for Soul Development.

Formology.

Showing the necessity of forming a clear idea of what you wish to be. Also of the necessity of developing this idea. Full mental laws are given.

Power of Love.

One of the greatest powers in the universe. It shows how all things may be accomplished.

Christ and Osiris.

Showing how the principles of the Christ and Osiris were the same, and much of ancient initiation is also given.

Development and Employment.

Proving that it is not necessary for the student to give up honest labor in order to become a Leader or Master.

The Religion Demanded by the People.

Millions realize that a true religion—a religion of the heart and soul—is much needed. Many grope in darkness, never finding light. The beauties and practical points of this religion are clearly set forth.

Temple of Illumination.

Giving a discourse on the Temple of the Illumination of the Soul. The religion that millions demand, but have heretofore sought in vain. Leaders are wanted everywhere.

Healing.

True Soul Science. Giving concisely, but fully, instructions that are alone worth more than the cost of the book.

Prayer.

Explaining why prayer is, and is not, effective. It reveals this most important mystery.

The Book Itself.

The book is printed on laid paper, beautifully bound in silk cloth and side stamped in gold. It harmonizes with the first text-book, "Soul Science, the Way to Immortality." Price 75 cents, postpaid.

* * * * * *

SOUL SCIENCE THE WAY TO IMMORTALITY

THE COMING CHRIST

It is universally admitted among scholars that we are on the Threshold of a new Dispensation. This means that we are expecting a new Law, which shall govern all things. To state this more correctly, we are expecting a *new* interpretation of the old Law, an interpretation that is at once practical and mystical.

Centuries ago, when civilization had reached a state somewhat similar to the present, when the time was ripe for a new Law Giver, or a Master who should anew interpret the Law, Moses appeared to the civilization of that age.

Centuries later, when the dispensation brought about by Moses was nearing an end, and new expectations arose among the people, the Master Jesus appeared and gave a new Interpretation to the same Laws interpreted by Moses centuries before.

The old cycle is at an end, a new cycle has begun; and there is, among the people, anticipation of a new Age. As, in the long past, Moses gave a new interpretation to the people, Moses who had been taught and Initiated among the Egyptian Priesthood, and, as centuries later, the Master Jesus, also taught by that same Priesthood, then called the Essenes, so now, in the new Age, who other than the same School of Priesthood should give forth the New Interpretation of the Law?

"Soul Science, the Way to Immortality" is the first of the text-books given out by this many-cycle-old school. In this book will be found a great many of the Christic Interpretations in harmony with the coming Age; for in this book is pointed out "the Way, the Truth, and the Life."

Annunciation, or Conception.

When the Soul succeeds in arousing the Mind and the Will to a desire for Truth, for Wisdom, and for greater Love, it is planting the seeds, or the Conception. Man cannot, and will not, accept of anything until there is something within him which tells him that it is truth. Thus, when we turn from an old condition to a new one, from an old belief to a new belief, it is a condition of Conception that has taken place.

The Confession.

Sorrow for old deeds and turning away from them, accepting new and higher belief in a just Law, and living in harmony with the Law—this is repentance. It is a confession; for to give up the old, and accept the new, is to confess that the old was in the wrong.

Re-Birth—Baptism by Fire and the Holy Ghost.

Few know the mystery of the Baptism by Fire. In this book the mystery is made so plain that all can understand it. The Baptism by Fire is the coming into Conscious Sonship with the Father—the Birth of the Christ.

The Coming of the Christ.

The various theories and guesses of the unenlightened are completely changed into Light and Understanding, as the full truth is unfolded and the mystery concerning the Coming Christ is revealed. How will the Christ come? When will he come? Where will he come?

The Judgment.

The Judgment Day has been portrayed as a day of terrible trial. What is the Judgment? When is it? Are all judged upon one day afar off, or is there a judgment every day and for every one? The Judgment has no terrors for those who know. The Judgment is not a day to be thought of with terror, but is something that we can change if we will.

The Awakened Soul.

The Soul that has awakened knows its birthright, knows good from evil, false from true. There are no more terrors of the Threshold when the soul awakens from its sleep and unfolds in Light and Wisdom—when Illumination is reached.

Building of a Soul.

The mystery for the millions to know; for to know is to become *free*. There is a right way and a wrong way. The architect knows his plans of work, so should the soul builder. Every living human being must become a Soul builder in order to become Immortal. Many are building upon the sand, without knowledge of the rock of truth.

Works and Faith.

Where there is true faith, works will be manifested. Faith without works is dead. He who has true faith will do the works according to his faith.

Understanding and Love.

Those who know Love understand all mysteries. Love is the Key to Wisdom; and Wisdom unlocks the doors to Understanding.

Atonement.

The meaning of At-one-ment. Unless we become at-one with the Father, we cannot know the Christ. To know the Christ is to become Illuminated. None can reach Immortality except through the Atonement.

Crucifixion.

The real meaning of Crucifixion. Soul Science and the

Christic Interpretation alone can give the true meaning.

The Passover.

There are few who know the true meaning of the Passover. The Passover is not a feast to be held once a year, but has a deeper, a mystical, or occult, meaning. None can become Immortal, none can become one with the Father, unless they have gone through the Passover.

Illumination.

Illumination is the resurrection of the Christ. The Resurrection *always* comes after the Passover.

The Christ.

If we walk as he walked, we shall become like him. To walk as he walked is to obey the same laws that he obeyed and in the same way. Mere belief will not give us the Christ; but in believing and in doing alone is to be found the Christ.

Healing.

John the Baptist taught the Laws of the Mind, or Mental Healing; but Soul Science and the Christic Interpretation teach the Healing of the Soul.

The Book Itself.

The book is printed on laid paper, beautifully bound in silk cloth, and side and back stampel in gold. More than 200 pages. Price $1.50, postpaid.

* * * * * *

THE ILLUMINATED FAITH

ST. JOHN MYSTICALLY INTERPRETED

A test was recently made by the Temple of the Iluminati to find out what subjects most interested those whose names were on their mailing lists. These subjects included "Soul Science and Success," "Spiritual or Mystic Christianity," and the "Christic Interpretation." Out of five thousand names, the largest number was interested in Mystical Christianity; the next largest number was interested in the Christic Interpretation.

The book now offered to you is a complete and exhaustive Mystical Interpretation of the Gospel according to St. John, so well called the Philosopher of Love.

Christhood.

Throughout the lessons of the book, the subject of Christhood is exhaustively dealt with. Do not think that the method of attaining Christhood is only hinted at; for much more than a hint is given concerning the subject. Indeed, it is carefully emphasized from many points of view. The teachings of St. John are treated in their entirety, and are fully and completely explained so that all may live the Illuminated Life and become as the Christ.

Initiation.

Throughout these lessons it is clearly shown that Attaining the state of Christhood means that he who so attains has reached Mastership, or Initiation.

Soul Consciousness.

To reach Christhood is to become Soul Conscious. Those who reach Soul Consciousness reach what several well-known writers have named "Cosmic Consciousness."

Illumination.

Illumination is reached when the mind has become awakened and enlightened, and when through this awakening the Mind Forces are used in the building, or creation, of a Soul that is "Consciously Conscious."

The Goal.

St. John recognized the one great Law—that the goal of all human endeavor is to become a Conscious Soul, a Cosmic Being, and that potential Christhood is nothing less than this.

The Divine Law.

Unless man understands the Divine Law and obeys it, he can reach neither Christhood nor Soul Consciousness, and it was the labor of St. John to teach men this Law.

Love.

St. John has been called the Philosopher of Love because the base of the whole work in the redemption of man, according to his teachings, is *love.*

The Ancient Wisdom.

The whole Philosophy is based upon the fundamental principles as taught in the Ancient Wisdom by the old Masters. Each Law is made plain, and, in many instances, appropriate illustrations are used.

The Crucifixion and the Resurrection.

The old Theological explanations are no longer believed in by mankind, and advanced criticism does not accept them. In this book a clear explanation is given; and, in the light of the discoveries of the Æth Priesthood, it is shown, beyond the possibility of contradiction, that not only could Jesus, having become the Christ, arise from the tomb but that any man now on earth, if he will obey the Divine Law, can do the same.

The Book Itself.

The book is printed on laid paper, bound in silk cloth, and throughout is in harmony with, and a companion to, "St. Matthew." It contains 53 chapters or lessons, and can be used as a text-book in schools and colleges where "The Illuminated Faith' is taught. Price $1.25, postpaid.

* * *

THE ILLUMINATED FAITH

The Christic Interpretation of St. Matthew

Who does not know of the unrest among the multitudes of today? Who is not aware of the fact that the many have lost faith in the established church of the present day? Who is not aware of the clearly apparent fact that millions of people are seeking, here and there, for a new religion—a religion or religious teaching, that is practical and can be applied in all the walks of life?

Many think that the Bible is a useless book, that it contradicts itself, that in it are found teachings which have been clearly disproved by science.

But there is one thing these multitudes do not know. They do not know that there is nothing at all the matter with "the Old Book," they do not know that all that is in the book is actual, scientific truth. They do not know that the fault lies, not in the book, but in the *interpretations of the book.*

In the Christic Interpretation, a clear distinction is made between those teachings of the book which should be considered literally, and those which must be considered symbolically.

When this is done, we find that the teachings are practical, that they can be applied in ordinary life, and that to apply them means health, wisdom, peace of mind, and success in life.

The Interpretation of St. Matthew is the first attempt of the Illuminati to give to the seeking world a clear interpretation of that Gospel. The interpretations are such as can readily be understood by all. These Laws can be applied in every-day life; and to apply them is to find peace, it is to find new life, a new faith in God and His revealed teachings.

To obey the Laws as interpreted in this book is to find the Christ, to find Conscious Sonship with the Father, and to find a religious faith that nothing can shake.

The Higher Law.

The Higher Law governs the body, the mind, the spirit, and the Soul. A clear distinction is made between these four departments of man's being.

The Illuminati is the only school that makes this distinction, and shows the reason for it.

Development.

The wise know that it is not well to undertake any development unless one clearly understands what he is doing. To undertake to run an engine, without understanding the mechanism, and how to set it in motion, how to stop it, how to feed, and how to oil it, would be dangerous. It is just as dangerous to meddle with the human machine without an understanding of the Divine Law.

The Forces.

The Divine Law controls all the forces in nature. The Divine Law and the Natural Law are one; but the Divine Law applies to the things of the Soul, while the Natural Laws apply to material manifestations. To break one is to break the other.

True Guidance.

The book is a guide. It is such a guide as all need who desire to follow the Path to Life, and Light, and Love. Occult and Mystical Laws are clearly interpreted, and the reasons given.

Going Astray.

There is no danger of the seeker's going astray if he studies these Laws and obeys them.

The Forces and Their Use.

All forces are for use; otherwise, a Wise Creator would never have brought them into existence. Wisely used, they will enable the seeker to make all the resources of his fourfold nature available and productive, so that he may create and execute plans, make his way through obstacles, and realize his highest ideals; in other words, an intelligent application of these forces will enable him to *become* and to *accomplish.*

The Book for You.

The book explains, from various points of view, the Divine Law underlying all things; and, if you become thoroughly established in its principles, there will be little likelihood of reaction from the forces you set into motion by your intense desires.

The Book Itself.

The book contains 265 pages; is printed on beautiful laid paper, bound in silk cloth; side and back stamped in gold. Is a standard text-book to be used in Soul Science schools and colleges and in class work. Is used at the "Beverly School of Sacred Science" when in session. Price $1.50, postpaid.

* * *

CHRISTISIS

HIGHER SOUL CULTURE

The lessons on Soul Culture in this book are a happy combination of two important features: first, they afford instruction concerning the fundamental truths of life expressed in language simple yet comprehensive; second, they afford practical suggestions concerning the application of these truths to the development of one's Soul nature. Thus, they satisfy two needs of the honest seeker, instruction and self-training.

The book is not for the idle curiosity-seeker. It is for the one who is eager to find the truth and is willing to submit himself to patient self-training that the truth may be unveiled to his own consciousness.

These are rightly called lessons, in that they teach; they are rightly called "lessons in Soul Culture," in that they offer and explain simple practical methods by which the Soul Nature of man may be developed. It is a text-book, in that it gives a definite course of study, and gives general outline of a specific course of self-training.

It is a book for the teacher because it is an excellent guide, in that the expressions are clear, yet condensed, leaving room for the teacher to follow his own inspiration in expanding and in illustrating the principles taught therein. It is a book for the student who has no teacher, because the instructions are so clear that he need make no mistake.

Lesson One.

Teaching that within himself each one must seek for, and

find, all power. Telling what to do, and how to do it, in order to develop the likeness of the Christ, the true Christisis, within himself.

Lesson Two.

The beginning of wisdom and knowledge. Teaching the Science-Religion, the wedding of Science with Religion. The giving up of mere belief in the acceptation of reality.

Lesson Three.

Life is concentration. Concentration is accumulation. Accumulation is power. The Magnetic Center, its finding, development, and power.

Lesson Four.

The undeveloped soul within man, like unto a seed. The seeds that lie dormant, the seeds that spring up and die, and the seeds that spring up and grow. The Divine Spark within. The development of the Christisis. Man a creator. The esoteric teachings of the Masters.

Lesson Five.

The whole external universe is the outpicturing of the thoughts retained within the Infinite Soul. God pictures the universe in His mind, and it becomes. Likewise, man can picture a universe in his own mind and cause it to become manifest. Material success and spiritual success. True success is one. The religion-science world.

Lesson Six.

The Master of Mysticism, Jacob Boehme. "God introduces His will into nature for the purpose of revealing His power in light and majesty to constitute a kingdom of joy." Will, the lever that lifts in any desired direction. How to use the power. Two aspects of the force. The grand faculty.

Lesson Seven.

Mind, not magnetic. Mind is electric. The Soul is the Magnetic Center. Mind the dynamo. Mind an electrical generator. The laws of of creation. The great secret of personal magnetism.

Lesson Eight.

The physical plane. The earth plane. The Soul plane. Limitation is bondage. Limitation is not reality, it is not life. Life is universal, it is unlimited. We can draw from the Universal Center as much as we need. We are limited only as we limit ourselves.

Lesson Nine.

"I and the Father are One." "I am in the world, but not of the world." The proof that man may live on the earth plane, but not be of that plane. All states are but conditions of mind and soul. Man is limited only as he limits himself. The voice of conscience is the voice of God speaking within us.

Lesson Ten.

The new life. In trying to find the universal life, you try to find the Christisis. The Christisis is the Son of God. The Christisis is the unity of man with God. The Christisis is the wedding of Science with Religion. The becoming One. The Soul is the life of man. The body is simply the necessary vehicle through which to manifest.

Lesson Eleven.

Individual responsibility. No one can escape from the law of cause and effect. It is absolute.

The Book Itself.

The book consists of an Introduction and eleven lessons. One hundred and ninety-two pages, printed on one side of sheet only. Printed on 80-pound beautiful cream Alexander book paper, and bound in buffing, with back and side stamped in gold. It is the text-book of the third year's lessons.

This book may be bought separately. The price is $5.00.

* * *

THE DIVINE LAW

Inner Aspect

In this book, many of the aspects of the Divine Law are taught in their application to the life of man.

The Laws here taught have to do with the Mystical side of life, those things which concern the Soul, the Life after this; or, the Law concerning the present life in its esoteric sense, so that, when the present life ends, it will be actually a continuation of the present life on another plane of existence.

These Laws, as here taught, are practical. We know that they are practical; for they are, in nearly every case, answers to questions received from some perplexed student. These expositions of the Divine Law are answers to such questions as were received from students in the Temple of Illuminati. We therefore know that they are adapted to seekers' needs.

These expositions of the Divine Law formerly appeared in THE INITIATES, and are demanded in book form, in order that the student may have ready access to various phases of the Fundamental Law in its application to life.

CONTENTS

Initiation.

Around the word "Initiation" centers all the work that has to do with the student who takes up the higher Life, the life that is different from that which is ordinarily led by man. Moreover, there is no word in the English language which is explained in as many different ways as the word "Initiation." In this chapter, a sane, rational, and mystic explanation is given of the work of initiation; and to give careful study to the chapter, and to heed the instructions contained therein, would be the means of saving thousands from unnecessary suffering and from traveling the wrong path, a path which leads to disappointment.

The Cause of Suffering.

Man suffers. There is no gainsaying that point. But why is it necessary that he should suffer? Is there a good reason for it? What is the reason? Does man suffer for any other acts than those connected with the present life? Does he suffer for the sake of others? All these questions are fully answered and a reason given for it. No sincere student can afford to be ignorant of the great Law; for it will show him that both God and the Law are *just.*

Man in the Great Beyond.

What is the status of man in the Beyond? Is his destiny irrevocably sealed at the transition called death? After having lived a godless life during his earth existence, is he forever debarred from the opportunity to accept the divine standards, and to amend his ways in harmony with them? In this chapter, the life of man in the Beyond is made clear in every respect. He is taught the Laws and the conditions that make for the future, the life on the Soul plane. The Laws of growth and development are clearly taught; and he is shown just what is necessary in order to advance continually without being retarded by ignorance and false beliefs. This chapter alone is worth more to the sincere seeker than the cost of the book.

The Origin and the Seat of Evil.

Is there evil in the world? There are those, so-called teachers, who claim that there is no evil. This claim is based upon the fact that God made all things and that when he made them He made them good. The School of the Christic Interpretation admits this fact; but it recognizes the greater fact that, when God made man, he gave him free-will, the right to use things for good or for evil, and that a good thing can be used for an evil purpose. The Law is fully taught in this chapter, the reason and the cause for evil given, and clear instructions for the overcoming of evil through obedience to the Divine Law.

The Status of the Soul.

What is the Soul? Do all souls reach perfection? How are we to account for the different stages of development which different souls reach?

This is one of the most important chapters in the book. It is clear, sane, and to the point. It shows just what the soul is, where it is, and what it may be. It answers the question that is uppermost in the minds of the multitudes.

The Law of Freedom.

What constitutes freedom? This is the question of the ages. All men desire to be free, to do as they think they should do; but few really know what freedom means. Very often they free themselves from one bondage only to come under a greater bondage. The old saying, "Know the truth and the truth shall make you free," is full of meaning; but we must know how to search for truth, where to find it, and how to apply it.

The Law of Faithfulness.

What constitutes faithfulness? To whom should we be faithful? All Divine Laws center around one Being, the One Being manifested in two. God the Father, or call Him what you will, is the One Being; man is but a part of that Being. To be faithful to God means to be faithful to the self. Faithfulness to these means faithfulness to all else; and to be faithful in truth, is to be a success upon all three planes of being. Faithfulness to the object underlies all real things in life, no matter upon what plane man may be. Before he can attain full satisfaction, man must understand the Law of Faithfulness.

Protection Through the Divine Law.

Can the mind of man be free from the adverse influences of

other minds? Is it possible for man so to live, so to think, that he need not be affected adversely by the perverted wills of other human beings? These questions are agitating the minds of many, especially those who are becoming awakened to higher ideals of living and thinking, and are seriously perplexed over the possibility of becoming victims of unprincipled wills. In this chapter, the Laws are fully taught, and, if obeyed, there need be no fear whatever. Frankly stated, this chapter is alone worth more to the student of the Mystic and Occult than the cost of the set of books; for it means freedom from fear concerning all evil influences of whatever nature.

What of God, the Father?

In this age when unbelief seems to be rife, when men seemingly believe in nothing, not even in themselves, it is high time that consideration be given to that which our forefathers, in faith and love, called God. Men now, are beginning to pretend that there is no God, no beneficent force in nature. Such is not the case, and the Christic Interpretation believes that, when men are taught the truth concerning the Father, they will again believe, and, through their faith, manifest the goodness of the Father. False interpretations of mystic truth has been the cause of the present unbelief. A mystic and sane interpretation will bring men to have faith, and, through their faith, to manifest goodness, truth, and power.

Prayer and the Unity of Souls.

Is there power in prayer? Can Souls be united in a prayer, or a Sacred Mantram, and does such unity give power, or bring an answer from the source of power? These questions are fully answered. Moreover, this chapter, clearly shows the true method of prayer, which is, in fact, concentration. It shows why such concentration should be had, and why Sacred Mantrams do possess power.

The Unborn and the Divine Law.

There is no greater need than that of teaching prospective mothers the laws that concern motherhood, the law that makes it possible for them to have healthy, bright, and desirable children. There is a Divine Law which has to do with this; for this is the most sacred duty of mankind. The instructions given are clear and to the point. It is possible for every woman to obey them, and therefore possible for every woman to have children that are desirable and an honor.

The Book Itself.

The book is printed on beautiful laid paper, bound in silk cloth, and in perfect harmony with the books, "St. John," "St. Matthew," and others of the Christic Interpretation The price is $1.25, postpaid.

* * *

THE DIVINE LAW

OUTER ASPECT

This book is a companion to the book, "Divine Law, Inner Aspect;" but it deals more with the Laws that have to do with success in life than with those Laws which concern only the Mystical, or the Inner, Life of man.

However, it must not be understood that these same laws have not also to do with the Inner Life; for to break any Law that concerns the Physical being, or the material life, is also to break the Law that concerns the Soul; but these Laws have more especially to do with the things of the physical plane.

CONTENTS

The Leaders.

Men have said that in this age it is almost impossible for a man to succeed. The fact is, never in the history of the world was there such a demand for real, capable men and women. But they must be capable in the real sense of the word, they must be fully rounded out, proficient in the things they would undertake; and, above all, they must be loyal to that which they undertake, in other words, put their whole heart, mind, and soul into the work, and not attempt to dabble in this, that, and every other thing. The Illuminati, with its Christic Interpretation, needs leaders, true men and women; and there is power, contentment, and advancement for such.

The Confessional.

Can the confession, or rather, can any confessional have part in the work of the Illuminati? To answer this question, we need but ask another: Is it necessary for men and women in the present age to confide in anyone? Is it necessary for them, at times, to relieve the mind of pent-up feelings? We do not endorse the old idea of the confessional; but we believe that human nature is much the same today as in the fore time, and that men and women need those in whom they can confide, and from whom they can receive instructions and words of encouragement.

A Promise, a Pledge, or an Oath.

What of the promise, the pledge, or the oath, made by man? Is it to be upheld? Has it any place in the life of the modern man? These have been perplexing questions of many students; and the Christic Interpretation answers them clearly and fully and according to the Divine Law.

Destructive Effect of Negative Yogaism.

To the Western Mind, the terms, Adeptship, Mastership, Yogaism, Psychism, Yogi, Master, Adept, and Psychic, are apt to present vague and confused ideas. Moreover, in the present day, when destructive Occultism is being so widely taught, it is time to sound a warning so that the beginner may be protected from spurious occultism, from those teachings which would make him a mere machine, to be used by other beings, embodied and disembodied. The chapter is clear to the point, and spares no one, though absolutely impartial and just in its conclusions.

Why is Man a Failure?

What is it to be a failure? Why is man a failure? What constitutes a failure? When we know what it is to be a failure, the reason for it and what constitutes a failure, then are we also prepared to find the remedy and to apply it. When we teach man the reason of his failure in every walk of life, then we can also teach him how to succeed, and this is one of the greatest works of the true teacher. This chapter on the cause of failure should be read, studied, and its suggestions applied by every man and woman in the world. The Laws applied will lead from failure to success.

The Law of Vibration.

Every one interested in the Occult and Mystic desires to advance in the science and the art of Soul Culture. Soul Culture is based upon absolute law, just as the building of a house is based upon absolute laws, laws which are known to the architect. Unless the student fully understands the Laws of Vibration, he cannot make much progress; and, the sooner he understands that every thought, every desire, creates vibrations which help him either to build up or to tear down, the better

Magnetic, or Drawing, Power of the Mind.

In nature, magnetism is active force, or energy. It is a drawing, or attractive, power. It is a force that draws things to itself. It may attract life, or life-giving forces; or it may attract to itself that which produces death and failure. No one can be truly successful unless he possesses the power called "magnetism;" and the more abundantly he posses it, the more successful he will be.

Highest Magnetic, or Æth Power.

Within every living thing, there is a power, a force, called magnetism. This power, this force, this energy, may be in different states of manifestation: it may be latent, it may be inert, it may be in an active state; or it may be reversed—that is, the power may be negative and of no use to its possessor; or it may even be misdirected and thus be a positive detriment to the possessor so long as it continues to be reversed. Without positive magnetism, man is a failure, no matter what his status on the earth plane may be. Learn the Law and be free.

Thought and theÆth Forces.

In the forces produced by thought lies the secret of all power that man can ever obtain. By thought, we concentrate upon a given object; and, through concentration, we accumulate the power to obtain the thing desired. Herein is found the power that brings us either failure or success; and it is a lesson that all must learn in order to succeed.

Miracles.

The common error concerning miracles is to regard them as effects without causes, sudden vagaries of the Divine Mind. Effects without cause contradict nature and all natural laws. A single miracle of this class would destroy the universal harmony, and reduce the universe to chaos. It is customary among both the educated and the common classes to designate as miracles those things which the mind cannot comprehend. The chapter clearly explains the parable of the Master Jesus concerning the loaves of bread and the parable concerning walking upon the waters.

The Book Itself.

The book is printed on beautiful laid paper, bound in silk cloth, and in perfect harmony with the books of "St. John," "St.

Matthew," and others of the Christic Interpretation. The price is $1.25, postpaid.

SPECIAL

All the articles as they appear in these two books appeared in "The Initiates." We have about 100 copies of the "The Initiates" beautifully bound in silk cloth. While they last, copies may be had for $2.00.

By ordering a copy, you will have all that would appear in the two volumes besides some valuable additional matter. Order at once.

* * *

RAKADAZANISM

THE EXALTED LIFE

As the title indicates, this book deals with the Science and Art of LIVING—living the Highest Ideal possible to man. It pertains to the culture and normal development of man's entire being—body, mind and soul.

The book recommends itself to the true seeker particularly on this ground; it is the result of years of practical experience in teaching the Higher Life to students. Consequently it is not an untried theory nor something far removed from human need. It is largely composed of material that has already been used in personal letters to students in answer to their question regarding individual difficulties. It has satisfied the needs of others, why not yours?

The book recommends itself to the earnest seeker again, in the most helpful manner, in that it sounds a clear warning against certain erroneous teachings that may have come to the student and makes clear WHY they are erroneous. These suggestions and warnings alone are worth the price of the book to one who has wandered through many phases of modern teaching concerning the Science of Life; for fundamental principles are made so clear in this book that one can readily see wherein the error lies in other systems of Self-Culture. As one studies carefully The Exalted Life, something within says, "These principles and deductions *are* correct."

The book presents the philosophy and general principles

underlying Self-Culture, including Health Culture, Soul Culture, the natural method of Rejuvination of the body and consequent Regeneration of the whole being, leading to conscious Immortality of the Soul.

The chapter on "The Metaphysics of Regeneration and Immortality" deals with such unique topics as these (among others not to be mentioned here for want of space): Interpretation of the "Fall of Man;" Distinction between soul and spirit; First and Second "Fall of Man;" First and Second Resurrection of Man;" Correct use of the Sex Function in the process of Regeneration; Interpretation of the Tree of Life and the Tree of Death, the Flaming Sword, the Lifting up of the Serpent in the Wilderness; Women's exalted place in the work of the Regeneration of the race; Finding the Ineffable Light Within; The Bread and Water of Life; Physical and Spiritual Effects of the true exaltation of the sex forces; Correct Use is the Law in all things; Why a teacher is necessary in Soul Development; Soul growth must be gradual.

The chapter on "The Science of Youth and Regeneration" or "The Regenerate Life" is full of inspiration. It deals with the Laws that govern health, strength and beauty, under such topics as these: Consciously cultivating a youthful mind and body; Constant renewal of physical cells; Transmutation of red corpuscles into white; Sex power is Soul power; Proper use of generative forces in promoting youthfulness and long life; The Elixir of Youth may be a reality; The Gospel of Life; Thought attitude concerning age and death; Destructive effects of fear; Regeneration belongs to body as well as soul.

The closing chapter of the book deals with Hygienic Laws under such topics as, The Natural Food of Man; Bath for cleanliness and Bath for absorbing magnetism and for Soul-development; Correct Breathing; Value of Sun Bath.

This book will be warmly received by the advanced student; for it presents in a new light truths already known to him together with many new aspects of truth. To the beginner it is indispensable; for it will give him a correct start in regard to matters of fundamental importance. *This book is worth while.*

DESCRIPTION. The book has 180 pages. Printed on good book paper and bound in cloth with gold stamp on side and back. A limited de Luxe edition was issued. This edition is in beautiful Berkshire book paper and bound in silk cloth. The price of this to all is $10.00.

This is a strictly private book and obligation of silence is required from all who desire it.

* * * * * * *

"THE WAY TO LIFE AND IMMORTALITY"

No book ever issued by this house has sold so well, and given such universal satisfaction, as "The Way to Life and Immortality.

This has well been called the most important book of the Age. Those who are no longer satisfied with the present-day presentation of religion, science, and philosophy, and who believe that there is something greater, deeper, and more sublime in life than generally recognized, will find this just the book to enlighten them regarding that something Higher, something Deeper, and something more Sublime.

The teachings of the book are in entire harmony with the article on "The Divine Spark." In fact, this is the most important text-book of the Illuminati.

The book contains more than 200 pages, printed on fine paper, and beautifully bound in cloth. Price, $1.25.

* * * * * * *

"THE WAY TO GODHOOD"

To those who want to get away from the poor, "worm-of-the-dust" idea, inculcated by many of the churches, no book ever issued is as important as this. This book teaches man so to live that he becomes not only a man, but even more than man; so to live that he will reach toward Godhood, toward all that is desirable, all that is worth while.

It condemns the theory that man is a worm of the dust, and holds that man is not a weakling, but that he has within himself the germ of all strength; that he is not a slave, but a master; not a child of the devil, but a son of the Godhead.

It is a book for the present age. It teaches a sane, a virile, a powerful philosophy, and shows the way—to Godhood.

It is a companion work to "The Way to Life and Immortality;" and no sincere student should fail to obtain a copy of each.

Printed and bound in harmony with the other book. Price, $1.25.

Those desiring further information concerning one or both of these books before ordering, should write for circulars.

"THE ROSICRUCIANS; THEIR TEACHINGS"

It is now becoming an admitted fact, by those who have given any thought to the secret philosophies, that the Rosicrucian Fraternity has been the Mother-Father of all that is truly mystical.

The Fraternity is "as old as the hills," and has never ceased to inculcate a sublime doctrine, though often its work has been secret and silent for centuries at a time.

Now that a new awakening has come, this book, giving much of the fundamental teachings of the Fraternity, is both timely and valuable.

Book is printed on fine paper, beautifully bound, contains 212 pages, 6 by 9 inches. For a limited time, the $3.00 edition is being sold for $1.50.

"THE PHILOSOPHY OF FIRE"

It has been well said, that the Fire Philosophy is the basis of all religion, and of all religious mysteries. It is the underlying principle on which all secret Occult Brotherhoods are founded. This philosophy was the foundation of all ancient religious systems, and it is actually the life of every known religion at the present day.

No one who is interested in any of the mysteries, in any of the Fraternities that teach a part of the mysteries, can afford to miss reading this book.

In this work are given glimpses of nearly every mystic Order, of both ancient and mediæval times, tracing the teachings from their first conception on the lost Atlantis, up to the present time. Some of the subjects touched upon are the Ancient Mysteries, Secret Doctrines, Regeneration, the Finding of the Christ, the Templars and the Essenes, and Higher Initiation

Printed on fine paper, beautifully bound, 265 pages. Price, $1.50.

"THE MYSTERIES OF OSIRIS"

More than one-half of the Masonic scholars hold that the Masonic Ritual is nothing more nor less than a rewritten ritual of the Ancient Egyptian Order. Be this as it may, it is true that the mysteries of Osiris were among the most sublime that have ever been taught by, or through, the Ritual of any Order known.

This is a private work, and can be had only through an obligation of silence concerning its teachings. It should be in the library of every sincere seeker after truth, and in the library of every Mason.

The Great Lost Secret which was reflected in the Ancient Initiation was the knowledge of God and His relation to nature and to man, and the knowledge of man and his relation to God and nature. The ancient Magi, Initiates, had an occult but absolutely science, wherein *self-knowledge, God-knowledge,* and *nature-knowledge* were combined in an exact and mathematical system. Of the teachings of the Magi, the Hermetic and profane sciences which have survived, were mere fragments, and were in turn used as a vocabulary, more as a means to conceal than to reveal. It makes no difference whether we call these sciences Astrology, Alchemy, Magic, Mythology, Natural Sciences, Philosophy, or Metaphysics. The book, "The Mysteries of Osiris, or Egyptian Initiation," is not an exposure, but a true Key to unlock the Great Mystery.

In language as plain as it is possible to write of mystic subjects, free from jargon, the author has given us in this book a true history and explanation of the Great Initiation.

We cannot too strongly recommend a careful study of this valuable work.

Students of the inner knowledge will no doubt avail themselves of this opportunity, especially since the edition is limited.

The book is on cream queen laid paper, printed in blue ink, and bound in leather, gold stamp side and back, 260 pages, size 6 by 9 inches. Price, $5.00.

Write for special arrangements necessary to secure the work.

Address all orders to